Working World

Related Titles from
Georgetown University Press

Careers in International Affairs, Eighth Edition, Maria Pinto Carland and Candace Faber, Editors

Career Diplomacy: Life and Work in the US Foreign Service, Second Edition, Harry S. Kopp and Charles A. Gillespie

Working World

Careers in International Education, Exchange, and Development

SECOND EDITION

Sherry Lee Mueller
and
Mark Overmann

Washington, DC / Georgetown University Press

Library of Congress Cataloging-in-Publication Data

The Library of Congress has cataloged the earlier edition as follows:

Mueller, Sherry Lee, 1943–
    Working world : careers in international education, exchange, and development / Sherry L. Mueller and Mark Overmann.
      p. cm.
    Includes bibliographical references and index.
    ISBN-13: 978-1-58901-210-3 (alk. paper)
    1. Job hunting.   2. Employment in foreign countries—Vocational guidance.   3. International education—Vocational guidance.   4. Globalization—Economic aspects. I. Overmann, Mark.   II. Title.
    HF5382.7.M84 2008
    337.702—dc22

                                                                              2007050931

Second edition ISBN: 978-1-62616-053-8

♾ This book is printed on acid-free paper meeting the requirements of the American National Standards for Permanence in Paper for Printed Library Materials.

15   14   9   8   7   6   5   4   3   2   First printing

Printed in the United States of America

Dedication

To the dean, faculty, and staff at the School of International Service, American University. Your work preparing leaders to be *of service* is an immense contribution to the university community, our country, and our fragile planet.

◊   ◊   ◊

To Barbara Gumbiner, my colleague and friend of thirty-five years, who shares and helped shape my commitment to mentoring and citizen diplomacy.

To the memory of my loving parents, who always encouraged me to explore the world, count my blessings, and give back.

Sherry Lee Mueller

To Mom and Dad, with love and gratitude for always helping me—and allowing me—to find my way.

Mark Overmann

Everybody says, "Do what you love." You'll know that you're doing what you love when you realize that your work is not just a job, but it's actually part of who you are.

—David Gregory
Moderator, NBC's *Meet the Press*, American University
School of International Service Commencement Address, 2007

Don't ask yourself what the world needs. Ask yourself what makes you come alive, and then go do that. Because what the world needs is people who have come alive.

—Howard Thurman
American author, philosopher, theologian,
educator, and civil rights leader

I don't know what your destiny will be, but one thing I know: the only ones among you who will be really happy are those who will have sought and found how to serve.

—Albert Schweitzer
German theologian, musician, philosopher,
physician, and medical missionary in Africa

Contents

Preface

W*orking World: Careers in International Education, Exchange, and Development* is intended to be a unique resource and a useful tool for job seekers in international affairs, particularly those interested in international education, exchange, and development. It is designed to streamline and clarify the initial stages of career research and help you put your job search in a broader perspective. The approaches and lessons shared throughout the book have evolved during the course of a rewarding career.

About thirty years ago, as a new director at the Institute of International Education (IIE), I was amazed by the many requests for "informational interviews" that I received from job hunters. In the intervening years, the requests grew exponentially. Motivated originally by a desire to save time while still providing sufficient help, in 1982 I initiated the Roundtables on Careers in International Education and Exchange.

These were not the first international career roundtables in the Washington, DC, area. In 1976, Geri Critchley, then codirector of the Experiment in International Living's Washington, DC, office, facilitated a weekly roundtable for job seekers. Several years later, Geri and Dick Irish (author of *Go Hire Yourself an Employer*) conducted monthly job conferences at the TransCentury Foundation.

Alex Patico and I conducted the IIE monthly roundtables for several years. In 1986, Archer Brown and Lorenda Schrader, at NAFSA: Association of International Educators, joined us by hosting the roundtables on alternate months.

Individuals seeking career guidance were invited to the IIE or NAFSA conference room on the third Thursday of each month. At the roundtable, each participant shared his or her educational and professional background and described the types of positions sought. Then the facilitators and fellow participants offered suggestions and contributed ideas for the job search. The roundtables proved much richer than one-on-one interviews because of the synergy that so many perspectives generated. A group inevitably has more knowledge of relevant job openings and successful job search tactics than one or two individuals. Collectively, roundtable participants could recommend more resources to explore and offer contrasting analyses of trends in the field. In addition, the participants did not feel so alone as they interacted with others who were going through the usually solitary activity of a job search.

I gradually realized that the roundtables were much more than a time-saving device for a new manager. They were a particularly useful mechanism for recruiting new staff as well as a tremendous source of information about job seekers, the job search process, and job opportunities in the fields of international education, exchange, and development. The practical ideas, down-to-earth suggestions, and diverse resources offered in my first book on careers, published by NAFSA in 1998, were based on my experiences in working with hundreds of job seekers in our field for more than fifteen years.

I presented that book to each intern at the National Council for International Visitors (NCIV) as a farewell gift and to other young people whom I wanted to encourage to enter these fields that I found so compelling. Years passed. My supply of books dwindled. Even before I gave the last of them away, I realized how outdated many of the resources had become. The need for a new book was great not only because of the way the internet had greatly altered the job search process, but also because the fields of international education, exchange, and development had expanded and evolved. In addition, there were other, more nuanced lessons about managing a career that I wanted to share.

Just as this determination to write a new career book blossomed, I was fortunate to have a young colleague on the NCIV staff who is an extraordinary writer. Mark has an agile mind, an ability to analyze his own experiences, and an engaging personality. Among other responsibilities at NCIV, he produced various publications and served as the editor of our newsletter. He was especially adept at keeping me on schedule in writing my monthly column for the *NCIV Network News*. I was consistently impressed by his editorial suggestions.

I must confess that my initial motivation in inviting Mark to coauthor this book was to keep him at NCIV as long as possible because he was so talented and he helped me be more productive. It was only later—after we started our active collaboration and the ideas ricocheted between us—that I perceived the real value of juxtaposing his perspective as a young professional with my career veteran voice.

One of our spirited discussions prompted our decision to include the profiles of outstanding professionals interspersed throughout part II. We realized that the book would be greatly enriched if we collected the views of others whose achievements we admired. We included highlights of their careers, and we asked them to distill lessons about networking, mentoring, and other topics that we discuss in part I.

Georgetown University Press published the first edition of *Working World* in 2008. Again, years passed. Changes abounded in the fields, in the use of social media, and in Mark's and my professional lives. The time was ripe for this second edition.

The book begins with some basic concepts to keep in mind as you develop your career philosophy and goals. The second section consists of selected resources that will help you plan the next steps of your job search. In between, you will find the profiles of potential role models. You can learn much from their impressive cumulative experience and reflections. The book is designed to be a coherent whole with each chapter building on the preceding one. However, you can also pick and choose, as each chapter is able to stand alone.

Mark and I welcome your comments as well as your recommendations and suggestions for additional resources to be included in future editions. We hope this book will help you chart your course and shape your career in these growing and increasingly challenging fields.

Acknowledgments

W E ARE MOST GRATEFUL to the interns and volunteers of the National Council for International Visitors (NCIV) who helped compile and annotate the selected resources in the first edition of this book, which was initially assembled as a handout for career round-table participants. In particular, we benefited from the conscientious research, editing skills, and enthusiasm of Chris Bassett, Alexander Hunt, Joanne Tay, and Melissa Whited.

For the second edition, special thanks go to Briana Cappelletti for her hard work researching and fact-checking, her constructive questions and suggestions, and her can-do attitude. We are grateful to Frank Kasell for his detailed copy editing and for the polish he brought to the book.

We extend a special thank you to Richard Brown, director of Georgetown University Press, for believing that a second edition of *Working World* will provide valuable guidance and inspiration to those seeking international careers.

Mark: I am grateful for the support that my colleagues—most notably at NCIV, Georgetown University, and the Alliance for International Educational and Cultural Exchange—have given on this book project, as well as for all that they have taught me about what it means to create a rewarding career in these exciting fields. My gratitude goes to Michael McCarry at the Alliance for his support and flexibility as we finished this project. I am indebted to Tate and Tuey for their company and insightful editorial suggestions. My most sincere thanks must go to Sherry for inviting me to be a coauthor on this book, for our work together on this second edition, and for continually imparting valuable lessons, large and small, that make me a better professional and a better person. And last in this list but first in my life, my love and thanks go to my wife Katie for her support and her encouragement, and for always making sure I was up in the morning to do what needed to be done.

Sherry: Heartfelt thanks to my family for their love and steadfast support throughout the writing process—in particular, Jeff Lee, Kathy Kolacinski, Gisela Leusink (my Experiment "sister"), and Jamey Eklund. You are my anchors. I'm grateful to Mary, Sheri, Betsy, Katey, Carol, Peg, and Herb for their enduring friendship and unflagging encouragement. Thanks to Rima for the delicious food she prepared that kept Mark and me going during our collaboration sessions. I would also like to acknowledge my remarkable mentors, Bill Olson and Nancy Friedersdorf. And thanks to Ellie and Mimi, whose companionship during the writing and editing process was much appreciated and never failed to elicit smiles.

A salute to Mark, my coauthor, for his commitment to excellence. It is truly a joy to work with him. Finally, I want to convey my gratitude to the NCIV board chairs I was privileged to work with during my almost sixteen years as president of that nationwide network of citizen diplomats: Bruce Buckland, Sandy Madrid, Alan Kumamoto, Phyllis Layton Perry, Jim Stockton, Larry Chastang, and Alexander Durtka. They valued initiative, modeled leadership, and contributed in many ways to my professional growth and current view on what it means to embrace a cause.

Introduction

Idealists Preferred

For most of our adult lives, we spend more time at our workplaces than we do in our own homes. Pursuing a career means making a series of choices that determine what we do with most of our waking hours. Inevitably, each choice we make exacts a price. The key is to be as aware as we can possibly be—up front—of the trade-offs our choices generate.

Some people can be quite comfortable working within the large, elaborately structured bureaucracy of a government department or multinational organization. Others feel much more at home in a smaller, less structured, nongovernmental organization. For some, with pressing student loans or a family to support, financial compensation is a primary concern. For others, salary and benefits are trumped by other considerations. There are no right or wrong answers here—just the awareness that a job search requires engaging in serious reflection, knowing your preferences, and understanding the circumstances in which you do your best work.

The purpose of this book is to equip you to make wise choices. Whether searching for that first entry-level job, making a midcareer change, or considering encore employment, it is vital that you make conscious choices and consider carefully the wide array of options within the fields of international education, exchange, and development.

The Changing Global Context for International Careers

The world has changed in fundamental ways since the first edition of *Working World* was published in 2008. The evolution of social media continually pushes us toward new and different ways of connecting, networking, and searching for employment. The profound economic downturn has caused job searches to be longer and more difficult and, in some cases, has prompted us to recalibrate the kinds of positions (and salaries) we are willing to accept. Geopolitical events (such as the Arab Spring uprising, greater emphasis on US–Asia relationships, and shifting immigration patterns across the globe) illustrate the growing need for expertise in the fields of international education, exchange, and development.

Indeed, the precise definition of an "international career" is elusive. The distinction between "domestic" and "international" has become increasingly anachronistic, and the complexity of many organizations in these fields defies easy categorization. The fields are amorphous—constantly changing, resettling, then shifting again.

Our basic assumption in this book is that international education, exchange, and development involve moving people, information, and sometimes supplies across national borders for educational or humanitarian purposes in order to build more effective communications, to tackle global problems, and to create the web of human connections so critical to existence in the twenty-first century. Each of these fields operates in a unique space and focuses on distinct goals. Yet international education, exchange, and development naturally fit together not only because of the professional interactions that regularly occur across the fields, but also because the work done by many organizations encompasses all three. In addition, and perhaps most importantly, the fields are all dedicated to improving the quality of life on our fragile planet.

Illustrative positions and organizations in these fields include

- A Peace Corps volunteer in Paraguay
- A program manager for Save the Children in Bangladesh
- The president of the International Visitors Center of Philadelphia

- A work and travel program manager at InterExchange in New York City
- A development consultant to a USAID contractor working in West Africa
- The manager of an Institute of International Education–administered project for teachers in Japan
- A cultural attaché at the US Embassy in Bulgaria
- A program coordinator in the American College Program at the University of Fribourg in Switzerland
- The exchange program director at CENET: Cultural Exchanges Network in Cape Girardeau, Missouri
- A program administrator of Palestine/Israel exchange programs for the Mennonite Central Committee in Jerusalem
- A program coordinator based in East and Southern Africa for the International Foundation for Electoral Systems (IFES)
- An expatriate professor at the Yamaguchi Prefectural University in Japan
- The vice president for business development at Creative Associates International, a for-profit development firm headquartered in Washington, DC
- The director of the Hong Kong-America Center based in Hong Kong
- The president of the Stanley Foundation in Muscatine, Iowa

Jobs in these fields are found in every sector. An increasing number are with nongovernmental organizations (NGOs), nonprofit organizations, private voluntary organizations (PVOs), educational institutions, and other agencies (Lester Salamon at Johns Hopkins University has defined this expansion as the "global associational revolution"). The overriding reality pertaining to most of these jobs is that the financial rewards are modest compared with those in the corporate sector and for some governmental positions. Most individuals aspiring to work in the fields of international education, exchange, and development are motivated more by a desire for psychological satisfaction than for financial gain. They are genuinely idealistic, wanting to make a positive difference in the world and a contribution to a constructive result.

For example, we know a program officer at the Meridian International Center who is absolutely committed to helping the foreign leaders from the Middle East participating in the US Department of State's International Visitor Leadership Program (IVLP) understand the United States and its democratic institutions. He is also determined to help US citizens comprehend the complexity and historic circumstances that drive so many of the events in the Middle East. It is unlikely that his efforts will make him rich in monetary terms, but he is blessed with many psychological rewards as the impact of his work becomes apparent at home and abroad.

One example from Sherry's own career may help further illustrate what we mean by psychological satisfaction. Sherry described this experience in her first book on careers:

> Some years ago, before apartheid ended in South Africa, I was watching Ted Koppel's show *Nightline* on television. The format was a town meeting concerning South Africa. As I watched, I realized I knew one of the men being interviewed. He was the current minister of education of South Africa and was arguing for the end of apartheid. I had served as his program officer at the Institute of International Education twelve years earlier when he was a participant in the US Information Agency's International Visitor Program.[1] I remembered sending him to communities in Alabama and Oklahoma to study successful integration efforts in the United States. The realization that in some small way my work may have helped nudge a South African leader toward ending apartheid was powerful indeed. This experience was just one of many times I have known without a doubt that I chose the right career.

The title of this introduction, "Idealists Preferred," reflects the basic assumption underlying this book: people drawn to careers in international education, exchange, and development want to have a positive impact. They envision their careers making a tangible difference in our turbulent world. There is an oft-quoted adage: "You are either part of the problem or part of the solution." People drawn to these fields want to be part of the solution.

"Idealists Preferred" was inspired by the original advertisement used to recruit Pony Express riders in 1860:

"Wanted: Young wiry, skinny fellows under the age of 18. Must be expert riders willing to risk death daily. Wages $25 per week. Orphans preferred."

Over the years, Sherry has often quoted the original advertisement in speeches she makes on citizen diplomacy, the concept that each individual has the responsibility to help shape foreign relations. Then she recounts a revised version of the advertisement that she suggests her audience has already answered:

"Wanted: Young at heart of all ages. Must be well-organized, eager to learn, and willing to risk breaking stereotypes daily. Wages—won't be discussed. Idealists preferred."

In fact, this revised ad is one that most people drawn to careers in international education, exchange, and development have answered, at least on a subconscious level. They are idealists. They desire to make a positive difference—to be a force for good. They are motivated by the notion of service. It is no surprise that one of the most popular job search websites for the fields is Idealist.org.

A Job versus a Career

A job comprises a set of responsibilities you accept at one point in time. A career is the trajectory of your cumulative efforts. It describes your accomplishments in a series of jobs—the impact you have made. As noted at the outset, charting your career is making a series of choices that determine what you do with most of your waking hours. These choices determine the context for your potential achievements. Each choice we make precludes others. We should be knowledgeable about the trade-offs our choices involve.

Whatever stage of life you are in, this book is designed to help you fashion a career that enables your idealist inclinations to thrive. When structuring this volume, we kept in mind that your job search and career development can be a demanding, time-consuming process. Thus, the whole book need not be read from front to back or cover to cover. Rather, it is divided into clearly marked and easily digestible chapters and sections, each of which can be read or skimmed alone.

Part I: Shaping Your Career Philosophy

Part I suggests a way of thinking about your career and leads you to consider a variety of activities that comprise career development. Although our focus in this book is primarily on the fields of international education, exchange, and development, the approaches discussed in part I can be useful to career seekers in many fields.

We first examine the need to identify your cause. Although your cause may evolve, grow, or change over time, it is the underlying force that drives your career. We agree with journalist David Gregory's observation, quoted at the start of the book:

> "You'll know that you're doing what you love when you realize that your work is not just a job, but it's actually part of who you are."

As you work, if you are typically oblivious to time rather than watching the clock, this is a good signal that you are doing what you love. Athletes call it "being in the zone." You are so caught up in what you are doing and derive so much satisfaction from it that you would keep that occupation even if you won the lottery. Identifying your cause will help you find a job that becomes a part of who you are.

In chapter 2 we turn to the frequently mentioned yet seldom analyzed art of networking. The size, quality, and accessibility of the network of colleagues at your disposal are key elements in your job search and career development—and of real value to a potential employer. There are many methods and approaches to networking. Several are discussed in this chapter. We also emphasize that the potential benefits of networking are not always clear when a new relationship begins.

In chapter 3 we encourage you to consider the value of having mentors, as well as the gratification of serving as one. The kind of personal tutoring mentors provide and the example they set are invaluable as you chart your career path. In addition, mentors often act as your best and most enthusiastic references. Some people have clearly identified mentors in their lives while others do not. Either way, most professionals have benefited from the wisdom and guidance of a friend or colleague at some juncture.

In the last chapter of part I we explore the important idea that pursuing a career is a continuous journey, not simply something a person does intermittently while engaging in a job search. We also tackle the concept of professionalism. People are frequently admonished to "act like professionals," yet the exact meaning of this phrase can be elusive.

Part II: Selected Resources and Profiles

Part II is designed to help you map out the next steps on your career path and appreciate the many different routes that are available. Here you will find selected resources to aid you in your pursuit of a career in international education, exchange, and development. It is important to note that the resources contained in this section are indeed "selected." That is to say, our lists are not exhaustive on any specific topics, fields, or organizations. The resources in this section, however, are a kind of compass. We view them as the best tools available to point you in the right direction as you make your career choices. For this second edition we surveyed more than a hundred professionals in the fields (of varying ages and in different phases of their careers) to find out their favorite job search and career development resources. Their responses greatly informed and added significant value to this section.

Each chapter in part II is structured to allow you to quickly locate the information most useful to you. Chapter introductions are followed by short descriptions of illustrative organizations, as well as selected web and print resources to jumpstart your research.

Many of these resources overlap. For example, InterAction is a coalition of more than 150 development organizations offering numerous resources and job opportunities in the development field. It first appears in chapter 5 because it is a valuable tool to help in your general job search in international development. InterAction, however, is also an association for development professionals and a leading nonprofit organization; thus it is cross-referenced in both chapters 6 and 9. Its members also offer substantial volunteer opportunities in international development, so it appears in chapter 8 as well. NAFSA: Association of International Educators, a large professional association, first appears as a resource in chapter 5. The job registry hosted by NAFSA, however, is a popular resource for those looking for jobs or internships in international education, so a cross-reference is included in chapter 7. Given space constraints, not every conceivable cross-reference is included.

Because the resources listed in part II may overlap across many topics, chapter 5 contains resources designed to help you begin a more comprehensive job search. The chapters that follow are devoted to more topic-specific resources in the fields of international education, exchange, and development. Many of the organizations and associations included also host their own job search sites; practically all organizations list internal job openings on their websites.

Profiles

You will also find profiles of accomplished colleagues interspersed throughout part II. These professionals represent a variety of career paths within the fields of international education, exchange, and development. These colleagues are at varying stages of their careers. We intentionally interviewed promising young professionals and midcareer colleagues in addition to presidents, CEOs, and executive directors in order to present a richer collection of career advice that transcends generations.

We asked each professional a common set of questions. Each provided information on his or her career trajectory and distilled lessons learned about pursuing a career in international affairs. The topics broached in the profiles are those also explored in part I: finding a cause, the importance of networking, and the value of mentors. In some instances, the advice offered by these professionals echoes the recommendations we share on these topics; yet, in other instances, their thoughts do not mesh tidily with our own.

Thinking about the process of career development from various viewpoints is essential to sharpening our own skills of discernment. Making an informed choice comes not from hearing only one viewpoint but rather from examining a broad range of ideas and interpreting what is appropriate for us. Much like the career roundtables Sherry still leads, the synergy generated by the multiple perspectives is much richer than one or two opinions ever could be.

Combined Voice of a Career Veteran and a Young Professional

When American anthropologist Margaret Mead published her book *Culture and Commitment* in 1970, she conveyed her keen understanding of how modern culture has changed the way we learn and our sources of information. She reminded her readers that for centuries, young people looked to their elders as the font of knowledge. She also observed that this was quickly changing. People were finding many other sources of information. They were looking to their peers rather than to their parents. Think about how often in today's society an older person is dependent on a younger person to help solve some pesky computer problem or resolve a technical glitch. In some ways, the traditional approach to knowledge acquisition described by Mead has made a U-turn. The trend she identified years ago has accelerated.

We acquire knowledge and access information in multiple ways. This fact suggested to us that juxtaposing a career veteran voice with that of a promising young professional would produce a much richer experience for the reader than either author could alone. In the collaboration process, we discovered that our interaction helped each of us challenge our assumptions and develop our ideas with greater rigor. Discussing the generation gap between us helped us better understand the value of our respective approaches. We came to appreciate that, in a way, our collaboration process is just what needs to happen in workplaces as leaders strive to tap the valuable institutional memory and experience of older employees and blend it with the fresh approach and technological dexterity of younger colleagues. We hope that by guiding you to approach your job search with this realization in mind you will be better equipped to function in a workplace that requires intergenerational cooperation.

When using this book, determine what is best for you and choose the resources that most closely fit your career aspirations. But remember that just as creating a meaningful career is more than landing one job, your career exploration should include persistent research in more than one place. Take time to investigate all that *Working World* has to offer, and in the end, we hope that you will feel confident and better prepared for the exciting opportunities that lie ahead.

Note

1. The US Information Agency (USIA) administered US public diplomacy programs from 1953 to 1999, including international exchange programs after 1977. USIA was abolished in 1999 under the Foreign Affairs Reform and Restructuring Act. Since then, US government-sponsored international exchange programs have been administered by the Department of State's Bureau of Educational and Cultural Affairs. In 2004, the International Visitor Program (IVP) was renamed the International Visitor Leadership Program (IVLP).

PART I

Shaping Your Career Philosophy

CHAPTER 1

Identifying Your Cause

Introduction

People often ask, "What do you want to be when you grow up?" Children usually reply, "a fireman, a doctor, an actor, a musician, a princess, a basketball star . . .," perhaps recalling the hero in a recently viewed movie or naming the profession of a relative they admire. They have yet to realize that they will be asked this question repeatedly as the years pass. Responding to the question as children was just our first experience with identifying our cause.

Your cause is a major force that guides your career decisions. Whether clearly defined and structured, or perhaps hazy and still in need of refinement, your cause is, as Howard Thurman phrases it in the quotation at the beginning of this book, "what makes you come alive." In this first chapter we focus not on clearly delineating the steps up a structured career ladder but on helping you locate something much bigger—the force that will illuminate your career path.

Sherry approaches the quest to identify a cause from the perspective of "your place in history": how your search for a cause is inevitably anchored in the trends and happenings of a particular period. How will you find your place in today's historical context? What will historians say about your cause and career when looking back many years from now? Or more importantly, what would you *want* those historians to say? In Sherry's view, how you approach these questions will help you define your cause and develop your career.

Mark, on the other hand, approaches the issue of finding a cause from the postcollege question of "What am I going to do with my life?" For him, there is less focus on the bigger picture of finding a place in history and more attention to microlevel decision making, namely, figuring out what is right for you at this point and proceeding from there. Even if you are unsure of your exact cause or how you want historians to view your choices, Mark urges you to go with what you *do* know. Pursue your interests, follow your feelings, and listen to your gut. If a certain path is attractive at this point in your life, it is probably a good direction to take, even if you're not sure of your ideal destination.

Sherry: Your Place in History

There are certain forces at work—economic, political, military, and social factors—that make possible or restrict certain job options. Understanding these factors can help you approach your job search more realistically. Certainly the economic marketplace is vastly different for you than it was for your parents. I have often fielded the question, "How can I explain to my father why it is taking me so long to find full-time work when he found his first job right after graduation?" As economists debate whether unemployment is structural or cyclical, the reality for the job seeker is that it is (as some readers may be painfully aware) much more difficult to find a job—particularly that first job—at certain points in time than at others.

There are still many bureaucratic organizations with rigid hierarchies. Nonetheless, technological advances, current management practices, and economic strictures suggest that lean, downsized, and restructured organizations are the norm in both the for-profit and non-profit worlds and in some government agencies. In some cases the result has been the reduction of jobs in traditional institutions or an increase in one part of the world with a corresponding reduction in other geographic areas.

Paradoxically, there are fewer jobs at the top of many organizations (upper management), as well as fewer at the bottom (receptionists, secretaries, clerks). A job that represents a rung on the career ladder in the traditional sense is increasingly scarce; this concept may eventually disappear.

We tend to think of history as those events that occurred before we were born. In our textbooks, history seems to be a series of dramatic events, such as revolutions, wars, and social movements, all far in the past. We should bear in mind that some decades hence our time also will be a historical period. Historians will assign labels and designations, analyze trends, and otherwise describe the context in which we now live. Your effort to find your place at this particular point in history may be more productive if you start by viewing your career in a more holistic way. Instead of focusing on finding a job with clearly defined next steps in the same organization, focus on identifying your cause.

As Mark and I were discussing this chapter, we reflected on the historic context in which I started my career compared with the backdrop that existed when he launched his. As a farm kid from northern Illinois, I chose to attend the School of International Service at American University (AU). I didn't even know what the Foreign Service was, but what I did know was that serving internationally was appealing. A child of the Cold War, I graduated from college and attended graduate school in the late 1960s. Despite the assassination of President John F. Kennedy, the stirring words of his inaugural address continued to motivate many of my generation as we began our career journeys: "Ask not what your country can do for you—ask what you can do for your country." One of my favorite memories is handing out programs as an undergraduate at the AU commencement on June 10, 1963, when President Kennedy gave a seminal speech on foreign policy. He urged all to work together "to make the world safe for diversity." That admonition describes one of the causes I've embraced ever since!

The Alliance for Progress with Latin America and the newly minted Peace Corps were just two sources of job opportunities that beckoned at that time. There was a call to public service. We had not yet become as disillusioned with our major institutions or those in authority as we are today. Despite the hovering nuclear threat, it was in certain ways an easier time.

In the Cold War era, the United States was the "good guy." We were generally (in some cases grudgingly) admired. There was not a lot of ambiguity. In fact, the superpower prism was a somewhat comforting, if overly simplistic, way to view the world. The book *The Ugly American* by Eugene Burdick and William J. Lederer, published in 1958, was instructive and, in retrospect, one of the key factors that inspired my own career in international education and exchange. (I still require my students to read it.) Though a novel, *The Ugly American* nonetheless made trenchant observations about the need for cultural and political sensitivity, carefully tailored and appropriately scaled approaches to development, and behaviors that produce constructive international relations. These are still valid. The book helped me identify my cause. I wanted a career that would help project a positive image of the United States abroad and lead to new avenues of cooperation.

In the intervening years, the Vietnam War and other events produced disillusionment, distrust of authority, and a much more variegated and complex global scene. As I often jokingly reply to colleagues and friends when asked about my cause: "I am still idealistic; I still want to save the world. Only now, I realize just how reluctant the world is to be saved!"

Mark and his contemporaries faced this complexity and the crisis of credibility surrounding many institutions much earlier in their lives than I and many of my idealistic classmates did years ago. Ironically, given these conditions, the need for exceptionally able people in service-oriented fields, such as international education, exchange, and development, has never been greater.

What Do You Care about Passionately?: The "Magic Wand Test"

Ask yourself, "If I had a magic wand, what would I do to make a difference in the world?" Lead a Council for International Visitors; build schools in South Sudan; advise international students at a university; manage a development project to establish village health clinics; organize short-term exchange programs for parliamentarians, librarians, or farmers—these are all potential answers. There are many more. Part of the challenge is comprehending the array of options. Whatever cause you find compelling, chances are there are various organizations working to make a difference in that area. Your cause is their mission.

The impetus to get a job, or to find a new one, comes from various sources. Almost always, the urge to fashion a career with an international focus stems from a particularly positive international experience, such as living with a host family on an exchange program, hosting an exchange student in your own home, participating in a short-term development project overseas, serving as a Peace Corps volunteer, or studying abroad. The intense learning generated by the face-to-face encounters, the riveting conversations, and the dawning awareness of intriguing cultural differences and common human aspirations trigger our ambition to replicate this wonder-filled experience for others as well as for ourselves. The desire to help solve some global problem observed during the overseas experience may also inspire the determination to chart a career in international education, exchange, or development.

My own experience is a good example. At the urging of an AU professor, Alexander Trowbridge, I participated in an Experiment in International Living (EIL) program in 1963. (EIL is now part of World Learning—see chapter 9 for more information.) That eye-opening summer experience included living with a German family and traveling in Germany, Austria, and Switzerland with a group of German and American students. My host family exposed me to so many new and exciting experiences. It was a time of intense learning and adventure. My worldview grew and became more nuanced. I came home determined to be an EIL leader and take my own group of students abroad, which I did in 1969—a memorable trip to the Soviet Union. After visits back and forth over the years, my German "sister" remains a dear friend. That kind of deep connection across time and culture continues to be an immense source of learning and satisfaction. My passion became finding jobs that enabled me to give others opportunities for similar, enduring relationships that transcend nationality and other differences.

I literally do keep a "magic wand" on my desk. I use it to remind job seekers (and myself) that it is important to suspend limitations and reflect on what you would do if no obstacles existed. Your answer is an essential clue to identifying your cause. As you consider possible causes, note your natural preferences. What events and speakers attract you? What are your favorite courses? What topics are covered in the articles you read first—whether perusing an issue of the *Economist* or skimming a favorite online compendium of articles? Whom do you admire? What facet of their work prompts you to say, "I want to do that—that is worth my energy and effort"?

People thoroughly content with the cause they serve often avow, "This is my calling." My favorite definition of a calling is that place where your greatest passion and the world's greatest need intersect.

The rest of this book concerns the process of identifying those organizations whose mission you can embrace and learning how to present yourself to employers so they recognize that your cause—your calling—and their mission are congruent.

Get Specific

Once you have identified your cause, it is critical to answer three sets of questions:

1. Where (in what geographic location) do you want to work? The answer may indeed be "anywhere," but be sure that is your considered answer. There are many international jobs that do not require a perpetually peripatetic existence. Of course, others require worldwide availability, or the willingness to relocate to a specific project site or other destination. Clearly, if you are working for the Red Cross as a specialist in humanitarian assistance, you are required to go wherever the latest crisis has struck. Hurricanes, earthquakes, and conflicts determine your worksites. Some job seekers know they want to be in a particular country; others must stay in a particular locale because of obligations to a family member or because they need to be rooted in a place for their own identity and effectiveness.

2. How do you want to spend your days? What kinds of tasks do you enjoy most? What sorts of skills and talents do you offer? As Adam Weinberg told us in his profile interview, it is important to play to your strengths. To what extent do you want to interact with international clients? There are international jobs where minimal contact with internationals is the norm. If you want to be a foreign student adviser, and enjoy daily face-to-face contact with international students, then you may want to avoid a job where your only contact with international colleagues is electronic or by telephone—unless, of course, you see it as useful preparation for an aspiring foreign student adviser.

3. What type of organizational culture do you prefer? Do you thrive in a large, structured environment or do you shine in an environment where being a self-starter and having initiative is highly

valued? What type of supervisor motivates you to do your best? Many job seekers underestimate the role their bosses play until they are ensconced in their jobs. To the extent possible, you want to work for people who care about your professional growth and development, even if you sacrifice a bit on the salary side of the ledger. When you are interviewing for a job, you are actually interviewing with someone who reflects and shapes the culture of a particular organization. This is the person who will give you assignments. And this is probably the person who will provide a key reference at some point. The value of having a supervisor you respect, admire, and learn from is tremendous. In fact, it supersedes many other considerations, such as job title and pay.

Mark: What Am I Going to Do with My Life?

I taught English in the northeastern part of China after college. I found myself feeling pessimistic at that time, as evidenced by journal entries like this:

> I don't know what the hell to do about grad school—or my life for that matter. People tell me I shouldn't worry so much about the future because "life is what happens when you're busy making other plans." That's all well and good for John Lennon—but apparently he never had his dad hounding him day after day about getting a job. I'd really like someone to come along and just *tell* me where I need to be.

If you've ever, at least for a moment, wondered what you should do with your life, you aren't alone. At some point, everyone has had that feeling— that perplexing, sinking feeling. You know you need to move forward, but you have no idea which direction to go, or even where to take that first step. You're wondering, to paraphrase myself, "What the hell should I do with my life?"

I'm not always so negative. When I was studying in France during my junior year of college, I was more optimistic about my search for a life and career course:

> You never know where the wiry arms of the world are going to push you. . . . Many people saw my coming to France to study for a year as misguided and perhaps fundamentally against the purpose of my major, English. From time to time, I still doubt my choices both to come to France and to pursue English as a major. But, in general, I believe they were both wise choices because they challenge me and, quite simply, because they feel right.

Looking back, I'm sometimes surprised to see that I was so comfortable with "going with what feels right," especially at a time when I was feeling the growing pressure of making postgraduation plans. This sense of going with my gut stayed with me when I decided to go to China, or as my dad characterized it, "to put off the inevitable." Later, once I got back to the United States, I reflected in my journal:

What do I want to do? Where do I need to be? . . . In the movie *Forrest Gump*, Jenny asks Forrest, "Who do you want to be?" Forrest responds, "Aren't I going to be me?" And that hints at the key to it all. As I am going through all of this examination and self-discovery, making decisions about grad school and trying to answer those questions, I must remember to be true to myself. Shakespeare said it in *Hamlet* ("This above all: To thine own self be true!"). John Wooden said it ("You must have the courage to be true to yourself!"). Even Tom Hanks said it. Be true to yourself and you can't go wrong.

My career has not been strategically planned. Back in college, and immediately postcollege, I saw myself as a person of many interests but with few ideas about how to channel those interests into a coherent career. Even so, I always tried to go with what felt right. Often this mentality led to choices that seemed random to others, or not in line with the path I had seemingly taken. Somehow though, those choices felt right to me. I went with them. Studying abroad in France, even though I was an English major; spending a year in China, even though I had no experience with Asia or the Chinese language; interning at a regional newspaper, then a nonprofit organization, then the Embassy of France . . . I have no regrets about these choices. They not only gave me an array of diverse learning experiences that have shaped me in positive ways, but they also led to where I am now. Never doubt the inherent worth of variety in your experiences.

There is a certain element of optimism and whimsy that exists in the search for a cause and a career. That element shouldn't be ignored. Ralph Waldo Emerson describes it with no small amount of literary elegance: "A man should learn to detect and watch that gleam of light that flashes across his mind from within, more than the luster of the firmament of bards and sages."[1] In more mundane terms, what Emerson conveys is this: Don't necessarily be swayed by what everyone else has to say—go with your gut. Surely there are other considerations to take into account as your career unfolds, considerations that will be examined as this book progresses. Yet your gut instincts can often be your best source of direction.

So if I've been as successful as I claim at following my gut and doing what feels right, then surely I can easily articulate my cause, right? The mission that has thus far driven my career choices must be at my fingertips.

Well, I'm *now* finally at a place in my career where I feel that I can articulate my cause—why I'm doing what I do. But it hasn't been easy getting there.

What Do You Care about Passionately?: The "Million Dollar Question"

My friend Karl Dedolph—a grad school classmate at American University's School of International Service, now a senior manager at Accenture, and profiled later in this book—once asked me what I would do if I had a million dollars. I immediately thought of the movie *Office Space*.

Current college students might not have seen—or even heard of—this movie (I'm told this means I'm getting old). But if you have seen it, you know that its main characters are stuck in dead-end jobs. Cubicles are portrayed as prison cells. The boss, Bill Lumbergh, is so infuriating that he drives one of his employees to set the building on fire. During one scene, the main character, Peter, tells his coworkers that a high school guidance counselor once informed him that how a person answers the "million dollar question" says everything about the career path he or she should choose.

Peter's coworkers have a chance to answer the question. A character named Michael Bolton (no relation to the pop singer) thinks it's a worthless exercise. Another character, Samir, interprets it literally and describes how he would invest the money. Then it's Peter's turn to answer his own query. His response to this all-important, life-defining question? "Nothing. I would sit around all day and do nothing."

When it was my turn to answer the question, I hesitated. I had no immediate answer. Karl jumped in and said that he'd go back to Togo, where he served for two years as a Peace Corps volunteer, and build a school. He has a passion for West Africa, and the idea of one day constructing and establishing a well-functioning school that would provide a quality education for countless young people . . . that is a dream for him.

Sherry and I also reflected on the question when discussing this chapter for the first edition. At that time, when I tried to answer, I couldn't. Sherry, on the other hand, knew her answer without a doubt. She wanted to be doing exactly what she was: leading the National Council for International Visitors (NCIV). She wholeheartedly embraces NCIV's mission of promoting excellence in citizen diplomacy. If only we could all be as fortunate as

Sherry, I thought: to be in a position where our job and our passion correspond so unmistakably.

I was worried that I had no ready answer. As Sherry points out earlier in this chapter, your answer to the "Million Dollar Question" (or the "Magic Wand Test," as she phrases it) can greatly guide you in identifying your cause. I feared that because I had no answer, I also had no cause. Had I been bouncing from job to job, experience to experience, aimlessly going nowhere?

Now it's been more than a decade since I graduated from college. More than five years have passed since the first edition was published. So now it's much easier to realize that while I *was* going from one experience to the next, one internship to the next, one job to the next, that *didn't* mean I was headed nowhere. Rather, in my own personal, unplanned way, my experiences and choices, while not linear, were tied together by one thing: my passion for them.

My passion for writing and literature led me to major in English. An undefined but urgent need to experience new languages and cultures—to get outside my comfort zone—led me to study abroad in France and work in China. These life-changing experiences spurred me to pursue an international communications master's degree, and eventually internationally focused internships and jobs.

I realized when writing the first edition that my passions were somehow connected to my search for a cause. I thought: could it be so simple that the things I enjoy are directly related to my cause, or even *are* my cause? It seemed too easy but was impossible to ignore. I began to think that by doing things that I enjoy and by following my gut, regardless of whether I knew for sure the result of those choices, I would be able to identify my cause and fashion a rewarding career.

With the benefit of a few years of hindsight, I believe this thinking to have been true. It's now clear to me that through my work, I want to promote international exchange programs, study abroad, and language learning. I want to help facilitate for others the life-changing experiences I had when abroad. Now my cause seems pretty straightforward and clear.

I also recognize that finally defining my cause is not the end of something, but one step in a continuous journey (a concept we discuss in chapter 4). Sherry has told me that in her experience, causes rarely stay unaltered during the course of a career. Interests shift, personal situations change, new causes and corollary causes emerge. Five years ago, this may have worried me. Now I find it appealing. I realize that the future holds exciting and unknown opportunities and that by continuing to follow my passions and my gut—no matter how things in my life shift—I'll not be bouncing aimlessly, but finding my way.

Get Specific

Career choices not only have cause-oriented elements but task-oriented ones, too. Looking back on my internships and jobs, I realize I was gravitating toward organizations whose missions I admire, as well as toward jobs that offer daily tasks I enjoy. Balance your search for a cause with an honest and clear examination of what you like to do. Sherry poses the question in this way: "How do you want to spend your days?"

If you hate the idea of asking others for money, don't apply for a position with an international development organization as a fundraising professional, no matter how closely that organization's mission matches your own cause. If organizational skills are not your strong suit, avoid a job as an event planner, even if it is for an international education organization that perfectly complements your worldview. You may be able to convince yourself for a while that distaste for daily tasks comes second to fulfilling the mission. But sooner or later, enjoyment of your job will markedly diminish, and that will be a product of disliking and not being effective in your daily tasks.

If this notion seems a touch selfish, that's because it is. But to a certain degree, self-interest is necessary in your search for a cause and a career. By being self-aware in this way, you'll better serve your cause because you'll do your job well. And you'll do your job well because you'll be happy to perform the tasks involved. Search for jobs that will allow you to work for a cause you support and to do tasks at which you excel. This might seem like a simple point, but it's one that can easily be overlooked in the quest for a broad, all-encompassing cause.

This discernment should include an examination of the kind of environment in which you want to work. First, in what kind of organization, company, or firm do you see yourself thriving? A small NGO or a large consulting firm? A large NGO or a small consulting firm? A US government or multinational agency? A relatively small study abroad office within the edifice of a relatively large university? Will you thrive within, say, the structured bureau-cracy of the US Department of State or be successful—and satisfied—in a nimbler nonprofit? It's likely that you can be happy and successful in more than one of these environments. It may also be difficult to know what you prefer until you've had an internship or job experience in several of these contrasting environments. Indeed, one of the common threads you'll notice about the professionals profiled in part II is that many have worked in different kinds of organizations (and fields) during the course of their careers.

Second in this examination of environment, and in many ways particularly pertinent to our fields, is the question: where do you want to live and what kind of lifestyle do you want? Many of us gravitate to these fields because we've lived or studied abroad and see ourselves living (or frequently traveling) outside of our home countries as part of our careers. If this is true for you, it's essential to think about specifics. Where are you willing to travel and how frequently? Are you willing to work on projects in Serbia, Cuba, and Peru, as profiled professional Tom Garofalo did? How much of your time are you willing to spend on the road—25 percent? 50 percent? More? Deirdre White told us that she spends about 100 days a year traveling and finds it challenging. If you want to live outside your home country, where are you willing to live? Are you willing to intern in Cairo, then relocate to Tajikistan and Azerbaijan, as Alanna Shaikh did? If you're interested in the US Foreign Service, are you willing to relocate every few years, cede control of where you are posted to your employer, and, in many ways, allow your job to become your life? (Sarah and Amit Mathur told us that being Foreign Service Officers defines them and is a commitment to a lifestyle.) These questions may not have tidy answers—at first or ever—but they're important to consider as you ponder your career direction.

Risk Yourself

For young professionals, sometimes the most difficult thing is bringing ourselves to make choices at all. With no clear career destination in sight and no way of knowing if our choices are good ones, it can be easy for those of us without the experience and knowledge of someone like Sherry to become paralyzed by fear. However, as James Baldwin writes in *The Fire Next Time*, "One can give nothing whatever without giving oneself—that is to say, risking oneself."[2] Follow your gut. Be true to yourself. Risk, and choose.

Notes

1. Ralph Waldo Emerson, "Self-Reliance," in *The Norton Anthology of American Literature, Shorter Fourth Edition* (New York: W. W. Norton & Company, 1995), 492.
2. James Baldwin, *The Fire Next Time* (New York: Vintage International, 1993), 86.

CHAPTER 2

The Art of Networking

Introduction

Most everyone agrees that we ought to network, but we rarely reflect on how to do it most efficiently and with the most rewarding results. Is there a certain formula for successful networking? A certain type of event we must attend or a certain kind of person we should engage? A certain number of business cards we should collect?

Furthermore, we seldom stop to consider the question of what networking *is*, anyway. All professionals use the term, but the meanings they ascribe to it vary. Is networking only about going to events? Or does it have other facets as well? Conducting an informational interview? Talking to a stranger on an airplane or subway? Chatting with the friend of a friend at a happy hour? Networking could be any or all of these things. It should not be confined to only one of them.

A useful definition of networking is building a circle of acquaintances—colleagues you admire who know and respect your work and who are willing to help you in a variety of ways. Similarly, you respect them, admire their work ethic, and are willing to be of help. The emphasis must be on quality, not quantity. You may have many connections on LinkedIn, but how many will use their precious time to do you a favor?

For Sherry, going to networking events and putting yourself in contact with potential employers or other people knowledgeable about the fields of international education, exchange, and development is invaluable. Yet she also advises professionals to avoid viewing these structured events as the only times when they need to be "on." Rather, for Sherry, you are always networking or "forever at the crossroads." You are constantly being judged as a professional, and you never know when a seemingly innocuous situation may help you—or haunt you—in the future.

Mark is less comfortable than Sherry with the idea of attending a multitude of networking events. He explores the question of how a professional might effectively network if he or she is uncomfortable with approaching new people or plunging into a noisy crowd at an event. Although he does not advocate abandoning events altogether, Mark suggests being strategic about the events you choose to attend. Much like Sherry, however, Mark sees networking as more than just attending events or gathering as many business cards as possible. He believes that every day, "in your own skin," you are networking. He recognizes that you cannot ignore the value of building relationships or getting to know people, even if the professional value of a specific relationship is not immediately clear.

Sherry: Encountering Potential Employers and References

There is no substitute for putting yourself in the company of potential employers or other individuals knowledgeable about employment opportunities in your field. A productive way to do this is to join the professional associations most related to the cause you have identified. I joined the International Studies Association (ISA) as a graduate student and have remained a member in the intervening decades. My ISA membership and participation in national conferences (where I sometimes present papers) enable me to keep in touch with a wide array of respected colleagues and to better understand the evolving context in which I work. (Consult chapter 6 for an annotated list of major professional associations and the benefits and costs of membership.)

You also can attend conferences, lectures, and other program events related to your areas of interest. Sometimes you can convince organizations to waive registration fees at conferences or other professional development activities by volunteering your services. Participation in such events will enable you to gain vital knowledge about the field that is the focus of the sponsoring organization. You will learn more about the history of the field and key issues currently commanding the attention of its leaders, and, in some cases, you may acquire skills pertinent to your career in training seminars. You will develop a strong sense of the major players and the array of organizations offering employment. Those events provide useful opportunities to raise questions and to demonstrate to colleagues your own grasp of various issues.

I always encourage colleagues to have a first question ready at the beginning of the question-and-answer periods that are often part of such events. Be sure to identify yourself and then ask a carefully phrased, succinct question that enables a speaker to elaborate on a concept presented. It is a chance to demonstrate that you were paying attention, want to learn more, and are articulate. It also is an opportunity to help the organizers keep the event moving—and organizers will notice that you have contributed in that way. On the other hand, I also caution colleagues not to display insensitivity to others who have questions by dominating the discussion or monopolizing a speaker's time when he or she is answering individual questions during or after the formal part of an event. Questions are a way to demonstrate your consideration for others, not only a way to illustrate your interest in the subject matter.

Once you have determined that the mission of a particular organization and your cause are congruent, you will want to participate in that organization's activities and programs. Again, most organizations look for volunteers to help. Once the leaders of an organization know you embrace their mission and are a competent and diligent worker, you will have a distinct advantage when a job opening does occur. It is no mystery why many of the people I hired at the National Council for International Visitors (NCIV) were former interns, including Mark. We knew the quality of their work. They were familiar with our membership, technology, and office culture. Therefore, they required less training than someone completely new to the organization. They were known quantities. Hiring them was less risky for the organization. Hiring the wrong person is expensive—in terms of time, energy, and dollars. Managers are always looking for ways to minimize that risk. That is why direct experience with a potential hire or the unqualified recommendation of a trusted colleague is a remarkable advantage. In sum, networking is getting to know potential employers and potential references.

Who Are the Gatekeepers?

People often assume that networking is done only with "important" people—an erroneous assumption, for sure. Accept at the outset that anyone you encounter may be important to your career. If you are waiting to meet the director of a program at a major organization, it can be particularly useful to visit with the administrative assistant who may be stationed nearby. People lower in an organization's hierarchy are generally less guarded about the information they will share. As a consequence, you as the job seeker may get a more accurate picture of the organization's culture and staff from observing and talking to them than you do from the formal interview. Plus, one of these people may decide whether your call to his boss next week will go through. His favorable comments may help generate a second interview.

For another illustration of conscientious networking, consider events held at embassies, where everyone generally vies for the attention of the ambassador. In fact, this networking opportunity can often be better leveraged by seeking out the spouse of the ambassador or another diplomat, who is almost always just as knowledgeable and has time for more than a thirty-second conversation. Again, it might be this person's favorable observation to the ambassador that produces the follow-up meeting you desire. Extrapolate this advice. It's often easier and more productive to interact with a key staffer than with a senator or CEO.

Start a Support Group

The idea of participating in a support group is an important and seldom-discussed aspect of networking. When I was conducting career roundtables at the Institute of International Education (IIE), I often urged like-minded participants with similar goals to form an informal support group. When we are working steadily at a job, we take the workplace community for granted. It is only during periods of unemployment that we realize how much we have depended on the camaraderie of colleagues and the structure of the workday to give shape to our daily lives. The solitary nature of the conventional job search can be one of the most difficult aspects of hunting for a new position.

Support groups provide a context in which job seekers can help each other search for the right positions. These job seekers are generally at similar stages in their careers. They meet on a regular basis to exchange information, critique resumes, and conduct mock interviews. They provide the prompting and encouragement so necessary to persevere with a job search. In some cases, the support groups endure long after those jobs are found. The groups serve as a confidential forum to discuss career challenges or other professional, and sometimes personal, dilemmas.

"The Bee Gees"

An example from my own experience will underscore the value of having a vibrant support group. Mine came into being without a deliberate intention to start a support group. It is a classic illustration of the fact that your efforts to help others often result in unanticipated blessings.

In 1992, when I was the director of the professional exchange program staff at IIE, some of the young women who served as program assistants on my staff came to me and said they had few role models. Could I introduce them to other women forging successful international careers? I wanted to be helpful. We decided to have a potluck supper at my home so they could meet some of my women friends and colleagues who had fashioned fascinating careers in international affairs. There was the top woman at the Boeing Company, the head of a Japanese foundation, a Finnish Foreign Service Officer serving as a cultural attaché in Washington, a Middle East expert, the wife of a US Agency for International Development (USAID) Foreign Service officer who had to remake her career every time her husband was reassigned to a new location, and several others. I asked each to share with the younger women a thumbnail sketch of her career and two lessons she learned the hard way. It was a remarkably stimulating evening; I wish I had recorded the discussion. Everyone learned a lot, and several of the younger women on my staff were mentored by my more experienced colleagues. (The Chinese parable I refer to in chapter 4 was shared as a lesson learned by my friend who headed the Mitsubishi Foundation.)

An unexpected result of the gathering was that the professionals I had assembled as resources were captivated by each other's stories. The woman who worked at Boeing invited all of us to dinner the following month, and a tradition was born. We morphed into a support group that continues to this day. We meet monthly for dinner. Everything is off the record. We have created a safe place to process major job transitions and work-related problems. We have also celebrated a wedding and milestone birthdays and helped one or more members cope with the death of a parent, divorce, illness, and surgery. We serve as sounding boards and professional references for each other. This support group, dubbed the Bee Gees by one of our members (a reference in this case not to the musical group but meaning "the Big Girls"), has become a highly valued source of stability and support for all of us.

Look for opportunities to collaborate with others in this way. When I recently conducted a workshop on NGO leadership for a group of East Asian women taking part in the International Visitor Leadership Program, a Filipina participant described the value of her support group, "The Sacred Circle." Her group observes the same "off the record" rule as the Bee Gees. A support group can be an enduring and enormously enriching part of your life.

You Are Always "On"

Another admonition to remember is that you are always "on." You are always in the presence of potential employers, even if they are currently members of your own staff. One of the secretaries I hired years ago worked in White House personnel some years later. Had I been seeking a presidential appointment, her earlier judgments about how I treated her and her assessment of my professional abilities could have made the crucial difference in getting, or not getting, a job.

I remember the first time I was asked to serve as a reference for one of my former bosses. What a surprise! Back then I did not realize how quickly tables could turn. Someone you interview today may be called upon to judge your credentials for a position or a consultancy a few years down the road. Our lives are amazingly intertwined.

Forever at the Crossroads

We sometimes look back on a specific event—an interview or encounter—that resulted in a specific job offer. In our memory it is a kind of crossroads or pivotal moment when judgments are made and choices determined. In fact, we have many more of these crossroads moments than we realize. Let me use my own experience to illustrate this notion.

As I reflect on the process that resulted in the board of directors hiring me to lead NCIV, I was at a crossroads in my career, particularly on the day that I was interviewed by the entire board. As I looked around the room, I realized that I had known or worked with at least half of the board members present. In fact, long before that day, they had most likely drawn their conclusions about my competence and fit for the position that eventually came to mean so much to me. I was not aware of these crossroads when they occurred. Every time I interacted with one of these board members, each was making judgments about my skills and talents. Perhaps these judgments were subconscious, but they certainly played a role on the day of that fateful group interview.

Another example I refer to as "The Story of Frank." Frank was a summer intern at NCIV some years ago. I invited him to join me for a Youth Leaders International dinner. En route in my ancient Mustang, we encountered a mega traffic jam. We literally talked for more than an hour—about what Frank learned from teaching in China, his career goals, and his approach to one of his assigned projects.

I remember being so impressed with his values, ideas, and experiences. Later at the dinner, I watched him interact effectively with young people from sixteen countries. Toward the end of the summer, one of my staff announced she was leaving to get married. Guess who got the job? Yes, Frank, and probably the pivotal moment was that philosophical discussion in my car. My decision had already been made by the time of the requisite interview.

These stories are another way of illustrating the concept that you are always on and forever at the crossroads. We should also remember that plain good manners—treating everyone the way you would like to be treated—are a fundamental part of a successful career. Every day, each task you do and interaction you have is either increasing someone's confidence in your abilities or eroding it. Later on, that someone may play a major role in determining your future.

The Science of Record Keeping

I only wish that years ago some well-meaning counselor had told me how to maintain a database of the most useful connections made through networking activities, whether these individuals were encountered when I was a job seeker or as the incumbent of a particular position. If you assiduously follow this one piece of advice, it will be worth much more than the price you paid for this book. Each time you accept a business card from someone you find informative and interesting, or who is active in your field, record the details of the meeting and store them, with the contact information on the card, so they are easily retrievable.

Years ago I kept a three-ring notebook of annotated business cards and a Rolodex. Now an electronic database is essential—backed up, of course. For the exercise to be useful, you must record in each entry the date, place, and occasion of your meeting, along with a brief phrase that will help you recall the conversation or other details of your encounter. Meeting a colleague and being able to recollect an idea she expressed is ten times more valuable than just knowing you met her. It facilitates follow-up contacts and demonstrates your own intelligence and ability to listen (a sometimes underrated communication skill that is nonetheless valued by employers).

I cannot emphasize enough the value of a carefully annotated record of contacts. Too often, people collect business cards and toss them in a drawer, erroneously confident that their memories are more accurate than they later turn out to be. The quality and comprehensiveness of the contact information in your database are amazingly reliable indicators of your usefulness to an employer.

The Tyranny of Time

When you send any message requesting information or an interview, be conscious of the time the response might require. I remember (with a certain wistfulness) an era when the only methods of communication other than a meeting were the telephone, the US Postal Service, or (in some cases) telegrams. Now each day, any active professional is besieged by an alarmingly large volume of messages from a plethora of sources. On busy days I sometimes skip over messages not directly related to my daily work, musing to myself: "If this is really important, they will send it again." That is just a form of self-defense. I may be, as one of my professors once said, showing a "keen grasp of the obvious" when I offer this observation: the volume of messages we each have to field has risen astronomically, but we are stuck with only twenty-four hours in a day.

Over the years, when people have asked for my time to share career advice, I have often invited them to participate in a career roundtable so I can avoid the time-consuming, one-on-one interviews. There were a few exceptions. When a long-time friend or colleague whose cooperation I appreciated in my professional role (a board member, donor, or corporate partner) called and said, "my niece is studying international relations and she would like to meet with you," I would generally make time. Perhaps a grad student called and said, "I'm writing a paper on leadership. May I interview you about your leadership style?" Such a request was irresistible no matter how busy I was. There was a higher purpose. I was sure to learn something and it tapped my natural inclination to be helpful when someone is conducting research. If the student offered to bring cappuccino, I was hooked. That gesture told me they appreciated my time and wanted to reciprocate in some way.

Now, as an adjunct professor at the School of International Service at American University (AU), some of the papers I require are a kind of "assigned networking." For instance, for the research paper for my cultural diplomacy class, I ask my students to choose an organization that appeals to them and interview two managers there about how they measure success. I assist in scheduling the appointments as needed. This gives my students valuable networking practice and the colleagues they interview have the opportunity to reflect on the results of their work. Remember that reciprocity is at the heart of effective networking.

Mark: Do I Really Need Business Cards?

At the orientation for my grad program at AU's School of International Service, a faculty member told us to start networking and start networking now.

According to this faculty member, the most important first step for any grad student is to have business cards made. "Business cards?" I thought, "I'm here to further my education, not negotiate corporate deals or sell knives door-to-door (*as I once did for three days in a misguided attempt to make some summer money*). Why do I need business cards?"

The faculty member insisted.

"There are hundreds of events *every day* in Washington, DC. Go to them. Learn from them. But most important, network at them," he asserted. "Talk to those who are already in your field. Give them your business card. Follow up. Because when you've finished your studies and are determining the next phase of your career, it is these people who will be your most valuable resources."

I couldn't deny the logic of his point. We've all heard, "It's not what you know, it's who you know." Even though I'd just started a two-year quest to learn more of the "what," I decided I'd also make an effort to get to know the "who." I would get those business cards.

But this feeling of resolve quickly morphed into anxiety.

"Remember," he said, "you should try to attend a networking event every day. Only 25 percent of your graduate learning will come in the classroom; the other 75 percent will come from out there." He made a dramatic and expansive gesture, presumably indicating a place "out there," a place I had the growing feeling I had no idea how to find.

Could this have been right? Could I possibly be expected to attend one event *per day*? How could I manage this with a full grad studies workload? How could I even find one event per day I wanted to attend? I left the orientation dismayed and wondering what to do next.

Looking back, I think my alarm stemmed from a combination of two factors: exaggeration on the part of that faculty member, as well as my newness to the art of networking. I've since learned that while it's *possible* to attend one networking event per day (especially in event-saturated DC), it's certainly not practical. I've also learned that the first image many people envision when confronted with the term "networking"—shaking hands at receptions—is misleading. Successful networking is about much more.

Know Yourself before Networking

When I first moved to Washington, I did in fact attend a good number of networking events. I did not enjoy them. I handed out a few business cards from time to time (yes, I had them printed) but rarely followed up. Often I left an event without talking to anyone. I felt guilty. It made me question the purpose of networking. Why didn't I get more out of these events? Why couldn't I muster the courage to talk to anyone? Should I feel guilty because meeting people in a room full of strangers is not my forte? How is networking best accomplished? What purpose does it really serve, personally and professionally? Does one network simply to gain something? To secure an internship, a job, or a recommendation? Or are there other reasons to network? Is it an inherently selfish enterprise?

I've realized that I simply don't like networking events, at least ones where the primary purpose is to meet as many people as possible. To some, this kind of networking comes naturally. These extroverts walk into a room full of strangers and happily anticipate meeting colleagues and making new connections. Shake enough hands and who knows what might come your way.

For me, however, networking events are a struggle. I'm an outgoing person, but I'm reluctant to approach people I don't know. If I attend an event with a group of colleagues, I'll talk mostly to them. If I'm by myself, you might find me near the bar or slowly circling the room to avoid the embarrassment of standing alone. For better or for worse, this is me. Once I realized this, I stopped attending events altogether.

Yet, after a bit of time, I realized that just because going to networking events was not a favorite pastime, this didn't mean I should abandon them. Rather, I needed to be more discerning about the events I attended.

I liken it to being invited to a party. If I don't know anything about the person throwing the party, I probably won't go. If I know the host and have friends or interests in common with him, however, I'm more likely to attend and have a good time. The same holds true with networking events. I disliked going to those events that didn't appeal to my interests. But I did begin to appreciate events that piqued my professional curiosity and where I found people with similar interests. A specific example is the day I met Sherry.

I was in my first semester at AU, and Sherry, an alumna, came to give a talk on international exchange and citizen diplomacy. I'd recently discovered the work of the organization she headed, NCIV, and was interested in pursuing an internship there. I figured that by attending this event I could learn more about the internship. I had a specific interest in Sherry's work at NCIV. I also had a goal. These things made all the difference.

At Sherry's talk I was engaged. I took notes. I asked questions. Afterward I was compelled to hand Sherry my business card and ask about the internship. None of this felt forced; it flowed easily. When I eventually visited NCIV's offices for an interview, I again talked to Sherry. After my internship I kept in touch with her, occasionally e-mailing to stay on her radar: for help on a research project, to pass along an interesting article, or for advice on my job search. Eventually, just after I'd graduated, Sherry called. She knew I was looking for a position; she had a job opening at NCIV and thought it might be a good fit. She invited me to come for an interview. Soon after, I began a rewarding two-year stint at NCIV, my first "real" job out of school.

It's true that my networking encounter with Sherry was uncommonly successful. It led to both an internship and a job. Most meetings do not yield such tangible results. Certainly other factors influenced my ability to secure these positions as well: education, experience, timing, luck. But the point is this: When it comes to the art of networking, learn to recognize your own skills and comfort levels. If you're a person who enjoys working a room and introducing yourself to new people, by all means do that. But if you don't relish schmoozing, don't feel guilty or despair that you'll never find a job. Instead, choose the events you attend strategically—and consider other forms of proactive networking, such as the informational interview.

The Informational Interview

In the five-plus years since the first edition of *Working World* was published, I have remained convinced that networking is done best when it's unforced and we stay open to unanticipated connections. But I've also come to appreciate that proactivity in networking is essential. And, in my view, the most effective way to network proactively is through informational interviews.

When I was in college and wondering what to do with myself, I wish somebody had told me about informational interviews. I wish that professor had skipped the business card lecture and instead told us to set up interviews. As I approach midcareer territory, I frequently field requests from younger professionals who want to learn more about the work we

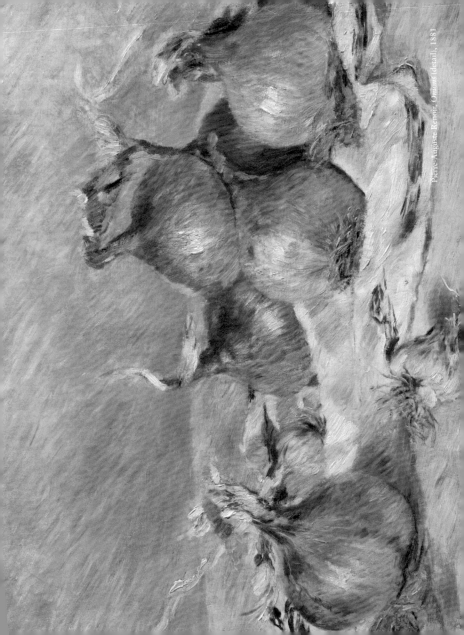

LUNDER CENTER AT STONE HILL

Opened in 2008 and designed by Tadao Ando, the Lunder Center at Stone Hill houses two sunlit galleries for special exhibitions, as well as the Williamstown Art Conservation Center, the largest regional conservation center in the country.

GALLERIES

GALLERIES

HUNTER STUDIO

WILLIAMSTOWN ART CONSERVATION CENTER

The Lunder Center at Stone Hill can be accessed by Stone Hill Drive, shuttle, or the walking paths that begin near the Manton Research Center and the reflecting pool.

RAW COLOR:
THE CIRCLES OF DAVID SMITH
July 4–October 19, 2014

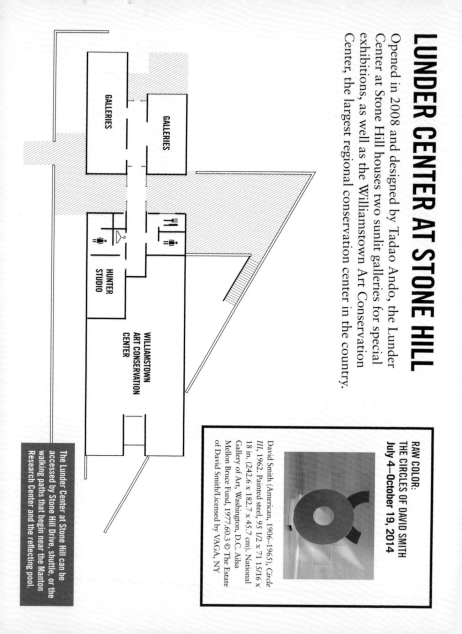

David Smith (American, 1906–1965), *Circle III*, 1962. Painted steel, 95 1/2 x 71 15/16 x 18 in. (242.6 x 182.7 x 45.7 cm), National Gallery of Art, Washington, D.C. Ailsa Mellon Bruce Fund, 1977.60.3 © The Estate of David Smith/Licensed by VAGA, NY

do at the Alliance for International Educational and Cultural Exchange (see chapter 6 for more information). The Alliance has a small staff, so it's unlikely we'll have a position opening or that an informational interview with me will lead to a job with us. We do have, however, a large membership of international exchange organizations, so I can answer questions about these organizations and introduce people to useful contacts.

Informational interviews can seem slow and frustrating, especially when you need a job, like, right now. But this is the most effective way for getting a personal, inside view of organizations and positions you might like to have. It also helps you "make your friends before you need them." There may not be a position open at a particular organization when you meet with someone there. But you've now established a relationship with that person, and when a position does become open—weeks or months down the road—you have that relationship to tap for assistance.

Just as networking is an art, so is effectively requesting and conducting informational interviews. Key points to remember include:

1. Informational interviews are best pursued through already established connections (i.e., asking someone you already know to make an introduction), but it's absolutely appropriate to approach someone you've never met, provided . . .
2. . . . you are respectful of their time. I believe that the majority of professionals in these fields are willing to help. However, you must, from the start, show respect for their time, always keeping in mind that . . .
3. . . . it's a process. Informational interviews are *not* about getting a job; they're about laying the groundwork that will enable you to move forward and eventually get a job.

REQUESTING THE INTERVIEW

Identify professionals doing interesting jobs at organizations you admire and where you might like to work. Don't choose the president or CEO; rather, target someone at a level closer to the positions you're seeking. These people are more likely to have time to meet with you; you'll also learn information more relevant to your own job search.

Once you've identified your targets, determine how to approach them. If you have a friend or contact in common, ask that person to introduce you.

Also consider asking your contacts to suggest other good prospects that were not on your original shortlist.

If you don't have a personal connection, then send a short e-mail (or LinkedIn message) to the target, briefly introducing yourself and explaining why you're reaching out. For example, note that you are a current student of international affairs and interested in pursuing a career in international education. Request a fifteen- to twenty-minute informational interview. Note that you'd like to hear about the target's work and organization, and ask a few career-related questions. Make this initial communication simple. It should require only a brief response. Follow up a week or two later, if necessary. No response does not necessarily indicate a lack of interest—it often means that the interview target is busy and your e-mail has slipped down in her inbox. A short and respectful follow-up is useful, as it bumps your request to the top of the pile.

REMAIN RESPECTFUL

Do your interviews in person, if possible; if not, then by phone. While e-mail is typically the best way to make your initial outreach, meeting in person for the actual interview is preferable for two reasons. First, it allows for a more personal connection. Second, it's easier for the person being interviewed. A fifteen-minute conversation doesn't require much prep. Writing nuanced insights in an e-mail, on the other hand, can take far longer—and can be far less appealing to someone who spends much of the day composing e-mails already. I recall receiving an e-mail from an informational interview seeker I didn't know. After a brief introduction, this person let loose with fifteen detailed career questions. He asked me to respond "within two weeks." I was incredulous and irked. I hit delete.

Be cognizant of time during your interview. If you promised you'd keep it to fifteen minutes, do your best to adhere to that limit. Also, be prepared. Come armed with a few questions you'd like to ask and one or two simple requests (i.e., "Can you suggest colleagues at two or three other organizations I should meet?"). I remember a recent informational interview where the job seeker had nothing prepared and seemingly nothing to talk about. I was left wondering why I'd bothered to interrupt my day. Make your informational interviews worthwhile for everyone involved.

REMEMBER, IT'S A PROCESS

I'll reiterate that an informational interview is not, in and of itself, about getting a job. It's about laying a foundation. It's about gathering information, making contacts, and widening your circle. A grad student once approached me for an informational interview and handled it all wrong. He focused the entire conversation on internship and job openings at the Alliance. Even after I told him that we had no openings and, because we're a small shop, were unlikely to have any soon, he continued in that vein. He was not interested in me, but only in what I might do for him. It was awkward and ineffective.

Informational interviewing is a process. When done patiently and strategically (with a requisite flexibility that allows unexpected connections to flourish), it is the best tactic for proactive networking.

The Promise and Perils of Social Media

Reflecting on the art of networking, Ambassador Kenton Keith jokingly paraphrased Woody Allen, saying, "Success is 99% showing up." The rise of social media has called into question exactly what "showing up" now means for networking. If you've only connected with someone via electronic means (like a LinkedIn request to someone you've never met), have you actually "shown up"? Have you actually cultivated a personal bond that will be helpful in your career contemplation and job search?

On these points I agree with Karl Dedolph, who told us in his profile interview:

> Social media is a certain form of networking, but to me, you network in person. You might set up a networking opportunity virtually, but if success is based on relationships, the only effective way to have relationships is in person. And that's a piece of advice that I give to people in any kind of work. If the opportunity is there to do it in person, then you do it in person.

Social media platforms have created beneficial ways for us to find potential informational interview targets, to reconnect with college classmates, or to stay in touch with former coworkers. But virtual connections can't—and shouldn't—take the place of personal ones. It's not enough to gain a connection on LinkedIn, a friend on Facebook, or a follower on Twitter. When this is the extent of your tie to this person, your network has grown in number only.

Remember that all social media presence now has professional implications. You're creating a perception of who you are via your social media channels. Make sure what you're projecting is consistent with who you are, what you believe, and the perception you want to convey (see chapter 4 for further discussion on the importance of perception).

While the misuse of social media can definitely damage your career, its constructive use has potentially powerful benefits. As Menchu Mendiola-Fernandez, the vice president of communications at The Washington Center for Internships and Academic Seminars (see chapter 7), told us:

> You also want to use social media to help you, and you can do this in a number of ways, including creating a brand for yourself. Your connections will see your updates, or your tweets, or your blog posts, and this can show that you care about what you are doing.

Posting, tweeting, and blogging on issues you're passionate about—and using social media to highlight this activity—can, as Mendiola-Fernandez said, "give people the perception that you are serious and professional." But be consistent and have a plan. Intentionality in your social media use can turn it from a diversion, distraction, and potential downfall to a powerful networking tool.

Every Day, in Your Own Skin, You're Networking

Despite my affinity for informational interviews and social media, I still believe networking can't be forced. Like informational interviews, networking is not, in and of itself, about getting a job. While a job, an internship, or some other career-propelling benefit may come out of networking, we have to understand that networking is not predictable. It's building a platform; it's not a lock-step formula:

> *Going to this event + meeting that person + applying for a job + sending a thank-you note* = **CAREER SECURITY.**

It rarely works this way.

If we view networking not as a grim necessity but as organically developing a web of reciprocal relationships, then we realize that we're networking all the time. Paul Binkley, former director of career development services at the George Washington University School of Public Policy and Public Administration and now an independent education consultant working in West Africa, phrased it in this way: "Every day you walk around in your own skin, you're networking." Every time we meet someone and a conversation ensues based on mutual interest, we're networking. Every occasion we meet a friend of a friend and talk about our interests or jobs, we're networking. Every day we do our work to the best of our abilities, we're networking.

Networking is an ongoing process with no end point. Larry Bacow, the president emeritus of Tufts University, told us that you have to take responsibility for your career, which includes being proactive and learning to "recognize opportunity when it walks up and hits you in the face." But as Dr. Bacow was also quick to point out, careers are often "a series of fortuitous accidents." You can't possibly map your entire career. Nor can you plan how your network will develop. Instead, let it develop organically, naturally, with genuine interest as a guiding principle.

"Get to know people for who they are," Belinda Chiu told us in her profile interview. "Some people you meet shut down when they think you can't help them now. You can tell when people turn off."

Malcolm Butler, former president and CEO of Partners of the Americas, put it another way: "There are a lot of relationships that are valuable to establish even if you don't know why at the moment. You don't have to have an agenda at any given point when establishing a relationship."

I take all of these points to heart. I never could have anticipated that getting to know Sherry would lead in the directions it has—namely, her invitation to coauthor this book. Also, I could not have known that when I first met Michael McCarry (my current boss), our relationship—based on a shared alma mater and similar interests, appreciation of humor, and compatible working styles—would lead to a job at the Alliance five years later.

As Sherry says, we're forever at the crossroads, forever in the position to take our careers in unexpected directions. We have to remain open to establishing the relationships that may take us in those directions, even if, at the moment, we've no way of knowing our exact destination.

CHAPTER 3

The Value of Mentors

Introduction

Several stories regarding the origins of the word *mentor* exist. The two most common have elements familiar to many people:

1. In Greek mythology, when Odysseus left to fight in the Trojan War, he entrusted his son Telemachus to his friend and adviser, Mentor. In looking after Telemachus in Odysseus's absence, Mentor's duties required that he be a role model, a father figure, an adviser, a guardian, a counselor, and an encourager; in other words, a mentor.

2. In 1689, the French writer Francois Fénelon was appointed royal tutor to Louis XIV's grandson, the Duke of Burgundy. In 1699, Fénelon wrote his most famous work, *Les Adventures de Telemaque*, which was both a continuation of the story of *The Odyssey* and a thinly veiled attack on the absolutism of Louis XIV. Using *Les Adventures de Telemaque*, with its main character named Mentor, as a primary text, Fénelon "mentored" his young pupil to grow up to become a just and fair ruler, unlike his grandfather.

   A third tale regarding the origins of the word, perhaps more farfetched, is certainly intriguing:

3. "*La Grotte de Niaux* is a prehistoric cave located high in the Pyrenees in southern France. After walking through silent and womb-like stillness, a visitor emerges into a large, domed space filled with paintings estimated to have been created somewhere between 12,000 and 9,000 BC. While most of the paintings depict horses and bison, there is one theme that is repeated in many

places. These paintings show a group of men taking children to what, at that time, was considered the edge or end of their physical world. The men exhort the children to be brave and expand their reach beyond the borders of the present world. Some believe that the origin of the term 'mentor' comes from what has been loosely translated in these ancient depictions as 'men' taking children on a 'tour.'"[1]

Regardless of the origins of the term, the concept of having a mentor to aid in successful career development has widespread acceptance. Professionals of all ages can benefit from the guidance of a more experienced, and often older, colleague who can provide advice, contacts, and encouragement throughout a career's progression. The way mentors are identified, utilized, and generally viewed, however, can certainly differ from person to person, from culture to culture, and from generation to generation.

Sherry is explicit in her use of the term *mentor* and in her view of the mentor–protégé relationship. She speaks often and reverently of her mentor, illustrates how she actively looks for opportunities to mentor her younger colleagues, and encourages young professionals to seek out a colleague or another professional to serve as a mentor.

Mark, on the other hand, is far more reticent about the term *mentor* and its implied relationship. In the early stages of his career, he had no one whom he called his mentor, nor had he ever actively sought one out. Yet he also realizes that, while he may not typically use the term or view the mentor–protégé relationship in the same manner Sherry perceives it, he has benefited a great deal throughout his career from friends and other professionals around him who have played this guiding role.

Sherry: Identifying Your Mentor

Mentors appear in our lives in various guises and at various times. In some cases, these nurturing relationships are literally lifelong. For example, I learned so much from my loving, disciplined, and congenial parents, who always insisted that I work hard and do my best. In other cases, mentoring may be limited to a particular period or the duration of a project. Some of us are particularly blessed (and this has been true for me) so that mentors seem to be a built-in part of our lives. The relationship may have evolved with no conscious effort on our part, and we may not realize how much we rely on this person's wise counsel, willingness to serve as a sounding board, and the lessons shared from his or her own career. Others consciously seek out mentors and deliberately tap into their expertise and guidance.

Whatever the case for you, having at least one mentor is critical to professional growth and development. Each of us needs a relationship with a respected, experienced colleague to help us spot pitfalls and encourage us to take on new challenges. A mentor is a person who believes in your talents and skills, who offers suggestions to strengthen them, and who has a way of helping you transform obstacles into opportunities. Your mentor must be someone with integrity, whose professional accomplishments and personal traits you admire and wish to emulate. Look around. Who fits that description for you? How can you become better acquainted with a potential mentor?

In a 2002 commencement speech at Dartmouth College, television icon Mr. Rogers asked the graduates some fundamental questions:

> Well, what is essential about you? And who are those who have helped you become the person that you are? Anyone who has ever graduated from college, anyone who has been able to sustain good work, has had at least one person and often many who have believed in him or her. We just don't get to be competent human beings without a lot of different investments from others.

He then told the graduates he was giving them an invisible gift—"a silent moment to think about those who helped you become who are you today." We should accept Mr. Rogers's gift—not just at graduation but frequently throughout our lives.

The following are a few examples from my own life—although I still expect that I will find myself mentored by new people in the years ahead. Already there are two professors at the School of International Service (SIS) at American University who are generous with their time and suggestions now that I am once again teaching. Our need for encouragement, new perspectives, and wise counsel never goes away, no matter what our age or career stage.

Sometimes it is only in retrospect that we realize we have been mentored by someone and that we view that person as a significant role model. To illustrate, I point to Vi Wellik, who owned and operated the Flying E Ranch for many years. My parents first took me to vacation at the Flying E, a guest ranch in Wickenburg, Arizona, in 1964. Friends and I still spend a week there each March. During these memorable ranch visits, each night at dinner Vi would ask new guests to say a few words about themselves and bid farewell to those guests who were departing the next day. I was relatively young as I first watched her and admired her extraordinary ability to make each person feel special and connected to the ranch. It was only about fifteen years ago as I was hosting a National Council for International Visitors (NCIV) dinner at my home that I realized I had been modeling myself after Vi for years. At that dinner, like many others, we followed a tradition referred to as "The Circle." Early during any party that I host in my professional role, I invite my guests to form a circle. After I offer a few words of welcome, each person identifies himself or herself and states his or her connection to the group. This tradition has enabled my friends and associates to make unforeseen connections and never fails to enrich the evening's conversations.

Fortunately, I realized what a powerful role model Vi had been for me and was able to thank her, both in person and in writing, before she died in 2004. To be able to observe, learn from, and acknowledge a mentor's contribution to your own life is enormously rewarding.

My primary professional mentor was Dr. William C. Olson. Bill died in 2012, and I was privileged to give a eulogy at both memorial services that celebrated his remarkable life. I first met Bill in the late 1970s when he became the dean of SIS, my undergraduate alma mater. Early on he recognized the need to establish an alumni association for SIS, and I was one of the alumni he recruited to help. Ultimately, I became the founding president of the association. In the process of working together, my relationship with Bill evolved in amazing ways.

I cannot remember exactly when I first referred to Bill as my mentor, but we explicitly recognized our mentor–protégé relationship for decades. In fact, Bill was a quintessential mentor to me—always encouraging me to stretch and grow, always providing significant opportunities to do so. He would pose questions that prompted and shaped my aspirations. One day he asked, "Would you like to be a member of the Cosmos Club?" Thanks to Bill's efforts in shepherding my nomination through the admissions committee, I was elected to membership in this revered Washington institution in 1991 and have enjoyed the benefits of membership ever since.

Bill invited me to teach a course at SIS as an adjunct professor. That led to my pioneering the first course on public diplomacy ever given at SIS. I taught that course throughout the 1980s—and learned an immense amount in the process. Although increased professional travel precluded my continuing to teach in the 1990s, that experience gave me invaluable background to return to the classroom after I stepped down as president of NCIV in 2011. In a fundamental way, Bill is responsible for my first "encore career" choice.

Another time, Bill said, "I'm putting out a new edition of my book. Would you like to have a chapter in it?" This allowed me to add another publication to my resume, while broadening my experience and exposure. Some years later, he queried, "What boards would you like to be on?" My first choice was the World Learning board, because participating in an Experiment in International Living program (EIL)—a World Learning program—had changed my life. Thanks in large part to Bill's support, I was elected to that board in 1999 and served in that capacity for twelve years. Serving on World Learning committees remains one of my favorite volunteer activities.

Over the years Bill served as a reference, made editorial suggestions for publications I wrote, and closely followed and encouraged me in my career. (He even donated to NCIV and read our newsletter, often commenting to me on various articles.) I asked him for advice on topics ranging from personnel problems to evaluating major professional opportunities. Always, I knew that I could count on his thoughtful analysis, broad knowledge, and carefully considered counsel. What an extraordinary gift!

In April 2007, the School of International Service presented me with their Alumna of the Year Award at a wonderful event held at the German Embassy in Washington. The venue was perfect because my first EIL program had included an extended homestay in Bad Godesberg, Germany. Of all the words of congratulations offered that night, it was Bill Olson's tribute that meant the most to me. This was because he knew every dimension of my career—and had helped me through the inevitable rough spots.

There was no way I could ever repay Bill. The only alternative is to do what many other professionals feel obligated to do—pay it forward. It was Bill's marvelous example and generosity that prompted me to invite Mark to coauthor this book. During our collaboration, Mark has learned much from me, and I have learned an enormous amount from him as well. The best mentoring relationships result when reciprocity is present—both parties are innately curious and want to learn from each other's unique vantage point.

Mentors are a valuable source of guidance and continuity. Over time, almost every career inevitably involves immense changes— sometimes sought after, and other times sudden and unexpected. The stability a good mentor provides is invaluable during these times of transition. Usually, mentoring relationships evolve from shared interests or participation in a project, much as my relationship with Bill grew out of our efforts to establish an alumni association. Sometimes, though, individuals actively seek out mentors. You should not be shy about asking someone to be your mentor. At a minimum, you will be paying a compliment to an admired associate. When your request meets with an affirmative response, you will have gained valuable help in making informed career choices.

When asking someone to serve as your mentor, be sure to explain your expectations and leave your prospective mentor with a graceful way to decline, in case he or she feels unable to meet those expectations. You might ask, "Would you be willing to have coffee with me once a month? I'm in the midst of making a career change, and I want to make carefully considered decisions. I realize that you have a busy schedule and might not be able to do this right now, but I want you to know how much I would appreciate your advice at this point in my career. If you're willing, I'll be pleased to buy the cappuccino."

Serving as a Mentor

Having been blessed with remarkable mentors and role models, I make an effort to be an active mentor to younger colleagues. I heartily concur with Larry Bacow, president emeritus of Tufts University, when he told us that the best way to pay back those who have mentored you is to "continue the tradition." At this stage in my career, it is a great joy to share some of the lessons I have learned the hard way and to encourage and enable my colleagues to pursue their professional development.

In fact, I consider being a mentor to others a professional imperative. At NCIV, whenever I attended events of any kind, I always asked if I could bring a guest. Then I made it a point to take a young person with me. I believe one of the reasons NCIV attracted such outstanding interns is that we had a reputation for getting them out of the office and being truly committed to their professional development. For example, when I was invited to speak at the Foreign Service Institute, I immediately asked permission to bring our summer intern as an observer. Not only did she have the chance to visit the campus of the National Foreign Affairs Training Center and witness a training session, but we also had time on the way there and when returning to talk about her tasks at NCIV, her career aspirations, and broader issues. All of us who are lucky enough to hold senior positions have an obligation to nurture and help develop the next generation.

Mark: The Seinfeldian View of Mentors

There's an episode of the classic sitcom *Seinfeld* in which a woman Jerry is dating, Abby, talks constantly about her mentor: the impact her mentor has had on her life and career; the advice her mentor has given her; her mentor's favorite restaurants, movies, and books. Jerry's bald and neurotic friend George Costanza can't quite get his mind around this concept of a "mentor":

> *George:*   I still don't understand this. Abby has a mentor?
> *Jerry:*   Yes. And the mentor advises the protégé.
> *George:*   Is there any money involved?
> *Jerry:*   No.
> *George:*   So what's in it for the mentor?
> *Jerry:*   Respect, admiration, prestige.
> *George:*   Pssh. Would the protégé pick up stuff for the mentor?
> *Jerry:*   I suppose if it was on the protégé's way to the mentor, they might.
> *George:*   Laundry? Dry cleaning?
> *Jerry:*   She's not a valet, she's a protégé.[2]

Much like George, I've struggled with the concept of a mentor. True, it's a common term, but not one that held meaning for me growing up, at least in a specific, personal sense. My parents never spoke of having mentors. No one ever encouraged me to seek out a mentor. I never had someone in my life that I consciously referred to as "my mentor."

Sherry, on the other hand, is very comfortable with the term. She speaks often of her mentor, Bill Olson, and she referred to herself as his protégé. They maintained a mentor–protégé relationship for more than thirty years. She openly searches for ways to be a mentor to young people around her.

So why the divergent perspectives? If I've never specifically looked for a mentor, does that mean I don't have one? Do I even need one? Or is it a concept that burned out before it reached my generation? Have mentors become irrelevant in a fast-paced, technology-dependent, and globalized world?

Attempting to answer these questions, I find it helpful to examine the characterization of the younger generation (broadly defined) as the "on-demand generation" (to borrow the term used by Arjun Desai, a Rotary Ambassadorial Scholar to Singapore and now an anesthesia chief resident at Stanford University School of Medicine). Younger people have come of age at a time when everything is at our fingertips. News, information, communication—it all happens in an instant. This sense of the urgent, of instant gratification, has permeated the professional arena. We want to do everything, and we want to do it now. We're confident and can-do. We're ready to perform the most demanding work possible and take on all challengers. This is not meant to imply that professionals of older generations don't want to perform challenging work or succeed in their careers—people of all generations are striving for success. But it's the on-demand generation who can't seem to wait for it. Sure, we might realize that we have a few things to learn, but there's no reason to pause and learn these *before* jumping into a position. Forget about paying our dues; we want to do it here, we want to do it now. Anything we need to learn, we'll just figure it out along the way.

Because of this mentality, we might be more inclined to view those who are older and more experienced simply as colleagues rather than mentors. Perhaps admitting that we have much to learn somehow diminishes our proven abilities and hard work. It stunts our movement, and the on-demand generation needs constant movement.

The irony is twofold. First, younger generations desperately need mentors to rid us of the notion that we don't need mentors (got that?). That is, we need mentors to help us slow down and realize that, in fact, we *don't* know everything, we *do* have much to learn, and it's okay to take the time to learn it. In fact, it will help us achieve all that we want to achieve.

Second, if there is one thing that mentors can do for their younger colleagues, it's to help them create movement in their careers, to help them grow. No matter how experienced, skilled, or confident a young student or professional may be, he or she will always benefit from the wisdom and experience of a colleague or friend.

So if I'm suggesting that the concept of mentors is *not* dead and that younger generations have a clear need for them, then why the discrepancy? Why does Sherry have someone who served as her mentor for a third of a century while I've scarcely used the term? In the end, I think the difference is both personal and generational.

There's the issue of terminology. Something about the concept of a mentor taking the protégé under her wing doesn't resonate with me. It feels dated, conjuring images of a stiffly formal relationship filled with protocol, rules, and expectations. Yet Sherry is quite comfortable with the term and image. I might refer to those who have helped me along the way with monikers like "friend" or "favorite professor" or "great guy," while Sherry prefers the term "mentor." One is not necessarily more accurate than the other. It boils down to your preference—a preference determined by personality or generation, or a little bit of both.

Just because I haven't approached things in the same manner as Sherry, however, doesn't mean that I haven't benefited from mentors in my life. Upon reflection it is clear (even obvious) that I *have* benefited from the advice, guidance, and counsel of various mentors, even though I have never consciously used that term. In fact, most young people have probably sought out a mentor or have mentors that are important in their lives. You may not call them mentors, but they play that role.

As an undergrad at the University of Notre Dame, I became close to the director of my study abroad program in Angers, France, Paul McDowell. Though I viewed P McD (as we called him) simply as a teacher and a friend, I now realize that he's a mentor. He has helped me greatly with my postcollege decisions and direction and continues to provide guidance, counsel, and friendship. In grad school I found myself repeatedly sitting in the office of my favorite professor, Christine Chin. Again, I viewed her as a friend and colleague more than anything else. Typically, I had a class-related question. More often than not, though, we ended up talking informally and frankly about my interests and possible career plans. While I would never have called her a mentor, in hindsight that's exactly the role she was playing. I was looking for someone to talk to, someone with experience and insight, someone with whom I felt comfortable sharing on a personal level—basic qualities of a mentor.

Sherry acted as an invaluable mentor to me during my time at NCIV and has continued in that role as I've progressed in my professional life. She has not only taught me more on the job than I can possibly relate, but she's also been extremely generous in recognizing my interests and abilities and providing me with opportunities to further them. My presence as a coauthor of this book is a primary example. My boss Michael McCarry has also been an invaluable professional mentor during my time at the Alliance. The tremendous growth I've experienced as a professional in my current position is in so many ways due to his advice, insight, and example.

I realize that my dad has always been a mentor, especially as I've progressed in my career. In times of deep career contemplation, he's always been there to act as a sounding board, to answer questions, and sometimes to be the devil's advocate. True, his idea of advice can be frustrating (I point specifically to the times during my job search when he asked me if I had a résumé and planned to wear a suit to an interview). But his experience—and, more importantly, his love—has always provided me with direction and stability that I sorely need and appreciate even more as time passes.

Mentors can come from all spheres of life: personal, professional, academic. A mentor can even be someone you've never met. In that same episode of *Seinfeld*, when first talking to Jerry about her mentor, Abby asks him if he has such a person in his own life:

> *Abby:* My mentor suggested that I move into equities, the best move I ever made.
>
> *Jerry:* Mentor? You mean your boss.
>
> *Abby:* Oh, no, no, no, Cynthia's just a successful businesswoman who's taken me under her wing.
>
> *Jerry:* Hmm. So Cynthia's your mentor.
>
> *Abby:* And I'm her protégé. You must have someone like that. You know, who guides you in your career path.
>
> *Jerry:* Well, I like Gabe Kaplan.

Jerry is being tongue-in-cheek when he mentions his affinity for Kaplan, an American comedian successful in the 1970s. This is a professional whom Jerry admires from afar but doesn't know personally. Even so, perhaps Kaplan *was* something of a mentor to Jerry as the latter developed his own career in comedy. While many people have mentors with whom they maintain a personal relationship, others, such as Charlie MacCormack, former president and CEO of both Save the Children and World Learning (see chapter 9 for more on both organizations), have found mentors in those they admire but never met: "I think it is essential that we get help and support from others more experienced than we are, and I think we can get that through direct advice, as well as through watching from a distance,"

MacCormack told us. "I think there are, therefore, people you see at a long distance that become indirect mentors. Certainly in my formative years, President Kennedy was one, and Martin Luther King Jr. was another, and Nelson Mandela has taken on that kind of role in past decades."

To some, people who have affected their lives, whether personally or from a distance, are called role models. Jennifer Clinton touches on this idea in her profile, saying, "You want to find people that demonstrate the kind of values that you have and the way you want to interact with people." Perhaps you might refer to them as "my colleague" or "my favorite professor" or "a great person" or "my friend." Regardless of the designation, they are still mentors and play a crucial role in your career development.

Serving as a Mentor

Sherry is conscious of being a mentor to young professionals. It is her way of continuing the tradition, of giving back for the help she received from her own mentors. When coauthoring the first edition of *Working World*, I questioned whether I was at a career stage where I could serve as a useful mentor. I wasn't sure at what age or point in my career the switch might flip and I could serve as a mentor. But I was sure that my need for mentorship far outweighed my ability to provide it.

Still, I did recognize that I'd been able to help a peer handle a situation because I'd recently experienced similar circumstances. I never saw myself as mentoring, but I believe I was at least being helpful by sharing my own trials and errors.

For example, when I was working at NCIV, a young woman named Michelline Granjean e-mailed me asking for help with her job search. Michelline and I didn't know each other, but she was finishing her master's in the same program I'd recently completed, and working for the same professor that I had. Because of these commonalities, and because Michelline was hoping to start a career in international education/exchange, she thought I would be a good resource. She asked for an informational interview (read more on this important networking tactic in chapter 2).

I really didn't know how I could help. I was barely two years into my own career—what did I know about helping other people get jobs? Getting one for myself had been tough enough. But I realized that *this* was exactly how I could help. I'd just been in Michelline's exact situation. I reflected on the difficulties I'd run into in my job search, the strategies I'd found most successful, and the job search resources I'd used most effectively (all of which are included in part II). It was this information that I passed along to Michelline. When she began to apply for specific jobs, I used my contacts to try my best to get her resume on top of the pile. It wasn't much, but others had done the same for me. It was the least I could do.

And then, a few years later, the switch flipped. I found myself in the curious position of being referred to by the exact term I'd always found so anachronistic. I volunteered for alumni mentor programs, first at American University, then at Notre Dame. I was assigned "mentees," undergrads with an interest in international affairs. I still worried whether I was cut out to be a mentor, whether I had enough experience in my own career to be useful to someone else. But in my interactions with my talented and passionate mentees, I found myself doing just what I had done for Michelline: passing along advice based on my own experiences, recommending job search resources, helping expand their networks, and acting as a sounding board. I was also surprised, but ultimately gratified, to see that the mentors in these programs were of all ages: from recent graduates to midcareer professionals to experienced career veterans. I realized that age doesn't necessarily matter in mentoring—nor does the terminology you use. Even if I didn't see myself as a mentor, I was still continuing the tradition.

Notes

1. From the October 22, 2004, issue of *The Mentor News* (available at www.mentors.ca/thementornews13.html).
2. From *Seinfeld* episode no. 140, "The Fatigues"; original broadcast date October 31, 1996.

CHAPTER 4

The Continuous Journey

Like Alice, most of us think we want to go "somewhere," and it takes some experience to learn that, in life, there is no "somewhere." There is only the road to "somewhere," and we are always on the way.

—David Campbell, *If You Don't Know Where You're Going, You'll Probably End Up Somewhere Else*

Introduction

Many of us have a tendency to think about career development in terms of conclusions—what we're going to do once we're finished. We consider our career paths, and our lives, in terms such as these: "Once I've finished my degree . . ." or "Once I've completed my exchange program . . ." or "Once I've accumulated five (or ten or fifteen) years of experience . . ." Yet we rarely reflect on the fact that we're never quite finished with anything. We may complete certain building blocks of our careers (such as a degree, an experience abroad, or a particular job), but, in a way, we never really "make it." Our career journeys are never over. As Larry Bacow, president emeritus of Tufts University, phrased it, "The only time that you can *really* describe your career is on the day you retire. Up until then, you're just making plans." And even when you retire, the opportunities for a postretirement or encore career are abundant, and sometimes financially necessary.

We are often inclined to view a job search as a series of activities that cease once a job is found. On the contrary, it is just as important to devote time to these strategic job search activities—defining your cause, networking, learning from mentors—once you have a job. If you consider your career a continuous journey of finding new and better ways to serve your cause, it is easier to understand why such activities must continue.

We have emphasized the importance of identifying your cause. But this is not a static activity. Causes do change. For instance, the first cause you identify—easing the adaptation process to a US university for international students as a foreign student adviser, or conducting training on health system management in Uganda as a young development professional—may evolve. Later you may be expanding the international dimension of a community college as its president or promoting best practices in health care as the communications manager at an international development organization. Whatever cause you embrace, and whatever accompanying aspirations are generated, a consistent way to think about your career will serve you well in your immediate job search and on your continuous journey.

In our respective sections in this chapter, we tackle the idea of the continuous journey in similar ways. Simply because a certain career activity has come to a close—because that building block has been laid and prompted you to make your next career choice—does not mean discernment can be suspended. Causes shift. Needs change. Maintaining a consistent way of thinking about your career will help you to deal with these inevitable transitions.

We also address the issue of professionalism. Our opinions about the details of professional behavior and what it means to act professionally often diverge—the issue of a professional dress code is one that we've had fun debating, and consensus still eludes us! Ultimately, we both agree that consciously honing certain professional habits is an inextricable part of your continuous journey.

Sherry: An Evolving Approach

It was in the midst of writing and compiling my first career book in the late 1990s when I realized that I had developed a structured way of thinking about careers in the fields of international education, exchange, and development. Furthermore, it was a constructive approach one could readily apply to a career in most any field. After facilitating many career roundtables, speaking on various career panels at NAFSA: Association of International Educators conferences and at local universities, and interacting with hundreds of job seekers over the years, there were distinct patterns and consistencies in the career advice I shared. When Mark and I met regularly to discuss the book and engage in the stimulating process of collaboration—volleying ideas back and forth—I realized that this deliberate way of thinking about careers had evolved even more in the intervening years as I accumulated more experience as a manager and leader of a nationwide network. Now back in the classroom, interacting with young people as they are starting their continuous journeys, I have become even more aware of my own preferences and predilections. I've given a lot of thought to what constitutes a viable career path and how to make decisions that lead to finding the best ways to embrace your cause.

In this chapter I share with you my approach to the continuous career journey. I do this not because I expect you to adopt it as your own but because I hope it will be catalytic and encourage you to consider your own career in a thoughtful, more philosophical way.

Career Choices as Building Blocks

I always encourage people to adopt a building block approach to their careers. This is the simple idea that early choices—interning with your member of Congress or serving as a resident adviser in your college dorm—are the foundation for later choices. Those early choices should be solid learning experiences that will not only appeal to a wide range of potential employers but will also serve you well as your career takes shape. There are certain building blocks—serving as a Peace Corps volunteer, a Fulbright scholar, or an Experiment in International Living group leader, for example—that I like to see on résumés of job applicants. Experiences such as these, as well as others that are comparable, convey to a potential employer that you have survived a vigorous vetting process. They also suggest that you can handle a challenging assignment overseas and have well-developed cross-cultural communication skills and a willingness to accept responsibility. Consequently, I always remind job seekers to highlight the fundamental building blocks on their résumés. In interviews they should be prepared to articulate the lessons they learned from these basic experiences and be able to illustrate those lessons with concrete examples.

Taking Risks

"Why not go out on a limb? That's where the fruit is."

—Mark Twain

This quotation reminds us that risk-taking is an essential part of any successful career. Several of the professionals profiled in part II have made a point to emphasize this fundamental fact. Allan Goodman, president of the Institute of International Education (IIE), expressed concern in his profile interview that today's youth are too fearful—less inclined to embrace the unknown than their predecessors. He urges young colleagues to experiment. Mark talks about the need for young professionals to take risks at the end of chapter 1. Careers in international affairs can, at times, put people into dangerous situations. Physical risks come in many guises. Other types of risks abound as well. Some might choose to accept a lower-paying job in tough conditions because they are truly impressed with those who will be their colleagues. Others may risk comfort because the chance to serve their cause is so compelling. Life is inherently risky. As those who opt for challenging assignments know so well, however, we humans are remarkably adaptable. We can get along quite well without many of the things we view as necessities in our home environment. In fact, the process of getting along without them and functioning well in a different country or cultural context builds our self-confidence, our capacity to make considered judgments, and our ability to get things done.

Lessons Learned

"That which hurts, instructs."

—Benjamin Franklin

Despite careful thought about the trade-offs involved in various career choices and decisions, we inevitably make mistakes, both large and small. I always told my staff to try and avoid mistakes, but when they happen—as they will despite the best of intentions—own up to them immediately. Together, we can work out a way to rectify promptly whatever problem was inadvertently caused. The key is to learn from mistakes of all types and realize that you are even more valuable as an employee because you can analyze your mistakes and apply that learning to the next comparable situation.

It is sobering to realize that I have learned the most—grown the most—from the job situations that seemed particularly problematic at the time. When things move along smoothly, we tend to take them for granted. Often it is only when we are coping with major difficulties that we consciously summon our problem-solving skills, engage in deep analysis, and use or combine our assets in new ways.

I remember one time when, as a relatively new manager, I hired a consultant to organize a seminar. I didn't know much then about monitoring a project and supervising a consultant. Thinking that she would handle her work the way I did mine, I blithely assumed she would be at the hotel to troubleshoot any problems that arose as the seminar participants checked in. It was only when I was called at home by irate participants threatening to return to their universities that I realized my mistake. Fortunately, before rushing to the hotel to salvage as much of the situation as I could, I had the presence of mind to notify the sponsor of the seminar and explain what had happened and what I was doing to remedy the situation. While I was on the edge of panic and envisioned being fired the next day, I certainly learned a lot from that episode. **Never make assumptions. Double-check *everything*.** To this day, a manager—in fact, any employee—without a prioritized checklist makes me nervous. This is just one example from my own career where a tough situation was inarguably instructive. The lessons live indelibly in my memory.

Remember the Chinese Parable

At the outset of this book Mark and I described a career as a series of choices that determine what we do during the majority of our waking hours. The implication is that usually we make the choices and are generally in charge of our own destinies. Sometimes this is true, but not always. Occasionally the choices of others seem to determine our fate. Economies take a nosedive. Staffs are reduced in size. Departments and entire organizations are restructured. New leadership imposes different requirements throughout an agency. Organizations are organic, after all, and subject to the same shifts, growth cycles, and metamorphoses as individuals. They, too, are buffeted by external forces. Sometimes our job search at a particular time is set in motion not by our own choices but by the decisions of others. Often this appears, at least at first, to be a tragic occurrence, but it need not turn out that way. As colleagues who were fired attest, they were forced to grow and stretch, learn new skills, and often found themselves in new jobs more satisfying than those they had assumed they wanted to keep.

The moral is that we cannot be sure if a particular career experience (or a personal one, for that matter) is in the longer term positive or negative. Remember the Chinese parable: There was a peasant family. One day their only horse and source of livelihood escaped—a "bad" thing. The next day the horse returned with another horse. Their herd doubled—a "good" thing. The next day when the eldest son was trying to ride the new horse, he fell off and broke his leg—a "bad" thing. The next day war broke out and the injured son was not required to fight—a "good" thing. You get the idea. The important thing is what we do when certain choices are made for us. We cannot judge immediately if an event is good or bad for the evolution of a career. The operative questions are "What lessons can I distill from this experience?" and "What do these lessons suggest for my job search?"

Professionalism

Frequently, people are designated professionals because they have attained certain academic qualifications or positions. They have earned medical or engineering degrees, for instance. Often, it implies that they are equipped to, and in fact do, handle specific responsibilities. Lawyers must have earned a law degree and passed the bar to defend clients in the courtroom. Professors of Russian must have a certain level of proficiency and command of the language. Only professors with PhDs are considered qualified to teach higher-level courses.

Nonetheless, in many offices, employees *at every level* are routinely admonished to behave professionally or act like a professional. In that context, professionalism is an unwritten code of conduct you are expected to observe. What it means to be professional may vary considerably depending on the field and the internal culture of the organization in question.

Regardless of your role within an organization, it behooves you to behave professionally. Whether or not your supervisor articulates just what being a professional means, she undoubtedly has a notion of appropriate behavior (even if subconscious) against which she judges your actions and those of your colleagues.

What follows is my own, admittedly parochial, understanding of this elusive concept. I offer it not as the ultimate definition of professionalism but rather as a way to help you think about your behavior—as a job seeker and as an employee in a specific workplace.

Character Counts—Honesty and Dependability

For me, and I would venture to say that for most managers, the first measure of professionalism is character. Above all, I want people on my staff who are honest and have integrity. I need to know that I can count on that person. If my assistant says she will be there at 7:30 am to be sure that the breakfast for a meeting we are hosting is indeed what we ordered and set up as requested, I can trust that she will arrive on time. If a colleague submits a receipt for a given amount, I know that is exactly the amount she paid for that taxi ride. If a colleague promised to complete a newsletter article or grant proposal by noon on Thursday, I have confidence that the article or proposal will be submitted on time. I no longer have to exert any mental energy considering those tasks. I can depend on these colleagues. They do precisely what they say they will do. They are professionals.

Ambassador Kenton Keith underscored this point in our profile interview with him: "No matter how good your excuse is, if at the end of the day you have not achieved what you committed to achieving, that's what is going to be remembered."

If a mistake happens or a problem arises, a professional quickly informs a supervisor so they can resolve the problem. A professional always passes along useful information promptly to those who need to know. And in certain cases, he makes sure he has done so in writing. The old paper trail concept may have morphed into an electronic record, but the fundamental principle is the same. Hone your judgment regarding who needs what information and when it is needed.

This is a much bigger challenge now than when I started my career because an avalanche of messages in many forms buffets us daily. Sifting through those messages and deciding which are relevant to various colleagues is an enormous task. Years ago I would return from a lunch meeting to find four or five pink slips on my desk documenting phone messages. My last year at the National Council for International Visitors (NCIV), an alarming number of e-mails and other messages had accumulated during a luncheon meeting.

In 1982, when I assumed my first managerial position, the comptroller of the Institute of International Education gave me one of the best pieces of advice I have ever received: "Remember, Sherry, never surprise anyone." This has been a guiding principle for me ever since. Whether it's reporting a problem or passing along information in a timely manner, don't let colleagues find out from other sources what should have come from you.

Doing Your Best

The second measure of professionalism for me is that I expect a member of my staff to do his best at whatever task is assigned. Whether taking notes at a hearing on Capitol Hill, organizing a national conference, or defrosting the office refrigerator, I expect a colleague to do these things to the best of his ability. I am a great fan of the legendary UCLA basketball coach John Wooden and his philosophy of leadership.[1] He coached his players to work hard developing their skills and to do their absolute best at every practice and every game, and he believed the score would take care of itself. For Wooden, success was not defined as winning per se—it was produced from the synergy of each person on the team giving his best effort each and every game, each and every shot. Winning resulted, but it was not the primary goal.

Attention to Detail

Intertwined with doing your best is attention to detail. If I see a typo or if poor grammar is used on a resume (or even in a LinkedIn profile), it is cause for rejection. My reasoning is as follows—if a person cannot muster the discipline to review her own resume or profile for misspellings (the documents that project her skills to a potential employer), how will she ever summon the discipline to produce error-free materials for our organization? Good writing and editing skills, as well as the ability to review work and catch mistakes (so I do not have to use my time to do it), are talents I value a great deal.

Being a Team Player

Another dimension of professionalism is being a team player. In every organization there are crunch times. A major one at NCIV is the month before the national conference. Everyone does what needs to be done to put on the best possible conference. It doesn't matter if technically a task is in—or not in—someone's job description. The important thing is that the entire team works together to produce the best possible event and experience for the conference participants.

Whenever I overheard one of my colleagues offering to help another so his deadline could be met, I knew that our office culture was evolving in a constructive way. One example I often used in interviews to describe this expectation was to say that you are hosting a meeting for eight people. There are only six chairs. I expect you to find the two extra chairs and not complain that "moving furniture is not in my job description." This basic concept that collectively we are all responsible for our organization and its work (not just for our slice of it) is an integral part of professionalism.

Curiosity—A Desire to Learn

A real professional always seeks opportunities to grow and learn. I tried to help the staff at NCIV understand the overall context for our work. I counseled them to approach their work in two ways. The first is that we each play a role and we do that to the best of our ability. Second, I always encouraged colleagues to study organizational dynamics. It is important to be able to discern whether a reaction to your work is directed at you. Perhaps this reaction would be directed at anyone playing the role you are playing. This idea of wearing a certain hat within an organization, plus being a student of the process, can help you react to some situations more calmly. It is useful to try to treat every situation as an opportunity for learning—not only about the specifics of a particular project but also about the context and culture within which the project is managed.

Dress

Be conscious of what the way you dress says about you and your attitude toward your job. Please note that these comments are directed primarily toward those working in an office setting. Clearly, if you are managing the delivery of humanitarian supplies at a refugee camp, your attire will be dictated by tasks, climate, and culture.

Even in nonoffice settings, however, I would argue that professionals should opt for more conservative attire. Some of my colleagues will undoubtedly conclude I am hopelessly old-fashioned when I say that sundresses (and similar garments), bare midriffs, short skirts, untucked shirttails, and flip-flops have no place in a modern office—even on casual Fridays. And I will confess that I have become an enthusiastic convert to casual Fridays, despite the fact that, when I started my first regular job at the Institute of International Education, I always wore jackets and skirts (sometimes with three-inch heels—what was I thinking?). At NCIV, each Friday I happily donned my jeans and tennis shoes. Still, coming of age literally in another century, it seems to me that casual Fridays—in some offices at least—have gravitated to sloppy Fridays. One's dress should never be distracting to others. I expected my staff to be dressed neatly at all times. I tried to convey this expectation during the interview process so no one would later say that she didn't know about my expectation and felt that her freedom of expression was unduly constrained.

The dress and image dimension of professionalism is especially important in international careers. Often we work with colleagues whose religious or other cultural beliefs mandate conservative dress. In my view, you should adapt to their norms rather than expect them to accept more casual standards. The office is not the beach, and professionals should dress accordingly. They should always be aware that the image they project reflects not only on their own judgment but on their organization as well. Only you can decide what you believe is appropriate attire for you in a given setting. Nonetheless, it is still prudent to be sure that your view meshes with that of your supervisor.

There is a useful way to think about dress, attention to detail, or any other aspect of professionalism I have outlined. As noted earlier, each action you take, as a job seeker or employee, will either build or erode the confidence of others in your judgment and abilities. As you contemplate any action, be sure to consider what it conveys to your potential employer or supervisor. These managers are the people who will serve as your references, decide the amount of your next raise, and identify professional development opportunities for you. They want to be reassured that you are worth the investment—that you are a true professional.

Don't Take It Personally

Such a glib, seemingly unfeeling phrase! It is easy to offer this advice as long as you are not the person who didn't get the second interview or the job that seemed like such a good fit. Yet this trite admonition—"don't take it personally"—has merit.

When I served as director of a relatively large staff at IIE and frequently hired new staff members, and later at NCIV, I often passed over job applicants who were capable people with impressive qualifications. In my experience, for each job opening there are a number of candidates who can do the job. Managers building a team of people with complementary expertise look for someone who not only can do the job but also whose background builds the strength of the staff as a whole. Please keep this in mind as you cope with the inevitable rejections an extensive job search entails.

What Do Employers Value?

We are often asked what it takes to succeed in the fields of international education, exchange, and development. What do employers value? In addition to professionalism, most employers seek these qualifications:

ACADEMIC CREDENTIALS

Most jobs have a minimum requirement. In some cases, an advanced degree may propel your resume to the shortlist. In other situations, "on the ground" experience will make hiring you more likely. Nonetheless, I encourage young colleagues to get the maximum amount of formal education that time, finances, and geography permit. It will never be cheaper. It will never be more convenient. Options such as American University's School of International Service Master of Arts in International Relations online program, which includes limited sessions on campus, are becoming increasingly popular.

The key question about earning a graduate degree is the same one you ask about any job: will it be rewarding to spend your time taking the prescribed courses and fulfilling other requirements? You want to earn an advanced degree because the learning involved excites you—not merely to acquire another credential.

What about a PhD? Clearly, if you want a career teaching on a college campus, it is a prerequisite. And it can be helpful in other roles where you deal with colleagues who hold doctorates. As a practitioner, technically I did not need the degree, but I am convinced that it often gives you more options and, in certain cases, gives you a leg up in the hiring process. One thing I didn't think too much about years ago in grad school was the fact that a PhD would enable me to serve as an adjunct professor in the 1980s and to again engage in that satisfying work in this encore chapter of my career.

Another factor to consider is that the alumni of your graduate school will likely be the core of your professional network. As a graduate of the Tufts University Fletcher School of Law and Diplomacy (and a member of the "Fletcher family," or "Fletcher mafia"), that tie has been important. Fletcher alumni have made special efforts to help me. (Ambassador Walter Cutler, who served as chair of the NCIV Advisory Council, is a Fletcher alumnus, and we often referred to our Fletcher connection while working together.) In turn, when a Fletcher alum asks me for a favor, I'm inclined to oblige because we share that common bond.

COMMUNICATION SKILLS

The ability to express oneself clearly and crisply in writing is fundamental. Many jobs involve writing grant proposals. All require communicating with stakeholders. As we are ever more inundated with messages from many sources, those who can draft messages concisely using attractive language have an advantage.

The ability to communicate well orally continues to be prized. Despite the electronics at our disposal, the skills to speak in public and to convey your ideas with compelling stories is sought after. Whether in a room of 500 people, via webinar or Skype, or around a conference table, those who are most articulate usually carry the day.

Finally, the listening dimension of communication is vital. Again, in our information-saturated workplace, the ability to distill the salient from the superfluous is essential. So many of the jobs in these fields involve building relationships. Productive relationships are always predicated on reciprocity. One small example: your thank-you letter for an interview will have greater impact if you recount several points the interviewer made. The thank you not only tells your prospective employer that you have good manners but it also demonstrates your important listening and writing skills.

DESIRE TO LEARN

This is probably the quality I value most in colleagues. The capacity to express genuine curiosity—authentic interest—in your colleagues from abroad and their cultures encourages cooperation. The relentless search for common ground undergirds fruitful collaboration. Those most effective in international careers have not lost their capacity for wonder.

Moving On

Knowing when to move on to the next chapter of your career is critically important. Too short a time in one position arouses suspicion and questions about your perseverance. Too long a time and your effectiveness has diminished. The exact time frames depend on the particular situation.

Sometimes leaving is prompted by the difficulty of working for a supervisor you do not respect, or by the belief that you can contribute more to your cause at a different organization. I remember my mom asking me why I left a senior position at one organization to become executive director for another while taking a $4,000 salary cut. I told her, "Mom, I'm not learning anything anymore." The challenge was gone.

That is what propels most of us to begin that job search. It was very difficult to leave my job as president of NCIV (after almost sixteen years), but I wanted to "finish strong." I wanted to leave the network I had come to love so much when people would be sad to see me go and not be wondering, "Is she ever going to leave?" No matter how good the fit, the time for the next chapter inexorably comes.

Discerning when it is time to make a change comes from pondering your career holistically. Ask yourself whether your cause, preferred tasks, and motivations have changed. As one colleague told us, if you look out the window and more often wish you would rather be out there than in here, it is time to make that move.

Work–Life Balance

When I presented some career seminars for the Foreign Policy Association, I was asked to comment on maintaining appropriate work–life balance. The trouble with the question is that the answer varies with one's personal preferences. Almost all of my adult life, I have been blessed to do work that totally engages me. My professional roles required hosting and participating in many events (including evenings and weekends). Wholeheartedly embracing my cause and building important relationships for my organization were enjoyable and, yes, time-consuming, activities. My professional life morphed into my social life. Some professional colleagues became lifelong friends.

For me the relevant questions have become: Are you spending enough time with family and friends? Are you exercising regularly? Are you getting enough sleep? No matter how much you love your work, you do it better when you take care of your health and interact with family and friends outside of the office.

Another related question I always pose when I conduct seminars on leadership for NGO executives is, "Do you have the discipline to disconnect?" Research increasingly shows that, much like accomplished athletes, we all need to rest and recharge. An instructive book on the subject is *The Corporate Athlete: How to Achieve Maximal Performance in Business and in Life* by Jack Groppel. I had the opportunity to discuss this issue with Jack. The research results he shared made me even more committed to my yoga practice and the healthful habits that are too often abandoned as 24/7 job pressures consume us.

A final bit of advice I often share, and try to follow myself, is: "Each day do something you don't have time for." If you wait until you actually "have time," you will miss some memorable moments.

Mark: The Never-Ending Job Story

A former member of NCIV's board of directors once told me that he regularly looks for a job. He often scans lists of available jobs in the fields of international education, exchange, and development, just to see what's out there.

"Why?" I remember asking. "Aren't you happy in your job?"

"I'm actually very happy in my job," he responded.

"Then why look for jobs if you aren't planning to leave your current one?" I wondered.

"I'm not looking for jobs that would be a lateral move or a moderate step up or because I need a change of scenery," he explained. "I look for jobs that are a stretch for me, that I may not quite be qualified for but, if given the opportunity, would work my butt off to succeed in. I'm always looking for the next way I can move on to bigger challenges."

For me, this story neatly illustrates the point that both Sherry and I stress in this chapter: Your job search never ceases. It's a constant activity, a continuous journey that will keep you on the lookout for new ways to challenge yourself and better serve your cause.

Moving On

The time came when, difficult as it was, I had to leave NCIV. I'd previously viewed landing my position at NCIV as the end of something—the end of a search, the end of a process, the end of wondering how I was going to pay my rent. A few years later, though, I learned that it wasn't the end of anything. Rather it was, as Sherry describes it earlier in this chapter, a building block of my career.

As noted in chapter 1, I had a variety of experiences throughout college and grad school that had no obvious pattern or path. But I was happy with these choices because they gave me varied, valuable experiences and were the foundation for my later choices. They were building blocks. It was easy to view them as such because they were impermanent, short-term opportunities. I knew from the start that, whether in three months, six months, or a year, I'd be moving on.

But when I accepted my position at NCIV, I didn't think about it as a building block. It was a full-time job; it was permanent. I suppose I knew I wouldn't be at NCIV forever. But I didn't much think about it. The fact that, at some point, I was going to have to make a choice and take another step forward in my career wasn't yet a concern.

And then, one day, I realized with a start that it was time to move on. At first I felt guilty, as if I were betraying Sherry, NCIV, and the whole field of international exchange. But this wasn't disloyalty—only a natural part of my career progression. It wasn't personal—I simply needed new challenges. Had NCIV been able to provide those, I'd have been glad to take on a new, expanded role. But because the organization was small—at that time, a staff of only eight—there was limited opportunity for advancement.

I also came to see that not only was this need for a new challenge natural, it was also beneficial to everyone involved. A new position would satisfy my need for something fresh and advance my career. This move would also benefit NCIV and the cause of international exchange. If I stayed in my job too long, I ran the risk of becoming complacent and allowing my performance to suffer, thus damaging NCIV's ability to serve its cause. When asked about moving on, Ambassador Kenton Keith put it this way in his profile interview:

> When you start thinking this is something you can do for another five–ten years—comfortably, with no particular effort—then it's time for you to be gone. You know when the job is no longer challenging for you, and you've reached the limit of what you can do with the resources that are available to you, then it's time to move on.

In searching for my next challenge, I started narrowly—looking largely at NCIV's partner and sister organizations in international education and exchange (some are listed in part II). This limited the possibilities, and the going was slow. I was encouraged to broaden my search, to think about potential new positions not only in terms of the cause they represented but also the skills I would learn. As Jennifer Clinton says in her profile, not every job will perfectly fill all of your "buckets" (i.e., embody your causes). But if a new opportunity hits at least one of your buckets and teaches you new skills that will transfer later on, then that opportunity may be a positive building block.

I broadened my search. While I hoped international exchange would remain a part of my career, I also wanted a position with a stronger communications focus and room to develop leadership and management skills. When initially interviewing for what would become my next job—as director of college communications at Georgetown College (the liberal arts school at Georgetown University)—I worried I might be compromising and abandoning my passion. Would I be happy in a job that didn't have a daily international focus?

In the end, though, I decided the position was right because it filled enough buckets. It would enable me to:

1. Build key skills, namely communications, writing, leadership, and management (supervising a small publications team).
2. Retain some involvement with international education by working with the dean on the College's outreach to China.
3. Support a mission I believed in. I was attracted to Georgetown College because I studied liberal arts at the University of Notre Dame. I strongly believe a liberal arts education has served me well, and that many other young people can benefit in a similar fashion.

When I left NCIV for my two years at Georgetown, I'd known it was time to move on. Moving on from Georgetown, however, was a very different process. It was only when the executive director of the Alliance for International Educational and Cultural Exchange, Michael McCarry, encouraged me to apply for an open assistant director position that I first considered leaving.

My discussion with Michael forced my hand. I was still enjoying, and learning from, my position at Georgetown and wasn't necessarily ready to move on. But I was intrigued by the possibility of working at the Alliance. First, I had to ask myself, "When *would* I be ready to move on, based on the growth potential of my job at Georgetown?" My gut told me nine to twelve months, tops. I wasn't itching for a change yet but thought I would be soon.

Second, I asked myself, "Where would I best be able to serve my cause?" As I discuss in chapter 1, identifying my cause has been an ongoing process, even a struggle. Around this time, though, I began to realize that the field of international exchange was where I wanted to be. Specifically, it struck me that my passion for the exchange programs I'd experienced was a clue to my cause. I wanted to be working on or with these kinds of programs.

Getting to these answers wasn't particularly easy. But once I'd considered them, it was clear. I needed to make a move and the Alliance was the place to go.

Key Career Building Blocks

After I was hired at the Alliance, it occurred to me that my first "interview" for the job had actually been five years earlier when I'd collaborated with Michael and shown him who I was through my work and actions. NCIV joined forces with the Alliance on various challenging projects. I enjoyed working with Michael in those demanding moments because we approached things in similar ways and because I learned a great deal from him. It was a relationship that developed naturally during the course of working together—unforced networking at its best.

At that time, I didn't realize that my relationship with Michael would lead to my next career step—or that his perception of me and my work would be so important five years later. Learning to recognize that perception is critical in the workplace is the first of several attributes essential for professionals in international education, exchange, and development.

RECOGNIZE THAT PERCEPTION MATTERS

Karl Dedolph told us a story about his first months on the job after grad school that illustrates the importance of perception. At one of his first client meetings, his boss gave him the opportunity, as a very junior consulting analyst, to present to their main client. He was nervous:

> Unlike most people who are nervous, who give off that sense of nerve, my counter is to try to be as relaxed as possible. Like over-relaxed. So instead of bringing energy and standing tall and looking the client in the eye, I slumped back in my chair. I crossed my legs. I lounged. After the meeting, our client pulled my boss aside and asked, "Is Karl sick? Is he physically ill? Because it sure seemed that way."

Later, his boss took him aside and said, "You've got one more chance, or you're out of here." Karl realized that how he was being perceived was blowing it for him—his body language, his nonverbal cues. It wasn't what he said, it was how he said it:

I had a quick and important lesson on perception. I realized that people remember these things. Differentiating yourself from your peers and advancing in your career often is subjective and based on people's perceptions of you as much as your actual work.

Early in my career, I, too, had small but meaningful lessons on the importance of perception. Three weeks into my job at NCIV, Sherry and I traveled to Denver for a board of directors meeting. A majority of the meeting was held on a Saturday. The board chair had determined dress would be casual. I put on a pair of khakis, a polo shirt, and black shoes—fairly dressed up for a dress-down day, at least by my standards. I even tucked in my shirt. I also decided to forgo shaving.

The following Monday, back at the NCIV office in Washington, Sherry and I met to discuss follow-up tasks from the meeting. As I sat down in her office with a fresh cup of coffee, she remarked that she liked the particular tie I was wearing. She then made another observation about my appearance.

"You're looking nice and neat this morning, too," she said. "You looked awfully scruffy on Saturday."

I blanched. I had no idea how to take this. Was it just a passing remark? Or rather a comment conveying Sherry's displeasure with my hiatus from the razor and an admonition not to let it happen again? Our meeting finished and Sherry never remarked again on my appearance, unless it was to comment on the fashionable tie I happened to be wearing.

The second example occurred not long after that board meeting. Sherry requested I write a follow-up e-mail to the board. Wanting to show my diligence, I wrote it immediately. I labored over the wording and tone. I knew it needed to be professional, but I'd also just discovered that the board was a laidback, personable group. I wanted to show that I, too, was laidback and personable and would prove to be an excellent colleague. So I chose my words and tone accordingly. Pleased with the amiable yet professional nature of the e-mail, I copied Sherry and hit send.

Later, Sherry told me in a respectful way that she thought the tone of that e-mail was too casual. A business-related e-mail to the board of directors of our organization needed to be more professional. "The members of the board are my bosses," she remarked, "and I need everyone on staff to treat them as such."

Both of these relatively insignificant events were meaningful learning experiences for me. While I'd thought the tone of my e-mail was appropriate, Sherry had not. While I'd thought there was nothing unprofessional about growing a bit of fashionable stubble from time to time, Sherry disagreed. Like Karl, I learned it's not always what you say, but how you're perceived.

I emphasize this idea not to say that first impressions are all that matter. I'm also not encouraging you to manipulate another's perception of you, or suggesting that you cultivate an image as a hard worker (whether you actually are or not). Rather, my point relates to one Sherry makes in chapter 2, and has made to me many times: you're always on. You never know who's observing. You never know who's storing away perceptions of you, good and bad. And you never know how those images might come back to help you, or haunt you, in the future.

CULTIVATE ADAPTABILITY

An important virtue as you progress in your career is not necessarily how you *conform* but rather how you *adapt*. Kowtowing to varying needs and expectations is less important than learning to work comfortably and successfully within various organizational and cultural constructs. Determine how you can work with colleagues of differing viewpoints and working styles in order to get the job done. Incorporate compromise into your daily routine. If another party is resistant to compromise, maintain your composure to work around and through the situation.

For young professionals, this process of adaptation can be especially challenging. As I discuss in chapter 3, my generation and the generations following us have an acute sense of urgency. We are on-demand. Consequently, when we enter the workplace, we're eager to bring our skills to bear on the tasks at hand. We don't necessarily stop to think about the need to adapt our performance and style to mesh with those around us or look to our more experienced colleagues for guidance.

Adaptation to professional environments is not an attribute reserved for young professionals. You must possess it and hone it even as you progress in your career. In fact, adaptation perhaps becomes even more important as you acquire additional responsibility and come into positions of leadership. Not only do you have to deal with irreverent young professionals like me who don't want to shave, but you're also required to be a leader for your organization. Leadership requires adaptation.

GO ABROAD, STUDY A LANGUAGE

Adaptability is one of many skills that can be cultivated while living within another culture. Studying abroad in France, teaching English in China, and learning French and Chinese: these experiences shaped the kind of professional that I am today and are the crux of my resume. They're the principal experiences that have shaped my cause and nourished my passion. Spending significant time abroad, and often gaining or polishing a foreign language in the process, are fundamental building blocks of a career in these fields.

The specific language skills and cultural knowledge gained are perhaps the most obvious benefits from time abroad and might end up being explicitly useful in your day-to-day work. If you work for, say, the American Councils for International Education, which focuses on exchanges with Russia and former Soviet republics, strong Russian skills and regional knowledge may be a prerequisite. If you're assigned to Peru to manage a Catholic Relief Services development project, fluent Spanish will likely be necessary. If you decide on the Foreign Service, previous linguistic knowledge—as well as the ability to quickly develop a working knowledge of new languages—is part of the job.

But more often than not, jobs in these fields *won't* require you to use language or regional skills on a day-to-day basis. I've had only one position—a three-month internship at the Embassy of France in Washington, DC—that absolutely required I speak a foreign language daily. I've traveled to China for work and was able to use my Chinese language and cultural knowledge in social settings—but it wasn't required for my daily work.

Even so, an experience abroad is essential for working in these fields. Hiring managers rarely give second consideration to a resume that doesn't have some kind of international exchange or foreign language component. But if the job they're hiring for doesn't require those specific language or regional cultural skills, then why the heavy emphasis on overseas experience? First and foremost, an international experience (or two or three) shows that you care deeply about the work you're hoping to do. It demonstrates that you've made it a priority to "get out there." It indicates you inherently understand the importance of the work (facilitating an exchange program, advising students who want to study abroad, planning logistics for an on-the-ground development project) because you've experienced it yourself.

Second, an experience in another country and culture teaches you skills that employers value and that will help you to succeed in your job: self-motivation, self-reliance, and self-confidence; time management, critical thinking, and the ability to work in teams; flexibility, adaptability, problem solving, negotiation, and compromise. Indeed, not only do employers in the fields of international education, exchange, and development prize these "soft skills," but increasingly employers in other sectors do too.[2]

As Sherry notes, though, in the job search process it's not enough just to *have* these skills and experiences. An experience abroad or language skills might help strengthen your resume in the eyes of a hiring manager and help get you the interview; do not assume the experiences will speak for themselves. You must be able to articulate *why* your time abroad or your language study has been so crucial for you—what you've learned from these experiences and how they'll help you succeed in that specific job with that organization.

CONSIDER A MASTER'S DEGREE—BUT WHEN?

One of the most common questions Sherry and I receive from job seekers is, "Do I need a master's degree?" followed closely by, "If yes, when should I get it?" My experience has shown that—for better or worse—an advanced degree is an increasingly essential building block of an international career. I don't believe I would've been hired for my current job without a master's degree (it wasn't the only reason, but it was a key qualification). The same holds true for friends and colleagues. An advanced degree is a qualification that, at a certain level, employers expect to see. This doesn't apply in all cases, and it certainly doesn't preclude professionals without advanced degrees from having successful careers. It does, though, strike me as the trend.

Some pursue a master's directly (or almost directly) out of college. This worked for me, and it works for others. Based on her ten years of hiring young professionals at WorldChicago, Peggy Parfenoff told us that she thinks, in many cases, getting your master's soon after you graduate can be beneficial. This gives you the time to burnish your academic credentials, develop your skills, and gain a variety of professional experiences via internships and fellowships.

Realize, though, that an advanced degree doesn't automatically entitle you to a more senior position. If you went to grad school more or less right out of college (meaning you have limited work experience), expect your first job, even with an advanced degree, to be entry level or on a lower rung (this was the case for me). Newly minted master's degree holders often (understandably) find this disappointing. They hope their advanced degree will automatically warrant a higher-level position. But, from the hiring manager's perspective, why should that be the case if those applicants have little to no practical work experience? Your advanced degree, especially if pursued shortly after undergrad, is not a panacea but a building block. It may take some time for that degree to pay off and to secure a position you couldn't get without a master's (it took me five years).

Others see gaining several years of work experience and layering a master's on top as the best way to go. Alanna Shaikh told us that she firmly believes professionals in these fields need a master's degree—but *not* immediately out of college. She notes that a recent college graduate may not know what kind of degree program is best for her:

> I applied to a lot of master's programs right out of undergrad, and if I'd been accepted, that would have been awful. The degree programs I was choosing did not coincide with what I'm interested in now.

It took Alanna several years of fieldwork to determine that global health is her passion and thus the field in which she should pursue a degree. And her process for knowing when it was time to go back to school went like this: "You'll hit a point where you'll top out and everything you can do with an undergraduate degree doesn't strike you as interesting any more. That's the time to go get your master's."

Second, Alanna believes that employers and hiring managers see a resume with "the whole package" (work experience + an advanced degree) as preferable to one that features two or more degrees but no practical experience. "You've got to have the actual experience to show them you can do the job, and then you've got to have the shiny credential and the up-to-date academic knowledge on top of that."

"It's Just the Bottom Rung of another Ladder"

Fayezul Choudhury, then vice president for corporate finance and risk management at the World Bank, told us a story that neatly summed up the main focus of this chapter.

On his wife's birthday in 1985, Choudhury spent nearly twenty-four straight hours at the office. At the time, he was working in London for a well-known international accounting and consulting firm. On that particular day, his wife dropped him off at the Underground station near their home at 3:30 am and didn't see him again until 2:30 am the next day. His wife was remarkably understanding and not upset with him for working on her birthday that year. Yet Choudhury said the experience unnerved him and spurred him to question whether this job was right for him.

Not long after, Choudhury received a promotion and was made a partner in the firm. "Finally," he thought, "this is proof that I've made it." A senior partner called Choudhury into his office and followed up this news of the promotion with a simple, "Well done. Carry on." No congratulations or praise for the hard work Choudhury had put in. Excited about the promotion but equally frustrated by the lack of enthusiasm from the senior partner about his accomplishment, Choudhury turned to leave the office. Just as he reached the door, the senior partner stopped him.

"Fayez," the senior partner called from his desk. Choudhury turned, an expectant look on his face. The senior partner finished: "Remember, you're not the only partner in this firm."

At that moment, Choudhury not only knew that it was time to move on, but he also came to realize a fundamental truth about careers: you've never really made it. The journey goes on.

"A number of pieces just fell into place for me," he recounted. "You have this notion that if you're a partner, or if you've reached a certain point in your organization or your career, you've got it made. But really, it's just the bottom rung of another ladder."

Notes

1. John Wooden and Steve Jamison, *Wooden on Leadership* (New York: McGraw-Hill, 2005).

2. British Council and NAFSA: Association of International Educators studies illustrate the importance of intercultural skills in the workplace and the value employers place on international educational experiences. See www.britishcouncil.org/employ abilityreport_us_canada.pdfandwww.britishcouncil.org/culture-at-work-research_march_2013.pdf.

PART II

Selected Resources and Profiles

CHAPTER 5

Your Job Search: A General Approach

Introduction

Cast the net wide. Search broadly. See what's out there.

One of the greatest myths regarding the job search, international or otherwise, is that you should only be looking for open positions. Clearly, the position you eventually obtain will have to be one that's available. However, in searching for those open positions, don't hesitate to explore the wide array of possibilities with an open mind. Check out jobs that you may not yet be qualified for but that you might someday be interested in. Dig deeper into organizations that don't have job openings at the moment but that have missions that excite you and that are doing work you would like to do.

Be alert to individuals doing work you find compelling. Ask them about their career paths. Sherry remembers meeting the executive director of the National Council for International Visitors (NCIV) shortly after she started working at the Institute of International Education (IIE) in 1978. Visiting his office and hearing him describe his work, she recalls thinking, "How exciting! I would like to have his job someday." Some years later, fortuitously, that dream came true.

Pay attention to the colleagues you naturally wish to emulate. Try to discern why their work is attractive to you. Ask them how they charted their career paths. What skills must you develop to compete for positions similar to theirs?

The career resources noted in this chapter can supply the specific details of available positions as well as give you a better idea of the enormous variety of jobs that exist. Many social media and career websites enable you to research jobs, companies, organizations, and industries.

Many provide articles and other advice for job seekers. The panoply of players on the international scene has expanded so much in recent decades that it is difficult for any one person to grasp the full range of possibilities. Using these tools to cast your net wide and discover what's out there will help immensely in this process.

This approach holds true not just for those who are in the market for a new job but also for those who will someday decide to change and seek greater challenges, though they are currently in a stable job and have no immediate intention of leaving. In some way, *everyone* is a job seeker. Some are active job seekers—those looking to start a new job as soon as possible—and some are passive job seekers, only developing a better understanding of their options.

Regularly perusing job boards will help you at that point when you do decide to begin an active job search; it will also assist you in thinking about your broader career development. To be fair, fifteen minutes spent one afternoon scrolling through a long list of job postings will not suddenly flip the switch and illuminate your lifelong career path. However, the cumulative effect of regularly gathering information and pondering your career will better prepare you for that pivotal moment when it is time to make the next move.

What Is Your Goal?

Keep in mind that *pursuing an international career* is not synonymous with *working abroad*. Just because a job enables you to travel doesn't necessarily mean it is the best opportunity to begin or continue your career in international education, exchange, or development. In the same way, even though a job does not have a travel component, it may still help to build your career in international relations in significant ways. Finding the job that enables you to visit exotic locales can be an exciting and worthwhile goal, but it is imperative to determine if this is *your* primary goal. What is more important to you? Traveling and working abroad in and of itself? Or creating a substantive career in international education, exchange, or development? These two can certainly overlap, and they often do, but they are not one and the same. In fact, given family commitments and considerations such as those described later by Luby

Ismail in her profile interview, the challenge may be to forge an international career that requires minimal travel abroad.

Be Realistic

Being realistic is key to distinguishing between working abroad and fashioning an international career. This is particularly true at a time of increased budget restraints for so many organizations. Finding a job that lets you travel extensively *and* work on substantive issues in the fields of international exchange, education, and development is not easy.

"Don't expect the moon just because you have a certain level of education or certain experiences," advised Paul Binkley, former director of career development services for the George Washington University School of Public Policy and Public Administration and now an independent strategic planning consultant working primarily in West Africa. "International development, exchange, and education jobs demand a vast amount of experience: experience abroad, languages, skills, etc. . . . many students would come to me wondering why they're having trouble landing that job they really want even though they have a master's degree or a certain level of education or have spent a year abroad. In this environment, these qualifications are not remarkable. They are expected."

This fact is not meant to deflate the hopes of recent college graduates and suggest that only those with master's degrees, five years of experience, and multiple international experiences can get a job. (Remember the old paradox of job hunting? Those with the experience get the job, but how can you gain the experience if you can't get the job?) What this means, however, is that it's important to have realistic expectations and understand that your dream job—the one with substantive responsibilities, a respectable salary, and business-class international travel—might not come right away.

"Remember that the vast majority of internationally oriented positions are located domestically," Binkley remarked, "so don't dismiss them. Everybody wants to go abroad, but finding a position that allows you to do this often takes a while. It's important to look for positions that give you experience, even if they don't send you abroad."

The Job Search in the Electronic Age

Thanks to the internet, the tools available for your job search expand almost daily. Online job postings, search engines, and social media bring with them the ability to peruse available positions in real time. Print resources, such as this book, are beneficial in their own right: they provide a broader context for your job search and easy-to-reference guidelines and resources. Online sources, however, are more dynamic. They are constantly (in most cases) updated and allow job seekers and other professionals to gain the most current view of trends within a given field, organizations experiencing turnover, and specific jobs available at that moment.

Online postings, job search engines, and social media are certainly valuable when you are actively searching and applying for positions. Yet these online resources should also be used at other times, well before the moment you actually *need* that next job. For example, you may be a student some time away from graduating and starting a new career. However, it can be instructive to scan job postings and perform random job searches, just to get a better idea about possibilities that might intrigue you. Follow an organization with an appealing mission on Facebook and Twitter. Check out the profiles of leaders you admire on LinkedIn. By doing this when you aren't under pressure to actually find, apply for, and obtain a job, you'll have an opportunity to see the range of positions for which organizations are recruiting (and the qualifications and skills they desire), to learn about new organizations, and to better reflect on and refine your own interests. The job search is an ongoing process of exploration and discernment.

University Listservs and Career Centers

In addition to career websites and job search sites, university e-mail lists (listservs) are still a great source of information about international organizations and position openings. Register for various listservs hosted by your undergraduate or graduate alma mater. There are likely many. At American University (AU), for example, there are hundreds, each devoted to a different topic. While a university-wide e-mail list may offer some useful job and career information, typically the e-mail list of the school, college, or department within the university that focuses on international topics of special interest to you will yield the most beneficial job information.

For example, on the e-mail list of the AU School of International Service, students and staff alike post job and internship openings regularly. In addition, several AU staff members who work in student services scour many of the job boards listed in this section (such as Idealist .org, FPA.org, and InterAction.org) and others and circulate a weekly job roundup on the e-mail list—essentially doing job searches for you. Like many universities, AU has its own institutional subscriptions to job boards that charge fees, allowing them to circulate information free to students and alumni. (Mark first learned about NCIV and internship opportunities there on the AU School of International Service listserv.) University career centers are also invaluable resources, not only for resume critiques, interview practice, and career counseling, but also for their online job boards and resume submission services.

E-Mail Is Not Always the Answer

Despite the fact that we are both enthusiastic advocates for the myriad web resources that will make your job search easier and more effective, we both caution that, in some instances, going electronic is not always best. More specifically, e-mail is not always the answer. Far too often, instead of considering our communication options, we simply fire off an e-mail. When it would be far more productive and downright easier to make a phone call, instead we'll spend twenty minutes composing an e-mail requesting information that takes two minutes to explain orally.

E-mail is a great way to inquire about job openings, ask for clarifications, and request informational interviews (Mark describes this effective networking technique in chapter 2). However, when you are in the later stages of the job search—following up on an application or an interview or trying to foster a personal contact at the organization that you hope will lead to a job—e-mail is not always the best solution. Not only does your e-mail run the risk of being lost among the avalanche of messages many professionals receive every day, but also the sometimes impersonal nature of an e-mail may have a negative effect. It is not only people of an older generation who may respond more favorably to a phone call or a handwritten thank-you note, especially after an interview. People of a younger generation respond to—and should be accustomed to using—these traditional modes of communication as well.

Regardless of the manner you choose—e-mail, phone call, or handwritten thank-you note—we cannot emphasize enough the importance of follow-up. Whether to a first meeting, a job application, or an interview, follow-up is essential. It is an opportunity to remind a potential employer of how well suited you are for an organization, as well as to demonstrate your writing skills. From her years of having a constantly packed schedule, Sherry can attest to the fact that following up will keep you on her radar screen and make it that much more likely that she will not only remember you but also will want to involve you in her work in some way. (Phone calls and handwritten notes are the best way to get her attention.) Mark has learned from personal experience that following up on a job application can make all the difference. After assuming his position as director of college communications at Georgetown College, he learned from his colleagues that his initial application was placed in the "maybe" pile. It was only after he followed up with a phone call that his application for that job was given a second look and moved to the interview pile.

Sometimes multiple methods of follow-up best demonstrate your interest and skills. After an interview, Sherry suggests e-mailing a carefully crafted business letter expressing your thanks and noting several points the interviewer made. Put "Thank You Letter from (insert your name)" in the subject line. Then send the original letter with a brief handwritten note via mail. This is an ideal way to emphasize your interest and illustrate both your writing and listening skills.

Get Involved

Job search engines and social media are wonderful resources, but they also can't replace a more personal, basic job search activity: networking and getting involved. It's still possible to get a job by sending in a blind application (when you don't know anyone at the organization and no one there knows you). You should never hesitate to apply if you find a position that truly excites you. It's easy to dismiss your chances of getting that job when you are an unknown quantity to an organization. You might tell yourself, "There must be *hundreds* of people applying and the organization doesn't know who I am. How am *I* going to get the position?" Yet you never know what can happen, and it certainly won't happen unless you apply. Sherry is fond of the quotation by the famous hockey player Wayne Gretzky: "You miss 100% of the shots you don't take."

However, you vastly increase your chances of getting that job if you make yourself a known quantity. Volunteer at conferences and other events. Organizations will be impressed by the initiative and commitment you show by volunteering your time for their cause. This will be remembered when positions become available. Network. Go to events sponsored by organizations in the field. Set up informational interviews with those who might be able to share insights about organizations of interest. By putting yourself in front of people already working in the fields of international education, exchange, and development, you're making it that much more likely that they will eventually involve you in their work.

And, of course, intern. It's no secret that, when positions must be filled, managers often think first of the outstanding interns who have already done excellent work in their offices. Those current or former interns are already familiar with the office systems and culture and require less training than other candidates.

But I Don't Live in Washington, DC, or New York!

You may also find, and perhaps become frustrated by the fact, that many of the organizations offering substantive jobs and internships in international education, exchange, and development are in large coastal cities such as Washington, DC; New York; and San Francisco. What, then, are those who live throughout the rest of the United States to do?

While it is true that cities such as Washington, DC, and New York have more international opportunities than most, many states and metropolitan areas have their own sets of international connections. You could even argue that some large cities and states conduct their own foreign relations. There are jobs with an international dimension at universities and colleges, world trade centers, in chambers of commerce, and in the offices of governors, mayors, and other elected officials. The jobs in the state and district offices of members of Congress are often dominated by domestic concerns. However, they also deal with various issues that we tend to consider international. As the distinction between domestic and international becomes increasingly blurred, many jobs will inevitably have a tangible international component, whether located in Bozeman, Montana, or Des Moines, Iowa.

You will find that job registries, such as Idealist.org and NAFSA.org, *do* have international job and internship listings in many cities. If you're interested in an organization located in Washington, DC, or New York, but are looking to intern in Denver or Cincinnati, contact those national offices anyway. Many organizations, such as NCIV and IIE, have member organizations or regional offices across the country. These organizations may have internship opportunities in their own offices, and, if not, they are plugged into the international pipeline in their particular city and can steer you in the right direction. And, of course, every pocket of the country has universities and colleges. As higher education becomes more internationalized by the hour and the competition to recruit international students escalates, the number of international opportunities on campuses will continue to expand as well.

The Promises and Perils of Social Media

While networking has been and remains an activity traditionally done face-to-face, online networking has evolved into an important asset in career development. LinkedIn, for example, has emerged as something that, as they say, everyone's doing. It's become a prerequisite to maintain a well-crafted and updated LinkedIn profile to complement your traditional resume. The site is an effective way to build a direct and stable connection to professionals in the fields—including close friends and colleagues; high school or college classmates you're looking to reconnect with; or someone you may have just met and hope to learn more from later. And while LinkedIn was originally conceived as a networking tool, it has also become a robust job search tool. Nearly every one of the more than a hundred professionals we surveyed for this second edition about their favorite job search resources mentioned LinkedIn.

Many of them also mentioned Twitter. In the years since its creation, Twitter has become much more than a social network. Millions of users are now able to follow organizations and interesting individuals to gain a better understanding of their work. Some organizations also post job openings or other opportunities on their Twitter feeds. Job seekers can find these opportunities by following the organization or by searching for particular hashtags or following certain accounts.

Other sites, such as Facebook, are used by some for career networking, though these social networking sites are not always ideally suited for the purpose. Though there is much promise in the online social media world for career advancement, it should be noted that perils abound too. Facebook, for example, can actually work against a job seeker if he or she is not mindful of the type of information posted on a personal page. Stories abound of employers getting the wrong idea about or changing their opinion of a potential employee because of questionable content on a social networking page. It's tempting to think that our personal and professional worlds are separate and strictly defined—however, because information is instant and always accessible, this is no longer the case.

One more cautionary note (and in a way, this admonition is useful beyond the social media context): just because it is possible to do something doesn't mean it is necessary or desirable. We have both received messages that can only be described as presumptuous. We often receive LinkedIn requests from professionals we do not know, without an attached note of introduction or explanation as to why we might want to accept the request. In one such request Mark received, this stranger *did* attach a note of introduction, but the tone was as if they'd been friends for years and he presumed that Mark would have no problem meeting for an hour within the next few days. Similarly, a professional Sherry did not know sent her a long e-mail asking for answers to a series of detailed career questions.

As you work to expand your network and reach out to professionals via e-mail and social media, be mindful of how you do so. Be sure to consider how much time you are asking for. Will your request be received with alacrity or dread? How well do you know this person? Has someone she respects suggested you contact her? Busy professionals have time to respond to only some of the onslaught of messages they receive daily. Why does your message warrant an answer?

Selected Resources

AidSource

Website: www.aidsource.ning.com

Twitter: @AidSource1

AidSource is an online networking site for individuals involved in international aid work. It contains extensive resources, discussion threads, and shared calendars. Free memberships are available to access all content on the website. *Web.*

Building Bridges: A Manual on Including People with Disabilities in International Exchange Programs, Susan Sygall and Cindy Lewis, eds.

Mobility International USA / National Clearinghouse on Disability and Exchange, 262 pages, 2006 (www.miusa.org) [also available for download at no charge]

This comprehensive manual features suggestions and ideas for including, recruiting, and accommodating people with disabilities in international exchange programs. *Building Bridges* also addresses cross-cultural issues and international service projects and includes an extensive resource section for further research. *Print and Web.*

Careers in International Affairs, Eighth Edition, Maria Carland and Candace Faber, eds.

Georgetown University Press, 432 pages, 2008 (www.press.george town.edu)

Published in cooperation with Georgetown University's School of Foreign Service, this book—now in its eighth edition—provides a wealth of insight and information on global careers and networking. The publication includes a selected list of organizations and businesses with brief descriptions and information about application processes. The editors review the challenges, possibilities, and realities of global careers. The book features chapter introductions by experts in the public, private, and nonprofit sectors. It contains nearly 350 profiles of international organizations, multinationals, banks, government agencies, and nonprofit organizations. *Print.*

Careers in International Business

See chapter 12 in this volume.

CEO Job Opportunities Update

Website: www.ceoupdate.com

CEO Job Opportunities lists executive-level job openings in associations, professional societies, companies, and nonprofit organizations throughout the United States. It also provides recruiting services and includes articles outlining business trends, recruitment strategies, and global economic issues. *Web.*

The Chronicle of Higher Education

Website: http://chronicle.com

The Chronicle of Higher Education discusses issues and events concerning institutions and trends in higher learning. The bulletin section lists job openings in various sectors of higher education, including internationally oriented jobs at colleges and universities. Visit http://chronicle.com for subscription information. *Print and Web.*

The Chronicle of Philanthropy

See chapter 9 in this volume.

Devex

Website: www.devex.com

Twitter: @devex

Devex (formerly the Development Executive Group) is a membership organization that works to bring efficiency to international development through targeted recruiting and careful analysis of trends, as well as other services. The Devex website hosts a free job board with more than 2,000 international development jobs posted and more than 50,000 visitors each month. *Web.*

DevNetJobs

Website: www.devnetjobs.org

Twitter: @devenetjobs

Devnetjobs.org is a resource for jobs within the international development and consulting sector. Individuals can opt for a free membership, which includes a weekly job newsletter; a "Value Membership" for customized job alerts and online searches; or the "Value Membership and Broadcast Resume," which sends information to headhunters.

Devnetjobs.org has more than 16,500 recruiters and 500,000 users. *Web.*

Directory of Executive and Professional Recruiters 2011–2012

BNA Subsidiaries, 1,000 pages, 2010 (www.recruiterredbook.com)

Executive recruiters can provide a channel to relatively high-level jobs that are, in some cases, not advertised on mainstream job boards and search engines. Published since 1971, the "Red Book" can aid your job search with its extensive list of recruiters and search firms, complete with contact information, to help you start networking with executive recruiters. *Print and Web.*

Encyclopedia of Associations: International Organizations and Associations

See chapter 6 in this volume.

Encyclopedia of Associations: National Organizations of the U.S.

See chapter 6 in this volume.

Foreign Policy Association

Website: www.fpa.org

Twitter: @fpa_org

The Foreign Policy Association job board is a free resource and contains job postings from international think tanks and foreign policy research organizations; nonprofit organizations in international exchange, education, development, and related fields; as well as a host of other policy, research, and internationally oriented fields. The board allows you to sign up for a free e-mail newsletter so that job opportunities are delivered directly to your inbox. The FPA website also includes announcements for boot camps and seminars on international careers organized by the FPA. *Web.*

The Foundation Directory

See chapter 12 in this volume.

Give and Take, Adam Grant

Viking Adult, 321 pages, 2013 (www.giveandtake.com)

Give and Take is a book that takes a new look at how individuals perform in the work place. Grant (Wharton's youngest tenured professor) proffers the assumption that all individuals are *takers, matchers,* or, rarely, *givers.* Through pioneering research and creative stories, the author argues that, contrary to popular belief, those who give unconditionally are not weak; in fact, they have the capability to become wildly successful. *Print.*

GoAbroad

Website: www.goabroad.com

Twitter: @goabroad

GoAbroad.com has the stated purpose of filling "an information void in the area of international student travel." The website was designed to provide a one-stop information center for students who wish to travel internationally and to link prospective travelers with organizations providing international opportunities and services. The site has an abundance of information regarding travel and living abroad, with details about travel insurance, phone cards, travel gear, and airfare, as well as links to connected sites with distinct URLs on topics such as:

* Studying abroad (www.studyabroad.com)
* Interning abroad (www.internabroad.com)
* Volunteering abroad (www.volunteerabroad.com)
* Working abroad (www.jobsabroad.com)

ICEF Monitor

Website: http://monitor.icef.com

Twitter: @icefmonitor

ICEF Monitor is a "market intelligence resource for the international education industry." Individuals can subscribe for free daily or weekly updates through e-mail, or follow the *Monitor* through Facebook and Twitter. The website integrates its information by topic—such as immigration and e-learning—or by region or country. *Web.*

Idealist

See chapter 8 in this volume.

IIE Network Membership Directory 2012: Directory of International Educators

Institute of International Education (IIE), 200 pages, 2012 (www.iie.org)

The IIENetwork Membership Directory lists more than 6,000 professionals (study abroad directors, international student advisers, university presidents, and many more) at more than 1,200 higher education institutions who are actively engaged in international educational exchange. Online access to the directory is reserved for IIENetwork members. *Print.*

Indeed

Website: www.indeed.com

Twitter: @indeed

The purpose of Indeed is clear from the get-go: with no highlighted features on its homepage except a job search function (enter keyword and city/state, hit "Find Jobs"), it cuts through the clutter present on some other job websites and provides pages and pages of available positions. Indeed searches thousands of major job boards, newspapers, associations, and company career pages—each search hit gives information about where that job was originally posted and when. Patience is required, however, as the volume of options that an Indeed search offers can be overwhelming. Much scrolling and scanning is required to find a job listing that suits your specific interests. *Web.*

Inside Higher Ed

Website: www.insidehighered.com

Twitter: @insidehighered

Inside Higher Ed is a one-stop shop for individuals interested in higher education. The website was created in 2004 by three executives who emphasize the principles of excellence, accessibility, and community. These principles underline the items offered on the website, which include blogs, opinion pieces, professional training opportunities, and a job board for individuals ranging from graduate students to university presidents. Access to the full website, including the job board, is free. *Web.*

International Career Employment Weekly

Website: www.internationaljobs.org

International Career Employment Weekly is a newsletter filled with current international jobs in the fields of international development, exchange, education, communication, health care, democracy building, governance, policy, environmental issues, and others. This newsletter has been published since 1991 and has more than 20,000 readers in approximately 160 countries. A subscription is required to receive the most comprehensive and up-to-date listings, though a limited list of "hot jobs" is accessible online for free. Subscription lengths vary from six weeks to two years. Reduced subscription rates are offered for individuals. The newsletter can be delivered via hard copy or e-mail, or it can be accessed directly on the International Jobs Center website. *Print and Web.*

International Exchange Locator: A Resource for Educational and Cultural Exchange

Alliance for International Educational and Cultural Exchange, 222 pages, 2011 (www.alliance-exchange.org)

The *International Exchange Locator* offers detailed information about exchange organizations and related governmental agencies including mailing addresses, websites, e-mail addresses, phone/fax numbers, exchange programs descriptions, and key staff members. Tables at the end of the book provide an overview of US Department of State Exchange Visitor J designations, as well as organizations offering programs in specific geographical regions and countries, academic levels (K–12, scholar, teacher exchange, and more), and cultural and professional exchange programs. *Print.*

Monthly Developments

Website: www.monthlydevelopments.org

This monthly newsletter, published by InterAction and started in 1985, provides in-depth news and commentary on global trends that affect relief, refugee, and development work. It features the latest information on the work of InterAction members around the world and keeps readers up-to-date on legislative action in Congress that could affect US foreign assistance. *Monthly Developments* also describes new resources for relief and development workers, professional growth opportunities, and upcoming events. It includes an extensive list of international employment openings. *Print.*

NAFSA Job Registry

Website: http://jobregistry.nafsa.org

NAFSA: Association of International Educators is a leading professional association, founded in 1948, that promotes the exchange of students and scholars to and from the United States (see chapter 6, Professional Associations). Its online career center has plenty of useful information for those interested in international education, and its free online job registry is the go-to resource for anyone looking for a job in this field, whether that person is interested in universities, nonprofits, teaching, or in student and scholar services. *Web.*

See the profile of Fanta Aw for more information. Fanta is president of the NAFSA board of directors for 2013–2014.

Practical Idealists: Changing the World and Getting Paid, Alissa Wilson, Ann Barham, and John Hammock

Global Equity Initiative, Harvard University, 228 pages, 2008 (www .practicalidealists.org)

Practical Idealists is based on the concept of expressing one's values and passions through careers and life choices. Wilson, Barham, and Hammock make it clear that it *is* possible to work for social change and to be paid for doing it. Drawing on interviews with forty "practical idealists," the authors highlight some of the rewards and challenges that individuals will face in their quest to be a force for good in the world. *Print.*

ReliefWeb

Website: www.reliefweb.int

Twitter: @reliefweb

ReliefWeb is an online gateway to timely information and is administered by the United Nations Office for the Coordination of Humanitarian Affairs (OCHA). Since its creation in 1996, ReliefWeb has published more than 500,000 reports on humanitarian efforts and events around the world. Beyond a wide range of up-to-date information, the website also offers a job board for internship and job opportunities around the world, as well as training that is hosted either online or on location. *Web.*

Simply Hired

Website: www.simplyhired.com

Twitter: @simplyhired

Simply Hired allows you to search by entering a keyword and a location. Searching thousands of job boards, newspaper classifieds, and other organization and company pages, this website presents you with a vast number of position openings that are closely (and often not so closely) related to your search requirements. This enables you to see the range of options but can be daunting due to the vast number of job listings you are required to review to find one that might interest you. Simply Hired also offers a free online resume-posting service, allowing you to post your CV on up to five major job boards (including Monster .com, CareerBuilder.com, and Job.com) at once. *Web.*

Transitions Abroad: The Guide to Learning, Living, Working, and Volunteering Overseas

www.transitionsabroad.com

Transitions Abroad is a bimonthly magazine that has been published since 1977. Now completely online, it contains practical information for independent-minded travelers. Each issue focuses on alternatives to large-group tourism, including living, working, studying, and volunteering abroad, as well as vacationing directly with the people of the host country. The magazine's emphasis is on enriching, informed, affordable, and responsible travel. *Web.*

Travel as a Political Act, Rick Steves

Nation Books, 209 pages, 2009 (www.travelasapoliticalact.com)

Famed travel writer Rick Steves emphasizes the importance of using travel to learn in an active way. He argues that travel can help everyone broaden perspectives, question assumptions, and understand the complexity of current events. Ultimately, active travel and the learning acquired through travel enables people to make more informed political decisions. This book emphasizes the importance of cultural exchange and citizen diplomacy in the twenty-first century. *Print.*

— PROFILE —

Alanna Shaikh

Director of Communications, Outreach,
and Public Relations for AZ SHIP
Abt Associates, Baku, Azerbaijan, 2012–present

Career Trajectory

Blood and Milk (bloodandmilk.org) and *UN Dispatch* (www
.undispatch.com), International Development Blogger,
2009–present

Abt Associates, Regional Monitoring and Evaluation Director, QHCP,
Tajikistan, 2010–12

UNDP/UNAIDS, HIV Consultant, Tajikistan, 2010

GiveWell, Research Consultant, Remote/Tajikistan, 2010

ZdravPlus, Technical Consultant, Tajikistan, 2009

MacFadden Associates, Country Assistance Coordinator, Washington,
DC, 2007–8

International Medical Corps, Senior Desk Officer, Washington, DC,
2006–7

Project HOPE, Deputy Chief of Party, Uzbekistan, 2004–6

Abt Associates, Country Manager, Turkmenistan, 2002–4

Academic Background

Boston University, School of Public Health, MPH (International
Health), 2001

Georgetown University, School of Foreign Service, BSFS (Bachelor of
Science in Foreign Service), 1996

How do you define your cause?

I am totally obsessed with global health. And I realize that's a big field to claim as a cause, but I am honestly interested in almost everything about global health.

What drew you to this cause and your field?

I've wanted to do this as long as I can remember. I remember being in 9th or 10th grade and already thinking I wanted to work in international development. I'm from Syracuse, NY, and I was heavily involved in Model United Nations. That put me in a group of other internationally minded kids; I am one of those people who gets to live her childhood dream.

How would you describe your field?

In the absolutely broadest sense, it's about trying to help everybody in the world reach a healthy and happy standard of living—about giving people the opportunity and potential to live fulfilling lives.

I don't see a lot of overlap between international education and exchange and international development. It seems to me development is about trying to support the poorest of the poor and finding a way to give opportunities to people who didn't previously have them. International education and exchange goes the other way, where it supports up-and-coming leadership in other countries. . . . So, I guess in that sense, it actually *is* a part of international development because it's building capacity. The poorest of the poor are not getting involved in international exchanges, but on the other hand, there are an awful lot of foreign leaders who have studied in the United States or elsewhere overseas, so exchanges do have an impact on international development by affecting the leadership.

How would you describe your career path?

I wandered around doing a lot of vaguely international things. And then I started my public health degree, and that snapped me on course. I had a global health-related internship while I was doing my master's degree, and then when I finished my master's I moved to Uzbekistan as an intern with a global health agency. I was offered my first paying job while I was there. I've been rolling happily along on a global health track ever since.

That international experience in Uzbekistan was the key that opened the door. That was the job that's gotten me every job since. I hate advising people to pick up and go somewhere without a job and find one, because it's risky. I've talked to people for whom it didn't go well. But that international experience is what makes people look at your resume twice, what makes you stand out from the other candidates. It's what proves you're really passionate about this line of work.

International development is an unbelievably competitive field. And I understand why. I absolutely love my job, and I can see why other people would want to do it. But because it's so competitive, the internships, initial jobs, or overseas experiences that you can line up in advance from the United States or your home country are insanely competitive. We're talking 10 selected out of 1,000 applicants—and that's for an unpaid fellowship.

Where did you "start" and how did it help you get to where you are today?

I was an intern in the Office of the President at the American University in Cairo, and I realized a couple of things. I found I was really well suited to living overseas and that I loved it. I also realized that I didn't want to work in university administration. When I looked at the jobs that interested me, pretty much every position required the master's degree in public health. So the internship helped me both to learn what I was good at and figure out what I wanted to do next.

What are the major day-to-day activities of your current position?

Abt Associates is a USAID (*US Agency for International Development— see chapter 10*) implementing partner. Right now, I'm working with a health sector support project in Baku, Azerbaijan. We work to support the Ministry of Health of Azerbaijan to provide better health care. That includes training trainers, training physicians, supporting the government in making better health policy, and helping the government develop information systems in order to track health care spending and health information itself.

It's office work. The management team is either in our office in Baku or in meetings with either USAID or different Ministry of Health departments. I personally do a lot of writing for the project. The project ends soon, and I'm involved in drafting our close-out documents to codify and present everything that we've learned so that we can pass it on to the Ministry of Health to use when our experts aren't in-country anymore. I also oversee all of the reporting to USAID and the internal writing for Abt Associates. And because I have relevant experience, I provide technical assistance and support to the maternal-child health team and the monitoring and evaluation director.

One of the first things I tell people who are interested in this field is international development work is office work. I know I had a romantic notion of what international development was when I started university. When people tell me, "I'm not suited for office work, but I want to work internationally," I tell them, probably the best thing to do is to go to medical school and work with international populations in the United States. It still has that intercultural experience, you're still doing good for an underserved population, and it will get you out of the office. But when you turn on CNN and see people wearing scrubs and handing out food to refugees in refugee camps, well, first of all, most of those people are local staff, and second, they still go back to their tents in the refugee camp and spend six hours writing up their reports about everything they just handed out.

What is your best advice for developing effective networking skills?

The key to networking is to think about it as being generous from your heart. It's not about meeting people and what you can get from them. It's about what can you do for them, how you can help them. If you're working in development because you care about altruism, then looking at your network in that way is a good place to start.

At some point you're a student—the key is to work that. Being a student is a special time in your life, and people respect that and find it interesting. You can actually e-mail people and say, "I'm a student and I'm really interested in your field, your organization, and your job. Can I buy you a cup of coffee and ask you some questions?" But be targeted and specific. When someone e-mails me and says, "I'm very interested in global health, can we do a phone call?" that's vague, and I really don't know where to start with that. But if he says, "I'm thinking of applying for jobs in Azerbaijan and I was hoping you could tell me what it's like" or, "I'm thinking of applying to Abt Associates, can you tell me if they're a good employer?", that's useful. That's something that catches my attention and makes me want to talk to them.

Do you have a mentor? How has he or she affected your life and career?

There are a few people I think of as mentors—although I think they mostly think of me as a friend. They are predominantly older women who are on career paths that I would like to follow. They are people I go to with questions and for advice.

One mentor—I call her my "Once and Future Boss"—I have worked for more than once in different positions. We always keep in touch when I'm not working for her. She is a very helpful resource. Another is someone I met because she came on a field visit to Uzbekistan when I was the country director for a project. It took time for me to realize that somebody so many levels above me was interested in me as a person and wanted to keep in touch. I remember she came in October and she sent me a Christmas card that year.

That's when I realized, she wants to keep in touch, I should keep in touch too!

Do you consider yourself a mentor to others?

I have one person who actually came to me and said, "Alanna, I don't know anybody else who works in global health. Can you be my mentor?" She also asked, "What can I do for you in return? How can I make sure it's fair?" And I told her, "that's silly, I'm happy to be your mentor, you don't have to do anything in return." But because she opened that door, when I do need help with something, something that somebody in their twenties would understand, I e-mail her and ask for help.

There are also different people that I've supervised who think of me as a mentor. It's not formal—they've never used that word—but we keep in touch. We talk frequently and, similar to the older women I mentioned, I do think of them as friends. But they are friends whose careers are more junior than mine.

How have you maintained a healthy balance between your work and personal life?

It cuts both ways. On the one hand, in the field of international development, I've found that employers are often more willing to compromise with you and are open to unconventional working arrangements. For example, I have an eighteen-month-old son. When he was born, he and a nanny actually came to my office with me. On the other hand, the time change is a killer; when you're just getting ready to leave work, people in Washington, DC, are just waking up and sending you e-mails.

For me, I mean, I don't know if it's a balance or not, but it works for me. Unless we're on an urgent deadline, I leave work on time and I go home. I don't stay late at work for minor things, and, until my kids go to sleep, I don't work. If I leave the office at 5:30 and get home at 6:00 and the kids are in bed by 9:00, wanting that one three-hour sliver to myself doesn't seem unreasonable.

You're very rarely going to have a perfectly balanced day, but it's like nutrition: you need to look at your whole week. Is your week reasonably well balanced? You have to remember that the balance is larger than a single day.

What lessons have you learned as your career has evolved?

Sometimes you make a big plan and it works; you have to stand and stare in amazement that you actually pulled it off. On the other hand, sometimes something you think is the best plan ever, you don't know enough to see the problems with it. So we are best served by figuring out what we love and making our choices based on determining the next step.

There is a difference between loving the organization and loving your job. You can be working with a fantastic organization doing fantastic things, but if you don't like your day-to-day activities, you're not going to be happy there. People confuse the organization with their specific position. As a rule, it's more important to look at what your average day is going to be like.

Any final advice?

I don't want to discourage anybody, but it is genuinely difficult to get your first job in international development. Usually, you end up working for free. That's bad in a lot of ways and has social justice implications that I don't like, but I can't personally fix the system. So I want to at least warn people that it's coming. You should think about your motivations and what really is interesting to you about this work. If there is anything else you can love as much, maybe you should do that.

— PROFILE —

Allan Goodman

President and CEO, Institute of International
Education (IIE), New York, NY, 1998–present

Career Trajectory

Georgetown University, School of Foreign Service, Washington, DC
    Executive Dean, 1996–98
    Professor of International Affairs, 1988–98
    Academic Dean for Graduate Studies and Faculty Development,
    1994–96
    Associate Dean for Graduate Studies; Director of the Master of
    Science in Foreign Service Program, 1980–94
    Associate Professor of International Affairs, 1980–87
    Adjunct Professor of Diplomacy, 1977–80

Central Intelligence Agency, Washington, DC
    Presidential Briefing Coordinator, 1979–80
    Special Assistant to Director, National Foreign Assessment
    Center, 1978–79
    Assistant National Intelligence Officer for Political Economy,
    National Foreign Assessment Center, 1977–78
    Analyst, International Issues Division, Office of Regional and
    Political Analysis, 1977
    Analyst, International Functional Staff, Office of Political
    Research, 1975–76

Stanford University, Hoover Institution on War, Revolution and Peace,
    Palo Alto, CA, 1974–75

Clark University, Chairman, Department of Government; Assistant
    and Associate Professor, Worcester, MA, 1971–74

Academic Background

Harvard University, John F. Kennedy School of Government, MPA, 1968, and PhD, 1971

Northwestern University, BS, 1966

How do you define your cause?

I've had many different causes, but in this field, my aim is to change the paradigm of higher education. International must become part of what it means to be educated. The vast majority of people don't plan on having an experience outside their own culture.

It's always troubled me that the majority of American citizens don't have a passport. We know from the IIE *Open Doors* numbers that fewer than 1 percent of Americans in higher education, at any given time, are going to study abroad—even though many more want to go and say they will as they enter university, but a lot of things happen in between. We've tried something that I call our "Passport Campaign," to encourage presidents of American colleges and universities, when they address the freshman convocation, to say "what you need to be successful here is not just a computer and your parents' checkbook, but also a passport."

What we've learned—or I believe I've learned—is that the model of the junior year study abroad, which IIE actually invented in 1923 with twelve colleges and universities participating, no longer works. The junior year is not the best time to go. Hardly anybody goes for a whole year, and what you really have to do is begin to plan for this when you're a freshman. Have a passport, plan whether your first experience is going to be a summer internship between freshman and sophomore year, or go for a Gilman or a Boren scholarship for your languages for your sophomore year. By the time you're a junior, you don't want to be away from campus, or you can't be away from campus if you're a varsity athlete or preparing for the MCATs. People tend to look at that junior year and find too many obstacles. So we need to start much earlier. The first step to get abroad is to get a passport.

What drew you to this cause and your field?

I never thought I'd have a passport. I never thought I would get to go abroad. And I really didn't think I was going to go to college either. I was lucky. I got a scholarship and I had great teachers who asked, "Have you considered this? Have you considered that? Why don't you try this?" I really fell into international work completely by accident.

Where did you "start" and how did it help you get to where you are today?

As an undergraduate, state and local government really fascinated me. I thought someday I would run for Congress. So I focused on domestic politics; the relationship between cities and their states is what fascinated me the most.

I won a scholarship to go to graduate school at Harvard and realized I needed a research assistant job—called "gophers" in those days—to make ends meet. I was told a professor in comparative government needed a gopher, and I said "Gee, I don't think I have any knowledge to contribute . . . I wouldn't even be a good gopher." But I was forced to meet this professor, and he was Samuel P. Huntington. Everything changed: my life, my work, my trajectory. He said to me in the second or third week, "By the way, do you have a passport?" I said, "No," and he said, "Well you better get one because we're going to take a trip around the world this summer."

My career advice here is to keep your mind open to the world. I meet so many students who are undecided, which is okay, but they refuse to try things *because* they haven't decided yet. They haven't decided if they want to be a diplomat, or a professor, or a consultant. Instead of exploring all three positions, they agonize over "which one am I going to marry?" And this isn't life-marriage. You need to have many options. You need to be flexible.

It's that empowering openness that I find missing in people today who are trying to make career choices. They think they have to solve and narrow before they actually do. We need to show them that if they've got a great education, they can *do* many things, in many different places: that's what it's all about.

How would you describe your field?

I think it's too soon to say now. A number of years ago, I think we'd have agreed that international education meant mobility. It meant student exchanges, and it meant tracking the numbers. And in the past decade or a decade-and-a-half, the definition and the concept has really dramatically expanded and changed—and it's still in the process of changing. It is mobility, branch campuses, global network universities, and curricular change. It is preparing the next generation for global citizenship.

And we're also on the edge of trying to figure out what distance learning and MOOCs (massive open online courses) mean to the world of international education and exchange. We're probably another five years away from really knowing how big the universe is, knowing the right descriptors, and characterizing it. There's always a risk that the world can turn inward. It has many times before.

How would you describe your career path?

Jagged and not based on any coherent plan. Being open to new challenges and new possibilities was something that Professor Huntington taught me.

What are the major day-to-day activities of your current position?

It's important to ask myself each day: Have I done enough with Congress in advocating for international exchange? Who am I going to ask for money? Do I remember what the vision is and what am I planning to do to execute the vision? If you're not focusing on the vision, then you're focusing on the tactical. And your job when you are president of an organization is to focus on the bigger picture: always try to move the organization forward, always think about what we ought to do and where we ought to be.

What is your best advice for developing effective networking skills?

I'll come back to something I said previously. I am struck in giving career advice that people starting out in their careers are not open-minded about what they could do, about what they could experience. That's a big danger.

Young people today are afraid. They are, after all, the first genera-tion that are guaranteed not to live as well as their parents. Kids are worried about getting into schools, they're worried about staying in school, about what jobs will be available when they graduate. There isn't a sense of opportunity, or of "let me explore the world." There is a profound sense of caution. We underestimate how worried this next generation is. And when you're worried, you're much less likely to say, "I'm going to try this. Or, at least, I'll apply for it."

I come back to this quality of openness. There isn't a course "Openness 101" at school. You need someone to encourage you: a professor, your parents, your significant other, a mentor.

Do you have a mentor? How has he or she affected your life and career?

Professor Huntington would be number one, but Peter Krogh, the dean at Georgetown University for whom I worked, taught me a huge amount. Admiral Turner at the CIA taught me a great deal about man-agement and leadership.

I learned to do the best job possible. Put excellence in your work ahead of everything else. I learned to get exposed to a lot of different issues and people. Ask short but good questions that you really need to know the answers to in order to do your work better. The more you speak, the less you're learning. Be very conscious in any space, in any dialogue—if you're the one speaking, you're not learning anything, so achieve the right balance between listening and talking.

How have you maintained a healthy balance between your work and personal life?

I think it's pretty unfair to ask that of a president, because you are the chief executive. You are responsible for the whole organization so you're never really off duty. I'm not sure CEOs can have a life–work balance. You just have to do the best you can.

What lessons have you learned as your career has evolved?

Keeping your job at IIE—or any place—requires two things. One is the ability to write a good paragraph or page, and no more. That's something that we don't teach in university. If you're not able to write an effective three-sentence e-mail, if you can't capture something thoughtfully and respectfully in a few sentences, you're going to have a problem.

Second, because we are a service organization, have the empathy or compassion to put yourself in the exchange program sponsor's shoes, or the program grantee's shoes, and try to solve their problems. And sometimes solving problems means getting multiple sources of advice.

I think good writing skills and the capacity for empathy are the two most important traits you can bring to the workplace, whether it's public or private, whether it's domestic or international.

CHAPTER 6

Professional Associations

Introduction

Becoming active in one or more professional associations will lead you to critically important avenues for networking and information gathering—two fundamental aspects of your job search. Professional associations (most of which have annual conferences), events, publications, and websites keep you abreast of what is happening in your specific areas of interest, who the leaders are, and where new jobs may be found. Many association websites contain information on training opportunities, as well as job banks, resume boards, and other employment-related services.

Membership in associations also demonstrates to potential employers a serious commitment to your career development. Most professional associations have membership opportunities available for students, often at reduced rates. Many allow job seekers to volunteer at conferences or regional meetings in exchange for waived registration fees. These conferences and other assemblies provide opportunities to present papers, participate in discussions, and raise questions. This is an ideal way to hone your communication skills, gain and share expertise, and interact with colleagues who share your specific professional interests.

In addition, the association field is the third-largest employer in the Washington, DC, area, after the federal government and the tourism industry. Associations not only offer career and job resources, they are also possible places of employment.

In this chapter you will find a selected list of professional associations with a focus on international exchange, education, or development, or a related field. A brief description of each association is followed by its membership categories (with costs, when available). This list is followed by additional resources that provide more information on associations, enabling you to research more broadly or find a specific professional association not listed here.

Sample Professional Associations

Association of International Education Administrators (AIEA)

Campus Box 90404, Duke University

Durham, NC 27708

Telephone: 919-668-1928

Website: www.aieaworld.org

Founded in 1982, AIEA's mission is to promote and improve international education administration. It provides opportunities for its members "to join forces, exchange ideas, share institutional strategies, and provide an effective voice on matters of public policy" through dialogues, workshops, scholarly journals, and a membership directory. AIEA holds an annual conference that attracts leaders from around the world to discuss current trends, challenges, and the future of international education.

Membership:

- Academic Institutional Membership ($400 per year)
- Other Organizations Supporting International Education Membership ($400 per year)
- Individual Membership: for individuals at colleges and universities with current institutional membership in AIEA ($100 per year)
- Unaffiliated Individuals ($400 per year)

AIESEC (International Association of Students in Economic and Commercial Sciences)

11 Hanover Square, Suite 1700

New York, NY 10005

Telephone: 212-757-3774

Website: www.aiesecus.org

Twitter: @AIESEC

Since its founding in 1948, AIESEC has grown into the world's largest student-based organization, with chapters in more than 113 countries and on 2,400 university campuses. The mission of AIESEC—a French acronym that stands for *l'Association Internationale des Etudiants en Sciences Economiques et Commerciales*, the International Association of Students in Economic and Commercial Sciences—is to contribute to the development of countries and their people with a strong commitment to furthering international understanding and cooperation. AIESEC works to "develop individuals, communities, and cooperation through global exchange" by facilitating work exchanges among its member countries. AIESEC provides opportunities for students to gain professional and cultural experience and access a global network through events and activities hosted by local chapters and work-exchange programs such as the International Traineeship Exchange Program.

Membership:

• Student Membership: available through a local sponsoring university—AIESEC's website lists sponsoring universities

Alliance for International Educational and Cultural Exchange

1828 L Street, NW, Suite 1150

Washington, DC 20036

Telephone: 202-293-6141

Website: www.alliance-exchange.org

Twitter: @AllianceExchnge

The Alliance for International Educational and Cultural Exchange is a nonprofit membership association dedicated to formulating and promoting public policies that support the growth and well-being of international exchange links between the people of the United States and other nations. Representing US-based exchange organizations, the Alliance acts as the leading policy voice for the US exchange community. The organization sponsors two annual advocacy days for its members on Capitol Hill to lobby for sound policies and more resources for federally funded international exchange programs. It also coordinates ongoing advocacy activities at the state and local levels. The Alliance compiles the *International Exchange Locator*, which contains entries for more than 300 exchange-focused organizations and federal agencies (*see chapter 5 in this volume*). The Alliance was established in

1993 through a merger of two organizations: the Liaison Group, which represented academic and professional exchanges, and the International Exchange Association, a coalition of citizen and youth exchange organizations.

Membership:

- Full Membership: intended for those organizations that conduct, facilitate, or support international exchanges (cost varies by organization size)
- Partner Membership: intended for companies, businesses, or organizations that provide services (e.g., insurance, tax preparation) to Alliance full members ($3,000 per year)
- Affiliate Membership: intended for exchange-related organizations or offices that wish to receive regular access to comprehensive information about policy developments that affect international educational and cultural exchange, but that are ineligible to become full members ($100 per year)

Mark is the assistant director and senior policy specialist at the Alliance.

American Association of Collegiate Registrars and Admissions Officers (AACRAO)

1 Dupont Circle, NW, Suite 520

Washington, DC 20036

Telephone: 202-293-9161

Website: www.aacrao.org

Twitter: @AACRAO

AACRAO was established in 1910 as a nonprofit, voluntary, professional association committed to supporting higher education and providing professional development opportunities to members. It comprises more than 11,000 higher education admissions and registration professionals who represent approximately 2,600 institutions in more than forty countries. AACRAO provides professional development services including national meetings and training events, grant and award opportunities, access to relevant publications and survey results, consulting services, online workshops, and a searchable job bank.

Membership:

- Individual Membership: open to high school registrars or counselors ($206 per year); retired AACRAO members ($103 per year); staff at international secondary or postsecondary institutions ($206 per year); and students at an AACRAO member institution ($25 per year)

- Associate Membership: open to voting members of AACRAO who are seeking employment ($206)
- Affiliate Membership: open to postsecondary degree-granting institutions ineligible for voting institutional membership (dues vary based on enrollment)
- Institutional Membership: open to postsecondary degree-granting institutions accredited by an agency recognized by the Council for Higher Education Accreditation (dues vary based on enrollment)
- Corporate Membership: open to individuals or organizations, whether for-profit or nonprofit, that provide products and services that assist or benefit the needs or purposes of AACRAO members (dues vary based on size)
- Organizational Membership: open to nonprofit associations whose interests are closely aligned to AACRAO, including state higher education coordinating boards and associations, accrediting bodies, and international ministries of education ($590 per year)

American Association of Community Colleges (AACC)

1 Dupont Circle, NW, Suite 410

Washington, DC 20036

Telephone: 202-728-0200

Website: www.aacc.nche.edu

Twitter: @Comm_College

AACC, founded in 1920, is an advocacy organization that represents nearly 1,200 two-year community colleges in the United States, Puerto Rico, Japan, Great Britain, South Korea, and the United Arab Emirates. AACC's mission of "building a nation of learners by advancing America's community colleges" is pursued via five goals: recognition and advocacy for community colleges; student access to learning and success; community college leadership development; economic and workforce development; and global and intercultural education.

Membership:

- Individual Associate Membership ($100 per year)
- Institutional Membership: open to two-year, associate degree-granting colleges (cost based on enrollment and varies from $1,300 to $69,900 per year)

- Educational Associate Membership: open to nonprofits not eligible for institutional membership ($715 per year)

American Association of Intensive English Programs (AAIEP)

AAIEP Central Office

PO Box 1158

Pacifica, CA 94044

Telephone: 415-926-1975

Website: www.aaiep.org

AAIEP, originally part of NAFSA, became a separate organization in 1988. AAIEP's goals include promoting professional standards, advocating the value of English study, and increasing the visibility of Intensive English Programs (IEP). More than 300 IEP programs are members. AAIEP advocates to ensure that only accredited language schools can offer certificates, and that short-term, full-time study in tourist visa status be permitted under the law.

Membership:

- Full Membership: open to US-based English programs ($200 application fee; $625 per year)
- Associate Membership: open to institutions and organizations that do not sponsor or provide English programs ($775 per year)

American Bar Association (ABA): Section of International Law

ABA Section of International Law

740 15th Street, NW

Washington, DC 20005

Telephone: 202-662-1660

Website: www.abanet.org/intlaw

Twitter: @abaesq

The Section of International Law, founded in 1933, works to educate lawyers on current developments in international law and practice, as well as to promote interest, activity, and research in international and comparative law and related areas. It is committed to the development of policy and the promotion of the rule of law on an international scale. It offers workshops and briefings on emerging issues in international law and is separated into divisions and subcommittees to accommodate specialized member interests. Categories include the Business Law Division, Public International Law Division, Comparative Law Division, and the General Division.

Membership:

- Section on International Law Membership ($175 per year; membership in the ABA is a prerequisite)

American Council on Education (ACE): Center for International Initiatives

1 Dupont Circle, NW

Washington, DC 20036

Telephone: 202-939-9300

Website: www.acenet.edu/programs/international

Twitter: @ACEducation

ACE is a major coordinating body for higher education institutions in the United States. Since 1918, it has provided leadership on higher education issues and influenced public policy through research, advocacy, and program initiatives. Through its Center for International Initiatives, ACE offers programs and services that support and enhance the internationalization of US campuses and works with international partners on higher education issues that have a global impact. The Commission for International Initiatives, an advisory body of ACE member presidents, guides ACE's work in this area.

Membership:

- Two-Year Institution Membership ($1,224–$3,641 per year; based on enrollment numbers)
- Four-Year Institution Membership ($1,353–$20,977 per year; based on enrollment numbers and total expenses of the most recent calendar year)
- Branch Campus Membership ($1,040 per year)
- National Association Membership: open to associations who work on the national level, and whose primary mission is higher education ($2,884 per year)
- Regional Association Membership: open to associations who work on the regional level, and whose primary mission is higher education ($1,444 per year)

- International Membership: open to international higher education institutions and international organizations that are concerned with higher education ($827 per year)
- Foundation Membership: open to those organizations that wish to support higher education ($2,364 per year)

American Foreign Service Association (AFSA)

2101 E Street, NW

Washington, DC 20037

Telephone: 800-704-2372 (within the United States) or 202-338-4045

Website: www.afsa.org

Twitter: @AFSATweets

AFSA was founded in 1924 as the professional association of the US Foreign Service. With more than 13,000 members, AFSA represents active and retired Foreign Service (FS) employees of the US Department of State and the US Agency for International Development (US-AID), as well as smaller groups in the Foreign Agricultural Service (FAS), US and Foreign Commercial Service (FCS), and International Broadcasting Bureau (IBB). AFSA's principal goals are to enhance the effectiveness of the Foreign Service, to protect the professional interests of its members, to ensure high professional standards for both career diplomats and political appointees, and to promote understanding of the critical role of the Foreign Service in promoting America's national security and economic prosperity. AFSA also acts in a labor/management-relations capacity as the exclusive bargaining agent for Foreign Service employees.

Membership:

- Active Membership: open to all Foreign Service personnel in the US Department of State, USAID, FAS, FCS, and IBB, based on FS paygrade ($86.70–$370.55 per year; $1,500 lifetime membership)
- Retired Membership: based on FS Annuity ($63.70–$167.20 per year; $1,000 lifetime membership)
- Associate Membership: open to anyone supportive of AFSA goals ($102.75 per year; $1,000 lifetime membership)

American Political Science Association (APSA)

1527 New Hampshire Avenue, NW

Washington, DC 20036

Telephone: 202-483-2512

Website: www.apsanet.org

Twitter: @APSAtweets

APSA, founded in 1903, is a professional organization dedicated to the study of political science, including international relations. It serves more than 15,000 members in more than eighty countries. The majority of APSA members are scholars; however, the membership also includes government officials, researchers, consultants, and NGO leaders. APSA provides members with services that facilitate research, teaching, and professional development and supports special projects to increase public understanding of political science. APSA maintains an online job bank, *eJobs*. APSA publications list employment opportunities, grants and studies, annual meetings, and publishing opportunities.

Membership:

- Professional Membership ($97–$316 per year, based on income; $3,000 lifetime membership)
- Retired Membership: open to those who have had membership for twenty-five continuous years ($40–$66 per year)
- Targeted International Membership: open to scholars in low/middle income countries ($40 per year)
- Family Membership: open to spouses and domestic partners of professional and life members ($29 per year)
- High School Teacher Membership ($45 per year)
- Student Membership ($45 per year)
- Unemployed Membership ($45 per year)

American Society for Training and Development (ASTD)

1640 King Street, Box 1443

Alexandria, VA 22313

Telephone: 703-683-8100

Website: www.astd.org

Twitter: @ASTD

Since 1944, ASTD has served professionals in the field of human resources and is dedicated to advancing workplace learning. ASTD's members live in more than 100 countries and connect locally in 120 US chapters and 16 global networks. Members work as independent consultants, trainers and suppliers, and in thousands of organizations of all sizes, both public and private. ASTD's website features a career center that offers a job bank, an ongoing education certificate program, career coaching and development publications, and a salary calculator.

Membership:

- Individual Membership ($199 per year)
- Senior Membership ($90 per year)
- Student Membership ($59 per year)

American Studies Association (ASA)

1120 19th Street, NW, Suite 301

Washington, DC 20036

Telephone: 202-467-4783

Website: www.theasa.net

ASA is open to all persons who "have in common the desire to view America as a whole rather from the perspective of a single discipline." It is dedicated to broadening and intensifying the study of American culture, history, and society. Founded in 1951, ASA has more than 6,000 individual members and 140 institutional members, representing a diverse cross section of fields such as history, literature, religion, art, philosophy, music, science, folklore, ethnic studies, government, communications, education, library science, popular culture, and others. On an international level, ASA encourages the exchange of students and faculty members, promotes the establishment of American Studies departments and associations abroad, and provides a communication forum for leaders of American Studies associations around the world. ASA offers a job bank, a Certification Professional in Learning and Performance Certificate (CPLP), and many other career development resources.

Membership:

- Individual Membership ($55–$120 per year, based on income level; $1,500 lifetime membership)
- Student/Income Under $12,000 Membership ($20 per year)
- Institutional Membership ($170 per year)

ASAE (American Society of Association Executives) and the Center for Association Leadership

ASAE and the Center Building

1575 I Street, NW

Washington, DC 20005

Telephone: 202-371-0940 or 888-950-2723

Website: www.asaecenter.org

Twitter: @ASAEcenter

ASAE is a membership organization that represents the association profession. It provides resources, research, knowledge, and advocacy to enhance the performance and power of the association and non-profit community. Founded in 1920, ASAE has more than 21,000 association CEOs, staff professionals, industry partners, and consultant members in more than fifty countries. The Center for Association Leadership, founded in 2001, provides information and training for the association community. ASAE and the Center together serve approximately 10,000 associations that represent approximately 287 million people worldwide. ASAE hosts a career center and job bank for the association profession at www.careerhq.org.

Membership:

- CEO Membership ($325 per year)
- Professional Non-CEO Staff Membership ($295 per year)
- Young Professional Membership: open to working individuals aged 30 and under ($100 per year)
- Consultant Membership: open to individuals who are not full-time ($425 per year)
- Industry Partner Membership: open to individuals who are part of nonprofits or are government employees ($425 per year)

ASEEES (Association for Slavic, East European, and Eurasian Studies)

315 South Bellefield Avenue, 203C Bellefield Hall

Pittsburgh, PA 15260

Telephone: 412-648-9911

Website: http://aseees.org

In 2010, the American Association for the Advancement of Slavic Studies (founded in 1948) changed its name to the Association for Slavic,

East European, and Eurasian Studies. ASEEES is a nonprofit, nonpolitical, scholarly society based at the University of Pittsburgh. It works to promote education and the spread of knowledge of the former Soviet Union and Eastern and Central Europe. With more than fifty member institutions both abroad and at home, six regional affiliates within the United States, and thirty-six organizational ties to scholarly societies, ASEEES works to lead open and thoughtful dialogue.

Membership:

- Individual Membership ($55–$200 per year, based on income level)
- Student Membership ($35 per year)
- Premium Institutional Membership ($600 per year)
- For-profit Institution and Foundation Membership ($400 per year)
- Nonprofit Organization Membership ($300 per year)

Asia Society

725 Park Avenue at 70th Street

New York, NY 10021

Telephone: 212-288-6400

Website: www.asiasociety.org

Twitter: @AsiaSociety

The Asia Society, founded in 1956, is a nonprofit and nonpartisan educational organization dedicated to fostering understanding of Asia. The Asia Society promotes communication between Americans and the peoples of Asia and the Pacific region. Through art exhibitions and performances, films, lectures, conferences, seminars, and programs for both students and teachers, the Asia Society provides a forum for presenting the uniqueness and diversity of Asia to the American people. The Asia Society is headquartered in New York. Regional centers are located in Washington, DC; Houston; Los Angeles; Hong Kong; and Melbourne.

Membership (at NY headquarters):

- Individual Membership ($65 per year)
- Student/Association/Senior Citizen Membership ($50 per year)
- Corporate Partner Membership ($25,000 per year)

Council on Foreign Relations (CFR)

The Harold Pratt House

58 East 68th Street

New York, NY 10065

Telephone: 212-434-9400

Website: www.cfr.org

Twitter: @CFR_org

CFR is a nonprofit, nonpartisan membership organization that aims to improve the understanding of US foreign policy and international affairs. Founded in 1921, CFR is home to a think tank dedicated to the continuous study of US foreign policy for the benefit of its members, as well as world audiences. By mobilizing resident senior staff, members, and other experts in dialogue, study, and publications programs, the Council serves as a forum for scholarship and policy analysis. The Council on Foreign Relations Press publishes *Foreign Affairs*, a leading print journal of global politics, books, and occasional policy reports on a broad range of issues. It produces "America and the World," a weekly radio series aired on National Public Radio.

Membership: Both individual and corporate members must be nominated by current members of the Council.

Council on Standards for International Educational Travel (CSIET)

212 South Henry Street

Alexandria, VA 22314

Telephone: 703-739-9050

Website: www.csiet.org

Twitter: @CSIET_Tweet

CSIET is a nonprofit organization dedicated to international educational travel and exchange programs for young people at the high school level. It functions in a leadership and support role for the youth exchange community with the ultimate goal of ensuring that young people have access to safe and meaningful international experiences. CSIET aims to identify organizations that demonstrate a commitment to good standards in youth exchange, dedication to developing and sharing best practices with the larger youth exchange community, and a belief in the educational value of youth exchange. Each spring,

CSIET publishes an *Advisory List of International Educational Travel and Exchange Programs* for the benefit of schools, students, and host families.

Membership:

- Educational Organization Membership: open to educational organizations that are not conducting youth exchange programs ($580 per year for voting membership; $205 per year for associate membership)
- Exchange Organization Membership: open to US-based exchange organizations that conduct international youth exchange programs for secondary-school students ($520–$9,975 per year, based on the number of secondary-school-aged exchange participants the organization has per year)
- Individual Membership: open to individuals who live in the United States ($80 per year)
- International Associate Membership: open to overseas international exchange programs who have been nominated for membership by a CSIET-listed organization ($685 per year)
- Corporate Partner Membership: open to commercial and business entities based in the United States that work with the international youth exchange community ($1,050 per year)

Devex

1341 Connecticut Avenue, NW

Washington, DC 20036

Telephone: 202-249-9222

Website: www.devex.com

Twitter: @devex

Founded in 2000, Devex is a membership organization that delivers business information and recruitment services to the international development community. Devex employs more than 100 staff in four locations including its Washington, DC, headquarters; Barcelona; Manila; and Tokyo. It aims to help the international community deliver foreign assistance effectively and efficiently. More than 500,000 individuals are registered with the organization, and more than 1,000 of the world's leading development consultancies and NGOs are executive members. A library of reports on development projects are posted on the website and a sixty-person team provides daily coverage of projects and news in the international development industry. The Devex online job board is a comprehensive listing of international development jobs.

Membership:

- Executive Membership: designed for senior managers and project directors ($99 per month)
- Career Account: open to professionals for job listings and career advice ($19 per month)

Foreign Policy Association (FPA)

470 Park Avenue South

New York, NY 10016

Telephone: 212-481-8100

Website: www.fpa.org

Twitter: @FPA_ORG

The mission of the FPA, a nonprofit educational organization, is to inspire the American public to learn more about the world. The FPA was originally founded in 1918 as the League of Free Nations Association to support President Woodrow Wilson's efforts to achieve peace. FPA organizes numerous events on diverse topics in international affairs, publishes and distributes books and other publications, sponsors the annual *Great Decisions* program, produces several free online newsletters, and hosts a resource library and a job bank on its website. FPA also offers Global Career Boot Camps that provide specialized seminars developed by practitioners in the field, networking opportunities, and career guidance.

Membership:

- Associate Membership ($250 per year)
- National Associate Membership: for those outside the New York City metro area ($75 per year)
- Student Membership ($50 per year; $25 per year outside of NYC)

Forum on Education Abroad

Dickinson College

PO Box 1773

Carlisle, PA 17013

Telephone: 717-245-1031

Website: www.forumea.org

Twitter: @ForumEA

The Forum on Education Abroad (FEA) is a nonprofit formed in 2001 with the mission of improving education abroad programs to benefit the students who participate in them. FEA goals include establishing standards of good practice, conducting research to assess outcomes, promoting excellence in curriculum design, and advocating for high-quality education abroad programs at all levels. Members include nearly 500 institutional members that collectively represent more than 90 percent of the US students who study abroad. The website offers free research and publications as well as information on events and a job board.

Membership:

- US Institution Membership ($696–$2,060 per year, based on number of students sent abroad annually)
- Non-US Institution Membership ($696–$3,606 per year, based on number of US study abroad students received annually)
- Affiliate Organization Membership ($1,030 per year)
- Individual Membership ($155 per year)

Fulbright Association

1320 19th Street, NW, Suite 350

Washington, DC 20036

Telephone: 202-775-0725

Website: www.fulbright.org

Twitter: @FulbrightAssoc

Founded in 1977, the Fulbright Association is a nonprofit membership organization of Fulbright Program alumni and supporters. The Association supports and promotes international exchange and the ideal most associated with the Fulbright name—mutual understanding among the peoples of the world. With more than fifty chapters across the country, the Association's central focus is to mobilize alumni and other supporters of exchange on behalf of this seminal program created by the late Senator J. William Fulbright in 1946. The Association engages in advocacy and provides mechanisms to take organized action on behalf of the Fulbright Program. The Fulbright Association hosts an annual conference on international issues; it also awards the Fulbright Prize to distinguished individuals who have done exceptional work in creating understanding among peoples and cultures. It is linked to seventy independent Fulbright Associations in other countries.

Membership:

- Individual Membership: open to those who have received a Fulbright Scholarship ($50 per year; $500 lifetime)
- Friend of Fulbright Membership: open to individuals who support the Fulbright ideals ($40 per year)
- Student Membership ($25 per year)
- Institutional Membership: open to institutions with close ties or interest in the Fulbright Program ($500 per year)

InterAction

1400 16th Street, NW, Suite 210

Washington, DC 20036

Telephone: 202-667-8227

Website: www.interaction.org

Twitter: @interactionorg

InterAction, founded in 1984, is an alliance of US-based international development and humanitarian nongovernmental organizations. With a coalition of more than 190 private and voluntary organizations (PVOs) operating in developing countries worldwide, InterAction works to overcome poverty, exclusion, and suffering by advancing social justice and basic dignity for all peoples. InterAction sponsors a broad array of programs and activities that focus on advocacy, development, disaster response, refugees, gender and diversity, and media. InterAction's monthly print newsletter, *Monthly Developments*—available for $40 annually—covers a wide range of issues in international development and includes an extensive listing of international employment opportunities (*see chapter 5 in this volume*). In addition, InterAction offers a free weekly listing of employment and internship opportunities in the international development and assistance field. Subscribers receive approximately twenty-five to thirty job announcements each week at US-based humanitarian and development organizations with positions available in the United States and overseas.

Membership:

- Organizational Membership ($2,000–$46,000 per year, calculated as 15 percent of assessable expenses)
- Associate Membership ($2,000–$20,000 per year, calculated on total expenses)

International Communication Association (ICA)

1500 21st Street, NW

Washington DC 20036

Telephone: 202-955-1444

Website: www.icahdq.org

Since 1950, ICA has been dedicated to advancing the scholarly study of human and mediated communication and to facilitating the implementation of such research findings. Members may join one of the Association's divisions or interest groups, which include interpersonal communication, organizational communication, intercultural/development communication, political communication, communication and technology, language and social interaction, journalism studies, and intergroup communication.

Membership (for US residents):

- Regular Membership: open to scholars and practitioners of communication research who have earned their PhDs ($150 per year)
- Student Membership ($75 per year)
- Sustaining Membership: includes a regular membership, one conference registration, and a $40 donation to the Student Travel Fund ($440)
- Life Membership ($5,000)
- Emeritus Membership: open to scholars who have been an ICA member for twenty continuous years ($50 per year)
- Institutional Membership: open to university departments, except libraries ($250 per year)

International Council on Education for Teaching (ICET)

National Louis University

1000 Capitol Drive

Wheeling, IL 60090

Telephone: 847-947-5881

Website: www.icet4u.org

Twitter: @ICET4U

Founded in 1953, ICET is an international association of educational organizations, institutions, and individuals working toward the improvement of teacher education and all forms of education and training related to national development. ICET promotes the cooperation of higher education and government institutions with the private sector to develop a worldwide network of international development resources. Their programs and services provide members with access to a worldwide resource base of organizations, personnel programs, research, and training opportunities.

Membership:

- Individual Membership ($50 per year)
- Institutional/Association/Ministry of Education Membership ($300 per year)

International Studies Association (ISA)

University of Arizona

324 Social Sciences

Tucson, AZ 85721

Telephone: 520-477-2050

Website: www.isanet.org

ISA, founded in 1959, promotes research and education in international affairs and strives to foster thoughtful discussion and systematic understanding of international issues. ISA, with 6,200 members worldwide in eighty countries, works to create a community of scholars dedicated to international studies. Sections and regional subdivisions as well as caucuses provide opportunities to exchange ideas and research with colleagues interested in specific areas within the field of international studies. ISA also sponsors an annual convention where papers, issues, and panel discussions are presented.

Membership:

- Standard Membership ($40–$330 per year, prorated according to income)
- Student Membership ($25 per year)
- Institutional Membership: designed for libraries and departmental access ($1,350 per year)

Joint National Committee for Languages-National Council for Languages and International Studies (JNCL-NCLIS)

4646 40th Street, NW, Suite 310

Washington, DC 20016

Telephone: 202-966-8477

Website: www.languagepolicy.org

Twitter: @JNCLInfo

Since 1976, the Joint National Committee for Languages, a nonprofit coalition of more than sixty national language associations, has promoted public awareness of language issues. It represents more than 300,000 professionals. The National Council for Languages and International Studies has worked to translate professional priorities into national policy since 1988. Together, these organizations work to ensure that all Americans have the opportunity to learn and use English and at least one other language. JNCL-NCLIS has many resources on their website, including extensive information on study abroad issues. They also provide information for grant seekers to access funding for language education.

Membership:

- Organizational Membership: includes organizations encompassing a variety of areas of the language field: the major and less commonly taught languages, including English and English as a Second Language, bilingual education, the classics, linguistics, exchanges, research, technology, and translation

Middle East Institute (MEI)

1761 N Street, NW

Washington, DC 20036

Telephone: 202-785-1141

Website: www.mideasti.org

Since 1946, the mission of MEI has been to increase knowledge of the Middle East among American citizens and to promote understanding between the peoples of the Middle East and the United States. MEI facilitates discussion among academics, government officials, businesspeople, and media representatives; supports research, writing, and public speaking on the Middle East; and hosts international scholars in Washington, DC. MEI also publishes the *Middle East Journal* and offers courses in Arabic, Farsi, Hebrew, and Turkish, as well as seminars highlighting the history, literature, and culture of the Middle East. In addition, MEI houses the largest English-language library on the Middle East outside the Library of Congress. MEI also sponsors conferences and offers internships to both undergraduate and graduate students.

Membership:

- Individual-Full Membership ($100 per year)
- Individual-Associate Membership ($50 per year)

NAFSA: Association of International Educators

1307 New York Avenue, NW, 8th Floor

Washington, DC 20005

Telephone: 202-737-3699

Website: www.nafsa.org

Twitter: @NAFSA

Established in 1948, NAFSA is a member organization that promotes sound policies in international education and provides professional development opportunities in the form of training, information, and other educational services. The organization is comprised of international program directors, foreign student advisers, study abroad specialists, English as a Second Language (ESL) program administrators, and international admissions officers employed at more than 2,000 US university campuses. NAFSA offers practical resources, relevant training and events, and the latest news in several specific professional areas: study abroad; international education leadership; international student and scholar services; recruitment, admissions, and preparations; and teaching, learning, and scholarship. The NAFSA website features a searchable job registry that is available to the general public.

Membership:

- Regular Individual Membership ($399 per year and $20 one-time processing fee)
- Associate Individual Membership: available to full-time students, retirees, and community volunteers ($133 per year)

National Peace Corps Association (NPCA)

1900 L Street, NW, Suite 205

Washington, DC 20036

Telephone: 202-293-7728

Website: www.peacecorpsconnect.org

Twitter: @pcorpsconnect

NPCA, a nonprofit organization of nearly 50,000 members and 157 affiliated groups, represents people who have served as staff members and volunteers in the Peace Corps. It is not part of the US Peace Corps, which is a federal agency. The mission of the NPCA is to lead the Peace Corps alumni community and others to foster peace by working together in service, education, and advocacy. It aims to educate the American public about other countries, promote policies consistent with Peace Corps values, ensure the continued success of the Peace Corps, and encourage Peace Corps alumni to engage in community and international service. The NPCA website hosts an online career center that is available to the general public, which features a searchable job bank and career advice from returned Peace Corps volunteers.

Membership:

- Current Peace Corp Volunteer Membership (free)
- First-Time Membership (first year free)
- Individual Membership ($35 per year)

Pact

1828 L Street, NW, Suite 300

Washington, DC 20036

Telephone: 202-466-5666

Website: www.pactworld.org

Since 1971, Pact, a global network of more than 300 organizations, has been working to build the capacity of local leaders, organizations, and communities in order to meet pressing social needs in countries around the world. With the goal of ending poverty and injustice, Pact's mission is to help build strong communities globally that provide people with an opportunity to earn a dignified living, raise healthy families, and participate in democratic life. Pact achieves this goal by strengthening the capacity of grassroots organizations, coalitions, and networks and by forging linkages among the government, business, and citizen sectors to work for social, economic, and environmental justice. Pact hosts a free job openings listing.

Membership: None indicated.

Peace and Collaborative Development Network

See chapter 9 in this volume.

Society for Intercultural Education, Training, and Research in the United States of America (SIETAR-USA)

8835 SW Canyon Lane, Suite 238

Portland, Oregon 97225

Telephone: 503-297-4622

Website: www.sietarusa.org

Twitter: @sietarusa

SIETAR-USA promotes and facilitates intercultural education, training, and research through professional interchange. The Society is composed of interdisciplinary professionals and service organizations that work to implement and promote cooperative interaction and effective communication among diverse peoples. Individual members represent more than sixty countries and come from a diverse array of fields: multinational institutions, NGOs, business and industry, consulting, training, K–12 and higher education, counseling, and all aspects of the media and arts. SIETAR-USA is a UN- and Council of Europe–affiliated nonprofit organization. SIETAR-USA hosts an extensive job board.

Membership:

- Full Individual Membership ($125 per year)
- Institutional Membership ($500 per year)
- Student Membership ($70 per year)
- Senior Membership ($70 per year)

Society for International Development (SID), Washington, DC, Chapter

1101 15th Street, NW, 3rd Floor

Washington, DC 20005

Telephone: 202-331-1317

Website: www.sidw.org

Twitter: @sidwashington

SID–Washington connects a diverse constituency of international relations practitioners, serving as a "knowledge broker" for ideas and best practices since 1957. SID–Washington is an educational membership organization that is a member of similar SIETAR societies spanning the globe. SID International is based in Rome (www.sidint.org). SID–Washington provides a space for dialogue and connects a dynamic community of individuals and institutions.

Membership:

- Institutional Membership ($500–$3,000 per year, based on revenue)
- Regular Membership ($75 per year)
- Retired Membership ($60 per year)
- Young Professional Membership: open to individuals ages 21–27 entering the international development profession ($45 per year)
- Student Membership ($35 per year)

Teachers of English to Speakers of Other Languages (TESOL)

1925 Ballenger Avenue, Suite 550

Alexandria, VA 22314

Telephone: 703-836-0774 or 888-547-3369 (toll-free in the US)

Website: www.tesol.org

Twitter: @TESOL_Assn

Founded in 1966, TESOL is an international education association with more than 12,000 members that is dedicated to the effective teaching and learning of English. TESOL promotes scholarship, disseminates information, and advocates credentialed instruction and quality programming. The organization publishes three serial publications and hosts an annual convention. TESOL also offers online and on-site professional development opportunities, as well as an online career center and searchable job bank.

Membership:

- Professional Membership ($98 per year; $65 per year for incomes less than $25,000)
- New Professional Membership: open to teachers who have been teaching for less than three years ($60 per year)
- Global Professional Membership: open to residents of countries with gross national income per capita of less than $15,000 ($35 per year)
- Retired Professional Membership: open to retired individuals who have been members of TESOL for five of the last ten years ($57 per year)
- Student Membership ($35 per year)

US Global Leadership Coalition (USGLC)

1129 20th Street, NW, Suite 600

Washington, DC 20036

Telephone: 202-689-8911

Website: www.usglc.org

Twitter: @USGLC

The mission of the USGLC, founded in 1995, is to make diplomacy and development a keystone of American international engagement. USGLC is a broad-based network of more than 400 NGOs and businesses, national security and foreign policy experts, and thousands of faith-based, community, and academic leaders in all fifty states. This coalition educates the American public on the value of smart power and works to protect national security, build international economic prosperity, and strengthen humanitarian values.

Membership:

- General Organizational Membership ($500 per year)
- Leadership Circle Membership
- Global Trust Membership
- Chairman's Caucus Membership
- Diplomatic Circle Membership
- Supporter Membership (free)

World Affairs Councils of America (WACA)

1200 18th Street, NW, Suite 902

Washington, DC 20036

Telephone: 202-833-4557

Website: www.worldaffairscouncils.org

Twitter: @WACAmerica

WACA was founded in 1918 in conjunction with the Foreign Policy Association. It comprises approximately 500,000 members participating in the activities of eighty-four councils and twenty-six affiliates throughout the United States. The World Affairs Councils system operates a speakers program that includes more than 1,200 events per year. Councils also manage international exchange programs, school programs, teachers' workshops, model UN programs, foreign policy discussions, national opinion polls, travel programs, young professionals' programs, conferences, and corporate programs. The system has six flagship programs: Travel the World, Global IQ with the *Economist*, *It's Your World* (NPR radio program), Great Decisions, World Affairs Today, and World in Transition.

Membership: Membership is available to organizations, as well as individuals in more than forty states, as well as Washington, DC, and Puerto Rico. Membership costs and benefits vary from regional council to council. Check specific websites for more information.

World Youth Student and Educational Travel Confederation (WYSE)

Keizergracht 174-176

1016 DW Amsterdam

The Netherlands

Telephone: +31 20-421-28-00

Website: www.wysetc.org

Twitter: @WYSTC

WYSE was created in 2006 by the merger of the International Student Travel Confederation and the Federation of International Youth Travel Organizations. This new organization continued the mission of "increased international understanding through the promotion of travel and educational opportunities for students and youth" by helping more than 10 million youth and students go abroad to more than

120 countries each year. WYSE also holds an annual World Youth and Student Travel Conference that brings together about 800 delegates from 120 countries who represent the youth, student, and educational travel industry.

Membership:

- Category 1 Membership: new organizations with low levels of industry activity (€450 per year)
- Category 2 Membership: applies to most organizations, except those with extremely low or high levels of activity in the industry (€1,250 per year)
- Category 3 Membership: reserved for organizations and trading groups with extremely high levels of industry activity (€6,500 per year)
- National Tourism Administrator, Official Tourism Organization, and Nongovernmental Organization Membership (€750 per year)
- Service Partner Membership: for organizations that act as auxiliary members to the youth travel industry (€1,800 per year)

Young Professionals in Foreign Policy (YPFP)

1800 K Street, NW, Suite 400

Washington, DC 20006

Website: www.ypfp.org

Twitter: @YPFP

YPFP is a nonpartisan, nonprofit organization founded in 2004. Embracing the expressed mission of helping to create the next generation of foreign policy leaders, YPFP organizes professional, educational, and social programs. YPFP has branches in London, New York, Brussels, and Washington, DC. A JobLink job board is available on the YPFP website.

Membership:

- Individual Membership in the United States ($35 per year)

Selected Resources

Encyclopedia of Associations: International Organizations

Thomson Gale, 2012 (www.galegroup.com)

This classic reference, now in its 51st edition, covers multinational and national membership associations from Afghanistan to Zimbabwe. It is published in three parts. Parts I and II, *Descriptive Listings*, provide annotated contact information, including US-based organizations with binational or multinational memberships. Part III, *Indexes*, contains geographic, executive, and name and keyword indexes to all of the associations listed in the first two parts. Prices vary by account type. *Print.*

Encyclopedia of Associations: National Organizations of the US

Thomson Gale, 2013 (www.galegroup.com)

This publication, in its 52nd edition, is a comprehensive source for detailed information on nonprofit American membership organizations of national scope. Each entry includes the organization's complete name, address, phone number, websites, founding date, purpose, activities, dues, and national and international conferences, together with the name and title of the organization's primary official. The publication also features an alphabetical name and keyword index so you can quickly locate the name and address of the organization you need to contact without consulting the main entry. Prices vary by account type. *Print.*

Marketing Source

Website: www.marketingsource.com/associations

The Concept Marketing Group offers a Directory of Associations that includes the full contact information for more than 50,000 professional, business, and trade associations, nonprofit organizations, and other charity and community institutions. Online access to the directory can be purchased in full for one month ($395) or one year ($995), or state-by-state for $50–$300 (depending on the size of the state), both of which include daily updates. *Web.*

National Trade and Professional Associations Directory

Columbia Books, Inc., 2013 (www.associationexecs.com)

This publication lists more than 8,000 national trade associations, professional societies, and labor unions in the United States. Nine indexes will enable you to look up associations by subject, budget, geographic area, acronym, and executive director. Other features include contact information, serial publications, upcoming convention schedules, membership and staff size, budget figures, and background information. This directory costs $299. *Print.*

— PROFILE —

Fanta Aw

Assistant Vice President of Campus Life and Director of International Student and Scholar Services, American University, Washington, DC, 1998–present
President and Chair, Board of Directors, NAFSA: Association of International Educators, 2013–14

Career Trajectory

American University, Washington, DC
    Associate Director, Intercultural Services, 1996–98
    Manager, Foreign Student Services, 1995
    Program Coordinator/Manager, International/Intercultural Student Services, 1992–94

Price Waterhouse and Ernst Young, Junior Auditor, Senegal, 1991–92

Academic Background

American University
    PhD (Sociology with concentrations in Social Stratification, Transnational Migration, and International Education), College of Arts and Sciences, 2011
    MA (Public Administration with a concentration in Organizational Development), School of Public Affairs, 1994
    BS (Business Administration and Accounting), Kogod School of Business, 1990

How do you define your cause?

I consider my cause to be promoting global citizenship. Part of that endeavor is increasing the intercultural competency of institutions that are engaged in international educational exchange. Intercultural competence is the ability to view the world from multiple perspectives. Those perspectives should be informed by interactions and social engagement. It's the ability to empathize with perspectives that may be, in some cases, radically different from your own. You may conclude that you do not agree, but you've taken the opportunity to hear and understand the other perspective.

What drew you to this cause and your field?

A confluence of circumstances. I'm originally from Mali in West Africa. When I was seven, we left home to go to Liberia. That was my first journey out of my home country. I was educated in French international schools, which had very diverse student bodies. This provided me with an educational background that was quite holistic. It opened up a world that was unknown to me. It allowed me to have an intellectual journey grounded in understanding multiple perspectives. I was able to interact with people on a daily basis who were from different cultures, but we could find common ground.

When I came to college in Washington, my undergraduate major was business accounting and finance. I picked this major because I wanted a mobile career. I knew that a career in business would give me the opportunity to live, work, and engage in other parts of the world. And accounting, in many ways, is a universal field, where I could be a practitioner and find my space and place, irrespective of where in the world I found myself.

How would you describe your field?

It's a quest for multiple truths. We are in the business of knowledge creation—searching for multiple ways to see, acquire, and understand knowledge.

How would you describe your career path?

Many people within our fields would say that their career paths are somewhat nontraditional. That's common among our colleagues. Landing where I've landed has been about finding my own voice and place. It is important to have the courage to, first, know and acknowl-edge your passion but, second, take that leap of faith that you will land in the right place as long as you follow that passion. When I reflect on my career, I was probably, all along, following my passion. It may not have been a direct road, but all the different components coming together explain where I am today.

My business background was incredibly important to me. I'm able to speak multiple languages; not just foreign languages, but also the language of finance. This has served me well in my work. Understand-ing budgets is essential to success in any field.

Where did you "start" and how did it help you get to where you are today?

I started by volunteering my time. As a student from abroad, the inter-national student office felt like a home. The programs that were being offered and the level of engagement with students and counterparts on campus made me feel comfortable in that space. Volunteering turned into a part-time student job. This allowed me to dabble in vari-ous areas; everything from putting together intercultural programs, to counseling students on basic resource needs, to assuming leader-ship roles. I advise people to, whenever you can, volunteer—give of your time. It is worth it. The learning is invaluable.

What are the major day-to-day activities of your current position?

I would break it into three segments. There's a lot of strategic plan-ning about which direction to take, about opportunities and deter-mining a potential course of action. There's a lot of high-level thinking that happens on a day-to-day basis, which I find extremely gratifying.

Second, trend analysis is big for me because it's about constantly taking the pulse of the field—finding multiple avenues for gather-ing information and data. These include talking to students and col-leagues to understand their perspectives, as well as engaging with external audiences about challenges in higher education in general.

And third is staff development—working with staff to assess how we continue to be cutting edge in the work that we're doing. How do we ensure that our work remains relevant to the particular audiences we serve?

Are you involved in community service?

The nature of our field is one where giving of your time, and giving back, is a core value. We don't get into this work because we make lots of money (*laughs*). Why do we do this work? We believe in its transformative nature and that we each have something to bring and to learn. From that perspective, it has always been plain to me that to be involved with my profession at its core is to volunteer time.

Serving as president and chair of the board of NAFSA (*see chapter 5*) is a volunteer position. It is a service to my community and my profession in many ways. It opens the door to shaping the future direction for new leaders who are passionate about this work and are trying to find their paths within the field.

What awards and honors have meant the most to you?

In the twenty-eight years that I've been at American University, I have received several awards for service in the university community, as well as recognition for my work as it relates to diversity and inclusion. That has meant the most to me. There's no better reward than to "just do your work." To give it your best, knowing that tomorrow there will be other lessons that you will learn.

What is your best advice to develop networking skills?

Networking is first and foremost about harnessing relationships in ways that are authentic and reciprocal. It is as much about giving as taking. When I think of networking, I think of it as every encounter we have with another person, whether a student, colleague, or stranger.

We learn about who they are, their travels, and potential common ground. That exchange alone affords us the opportunity to learn and grow, and then to create a "web of relationships." It's the web of relationships one develops that is a true test of networking skills and abilities.

Do you have a mentor? How has he or she affected your life and career?

Much of what I've learned about this field, and particularly my work with students, I learned from Gary Wright. He hired me, gave me the opportunity to find my passion, and was an extraordinary mentor. I learned by watching him. The most effective mentors are role models. Mentors teach you what matters and how to do the work well.

Other mentors have been people whose actions showed me what not to do. I am grateful to them as well, because working and interacting with them, I learned a great deal about what works and what doesn't.

Do you consider yourself a mentor to others?

"Mentor" is not a designation that we give ourselves; rather, it is an attribution that others perhaps make. I would hope that I've been a mentor to my students over the years. The chief indication that I may have been a mentor to them is that they keep coming back. They continue to value the relationship and to seek my advice on career decisions as well as personal matters.

I've worked with various staff members to help them find their next career moves. They continue to seek me out. I hope I've been a mentor to them.

How have you maintained a healthy balance between your work and personal life?

I'm not sure I'm a good model for that. The work life dominates. I'm learning from the younger generation about balance. This is a generation that deeply cares about work–life balance in ways that perhaps my generation and the generation before did not necessarily consider.

I'm getting better at it because I'm much more mindful. My motivation is to model good behaviors for my staff. It means taking vacations, it means listening more to my body. When I know it's time to slow down, I take that seriously. It means finding quality time to spend with friends and those I deeply care about. And being much more intentional about it.

What lessons have you learned as your career has evolved?

The importance of listening to your voice. You have to stop and reflect. In listening to your own voice you become less afraid. In becoming less afraid, I am willing to take risks that can take me down certain paths that otherwise I would have never taken.

I intentionally picked business and accounting as an undergraduate major because I wanted something that was universal that could take me around the world. I could have excelled in that profession. But I was able to listen to my voice that said, "Yeah, you could do this, but is this really where you see yourself five to ten years down the road?" I was willing to leave it behind and go into uncharted territory. I'm glad I did because going into international education was probably the best decision I've ever made.

Any final advice?

Remain consistent in your level of engagement and the quality of your work. Stay flexible. Like many of us, I stumbled into this field. The road is never direct. It's important to be flexible and comfortable with change. The more you understand and value that, the more likely you are to land where you need to land.

— PROFILE —

Belinda Chiu

Principal, Hummingbird Research Coaching
Consulting, Durham, NC, 2009–present
Executive Director, Zomppa, 2009–present

Career Trajectory

Duke University Talent Identification Program, Director of
International Programs, Durham, NC, 2008–9

The Phelps Stokes Fund
Special Assistant to the President, New York, NY, 2006–8
Program Officer, Washington, DC, 2004–6

Equals Three Communications, Inc., Research Analyst, Bethesda, MD,
2004

Center for Applied Research, Project Consultant, Cambridge, MA/
Philadelphia, PA, 2003–4

Dartmouth College Office of Admissions, Assistant Director, Hanover,
NH, 2000–2002

Dove Consulting Group, Inc., Senior Research Analyst, Boston, MA,
1998–2000

Academic Background

Columbia University, Teacher's College, EdD (Concentration in
International Education Development), 2009

The New School, Democracy and Diversity Institute, Transregional
Center for Democratic Studies, Cape Town, South Africa, January
2007

Tufts University, The Fletcher School, MALD (Master of Arts in Law and Diplomacy), 2004

Dartmouth College, AB (Government), 1998

How do you define your cause?

My cause, at its core, is unleashing potential: helping individuals discover how their natural talents can strengthen organizations and communities; encouraging others to perform as the best versions of themselves so that they can leverage organizations as platforms for inclusive social change and make a positive impact on the world; supporting others to craft their own career paths, aim for their own definitions of success, and challenge social expectations.

I have been very fortunate with my educational and professional opportunities, driving me to ask, "How do you offer everybody greater awareness of and access to life's opportunities? How do you create those opportunities?" I truly believe that when people are fulfilled, when they are pursuing the things they're most passionate about, change—real social change—begins. Perhaps that means they have to step "outside the matrix" and create their own mode of working.

In my own career, I've always looked for things I'm passionate and excited about. If I'm not excited to go to work in the morning or find a greater purpose, I won't do it anymore. If I'm not learning, I fall asleep. Interest and passion have always driven me much more than money. I figure money will follow when you're doing what you love.

What drew you to this cause and your field?

Being bicultural, I've always been aware that I straddle a couple of different identities. Code shifting happens all the time. Every day is almost a contradictory experience: simultaneously and effortlessly feeling very much a part of communities while fighting to prove a sense of belonging and not being "Othered."

Growing up, I became sensitive to people who are on the margins of society, whether it's due to their socioeconomic situations, the color of their skin, or their sexual orientation. There is a great deal of potential out there, but far too often folks feel restricted to explore their talents fully. Creating opportunities for people (and kids) to explore and take risks, to see how they can change the world for the better, is a pretty awesome process. Having awareness, confidence, and the support of others around us is so important. Providing these things for all people is my cause.

How would you describe your field?

Depends on the time of day or day of the week you're asking me! Maybe if I had to simplify it, I would describe my work as global human development. It encompasses working with kids to instill a curiosity and desire to live as healthy and responsible global citizens; researching how tribal colleges can best prepare their students for a global economy; identifying the next generation of global leaders; helping Fortune 500 companies create more effective leaders and teams; coaching individuals on moving past feeling "stuck" in their professional lives and taking ownership to craft a new reality instead.

How would you describe your career path?

Like an anthill or a beehive: tons of paths and ways to get around, but all toward a common center. Bumblebee was my nickname in college, actually (*laughs*). Bees seem to do the aerodynamically impossible. And that's my philosophy: we should always do the impossible.

A hummingbird is similar to a bee in that way. That's why I named my consulting company Hummingbird. Hummingbirds fly backward, forward, up, and down. They are small, agile, and powerful. Their wings make the infinity symbol—infinite possibilities. They go from flower to flower to pollinate. That's how I see what I do. I pollinate—help people find their authentic selves and, through that, a stronger connection with each other and the Earth, and recognize, "Yeah, this is possible!"

I decided not to follow the traditional academic route or development route. I needed a way to design my own path and define for myself what is meaningful in my efforts to contribute to the universe. This process is constantly evolving and very challenging. It requires a certain level of comfort with uncertainty and faith that things will work out. What I really enjoy is stirring people up! Maybe I should just say that I'm a troublemaker (*laughs*). But I like to think that, in my own way, I'm helping people and making a difference, however small.

Where did you "start" and how did it help you get to where you are today?

Family. My grandmother taught me the idea that if you are kind to everybody, the world will be kind to you. I try to approach life that way. You put good stuff out into the world and hopefully, that collective energy will help the world be a better place for all beings.

And then there's food. I just love food. I never thought of combining my passion for international development, equity, and social justice with food until later in my life. My cofounders of Zomppa are best friends from grad school. We are all committed to the role of international dialogue to drive positive change, the notion that such conversations cannot happen in silos, and the idea that food is a critical way to drive this process. One of the things I'm trying to do with Zomppa is not only to teach kids (ages four to eight) about healthy eating habits, but also to take them on a global journey in the process. While we focus on students from underrepresented communities, we embrace all kids. The key is to get children excited to learn about the world through experiential learning and play. In the process, they create healthy eating and living habits, develop greater curiosity about the world, and learn about their role as advocates. We're trying to create pro–social skills in young people and give them the sense that they have an active role to play in the world, that they have agency. They should never ever think that they are less than anyone else.

What are the major day-to-day activities of your current positions?

I'm not a nine-to-five office person. I need variety. That's why consulting has been really good for me. So it depends on what day of the week or time of year you're asking me.

Some days, I'm focused on the more academic side of my work: collecting and analyzing data; writing; presenting work at conferences; meeting other scholars and practitioners in the field to grapple with the nuances of global education.

Other times, I'm networking for Zomppa—finding community partners, figuring out ways to collaborate. I'm developing curriculum, designing programs, figuring out how to make it economically sustainable. Then I might switch gears to wear my college admissions hat, identifying promising young scholars.

Other days, I'm assessing the abilities of graduate students from around the world to handle conflict. Or facilitating a leadership workshop for upper-level managers at a global pharmaceutical company. Or focusing on some civic and community service engagements. I find myself at the airport a lot.

What is your best advice for developing effective networking skills?

Be authentic. If you're authentic about really wanting to get to know someone (not for what they can get or do for you, but for who they are and what they do), then folks respond accordingly. You never know who can "help" when you need it. Reach out. Talk to folks even if you don't think they are "relevant." A simple act that is often forgotten: thank them!

Take the time to talk to others who seek your advice. You'd want others to do the same.

People think that if they're more introverted or not good in crowds, then they're not good networkers. That's not true. You don't have to be the one who is shaking everyone's hand. Take the chance and start a conversation with the person standing alone at the cheese table—one person is all you need, and from that one person, who knows how many people you might get to know.

Do you have a mentor? How has he or she affected your life and career?

I have many. My first real mentor was Ed Dailey, an attorney and Dartmouth alum. He became, and still is, someone I respect very much. He's never let others define his path. In his "second life," he went back for a degree in divinity after decades of being a successful corporate lawyer. He consistently opposes things he believes are unethical. To have the guts to do this . . . even to this day, I wouldn't mind being fired as long as I know I'm standing up for something I believe in.

The former first lady of Dartmouth, Susan DeBevoise Wright, has had a great influence on me. Having her as a mentor was really important—to see a strong woman, leader, educator, wife, and mother who was comfortable in her own skin and made others comfortable in theirs. She encouraged me and pushed me to look beyond my self-imposed boundaries, to pursue what I loved.

Joan Gussow. She started the local/global food movement decades ago before it was cool. She is amazing. She is irreverent, bold, and speaks truth to power. She was the one that made me go "Aha!!!" and put all my interests together. I want to be her when I grow up.

Do you consider yourself a mentor to others?

I hope not (*laughs*)! When I was in my mid-twenties, I always thought people in their thirties knew *exactly* what they were doing. Now that I'm in my thirties myself, it still makes me nervous when people ask for advice. I want to say, "I don't know anything! Are you sure you want to ask me this?"

But I love working with younger people and emerging leaders. Nineteen- and twenty-year-olds are so idealistic . . . but at the same time, they're a bit scared because of the high expectations and because they *don't* yet know what they're going to do. Sometimes they're so stressed out about college or jobs . . . I love helping them see a broader perspective and challenge external expectations—that there is no one right path.

How have you maintained a healthy balance between your work and personal life?

It's a must! When you work for yourself, the work-life divide is less clear, so it's very easy to just work, work, work. I'm not always good about putting the work down, but I try. I like to play, too. I always make sure I eat well. Exercise. Watch my TV shows. Meet with friends. Take time for me. Last year, I took a month to walk the *Camino de Santiago* in Spain. I thought, "why the heck not?" Talk about finding your own path. The 500-mile walk is a perfect symbol of how individuals must follow their own paths, and all those paths create a communal synergy. Each person walks alone, but no one ever walks alone.

What lessons have you learned as your career has evolved?

Learn who you are. It's so easy to get caught up in what other people say—your parents, your friends, your teachers. It's important to listen to others because they give you perspective, but at the end of the day, your gut tells you what's right for you.

Take risks. Don't let fear stop you. Be smart about it, but don't regret not doing something. I don't want to be fifty years old, look back, and say, "Damn, I should have done it." If something doesn't work out, so be it. But I'm not going to regret missing an opportunity.

Make sure your work is aligned with your personal life and values. If something or someone is working contrary to your values and you are questioning ethics, walk away.

Don't be driven by the "golden handcuffs"—the title, the salary, the prestige. It's shiny and beautiful, but you can end up tied down to something you don't care about. Be driven by the possibility that the world can be a better place.

Any final advice?

Tell your story. Find themes in your resume and your experiences. I want to say to a lot of younger people, "I know you're smart, I know you're capable, I know you're talented, but so are a lot of people. What is *your* story?" This not only sets you apart from others, but this also helps you find your focus.

Be irreverent. Be a nonconformist—but not for the sake of non-conformity. Being a true individual means being part of a larger collective. Stay young. Look at things as a child might. It sounds immature. But it makes everything so much more fun. And possible.

CHAPTER 7

Internship Opportunities

Introduction

Internships are building blocks of a career. In many cases, they have become an implicit prerequisite for an entry-level job. Internships are the source of much practical training and office experience that employers seek. Employers want to be sure that potential hires understand the demands of the contemporary workplace and are not under the impression that the sometimes more relaxed deadlines of academic life apply in work situations.

Researching internships should be approached as seriously as searching for a relatively permanent position. You will be trading a precious commodity—your time—for valuable training in return for either no remuneration or, if you're lucky, a modest stipend. You want to make sure you choose to work in an environment where your supervisors truly care about your growth and professional development.

Exploitation? No, a Chance to Learn and Grow

Internships can provide skills training and other valuable learning that one cannot acquire in the classroom. Actual work situations in the fields of international education, exchange, and development may be quite different from what you imagine. The introduction an internship can provide to the daily tasks involved in a given job or organization is invaluable.

Some career websites and discussions warn students that certain internships might be "only for the benefit of the employer" and may not offer any useful or pertinent experiences. One such website goes so far as to say that unless an internship provides a valuable learning experience, such as skills training or exposure to a specific business culture, the experience might be "little more than exploitation." This seems to be overstating the case.

It's true that some internships in the field of international affairs pay little to no money—few internships are actually a source of significant income. It's also true that most organizations, especially small ones, greatly benefit from the presence of interns. We know from experience that the National Council for International Visitors (NCIV), the Institute of International Education, the Alliance for International Educational and Cultural Exchange, and many other international education, exchange, and development organizations could not function as effectively as they do without the talent and contributions of their interns. But this certainly is not tantamount to exploitation.

Many organizations that recruit and utilize interns greatly appreciate the sacrifices interns make in order to work in their chosen fields for little or no salary and attempt to repay them with quality experiences that include genuinely substantive work and opportunities to participate in events outside of the office. For example, in addition to the stipend it provides for its interns, NCIV emphasizes that they are not cheap labor brought in to do the menial tasks that no one else wants to do. Rather, they are an integral part of the staff. Though NCIV intern supervisors make certain that each intern knows some grunt work will be required—indeed, in a small office, *everyone* is required to do grunt work—it also strives to ensure that 75 to 80 percent of their tasks are substantive projects and research aligned with their interests. It's true that organizations want to benefit from their interns, but they typically want to see their interns flourish as well. Wise managers know that satisfied, well-trained interns are a valuable pool of future employees. They treat their interns accordingly.

A Good Internship Depends on You

Surely there are a few organizations and supervisors who are uninterested in the development of their interns. They may pile on mindless tasks, and an intern might spend a semester in front of the copier or doing interminable data entry. The first way to avoid such an internship is to ask questions. An internship posting can tell you only so much about the duties you'd be performing. A website reveals only what the organization chooses to convey. Remember that an interview for an internship is just as much about you judging a potential employer as it is about them assessing you. Come prepared with a list of questions and try to glean from your interviewers the type of tasks you'd be assigned. Try to get a feel for the working environment. What can you expect to learn in your time as an intern? Talk to current interns, if possible. Don't be shy about making it clear that, while you are excited to help the organization in any way you can, you are also looking for an experience that is both substantive and meaningful.

We always advise anyone going to an office for an internship or job interview to arrive early. This builds in a margin for delays so that you're sure to arrive on time, thus demonstrating your dependability. However, if you arrive early, you'll also have time to observe while waiting. Do they have time to offer a newcomer a smile and friendly hello? Is the receptionist polite and helpful? If the answer is yes, chances are your supervisor will be as well. An organization's culture inevitably reflects the examples set by those in charge.

Once you've accepted an intern position, it is also up to you to get the maximum benefit possible in exchange for your effort. Communicate with your supervisor regularly. Express interest in projects that captivate your attention. A meaningful internship experience comes not only from the tasks you're doing but also the people you meet. Extend your network as much as possible. Push yourself to meet others working in your specific field of interest. Interns find that contacts gained in such situations are often the most beneficial.

Not Just for Students

Internships are not solely for undergraduate students or recent grads. These demographics may make up the majority of intern applicants, but professionals further along in their careers also find internships valuable. Many of these professionals are either looking to change fields or have returned to graduate school and are using an internship for experience or academic credit. One of NCIV's interns we both worked with, Mory Pagel, had more than five years of experience in the field of international exchange before applying to NCIV. He had recently returned to graduate school to study international communication and sought an internship to provide him with a professional experience as well as academic credit. It is important, however, for nontraditional internship seekers to read the fine print of internship postings and make inquiries when necessary. Some internship programs accept only current students and recent graduates.

Finding an Internship

Just as you would in a regular job search, cast the net wide when searching for internships. By exploring the full range of internship possibilities, you will know what to look for in terms of tasks, what to settle for in terms of compensation, and be able to better weed out the duds from the true, substantive opportunities. Apply early and often. Application deadlines can often be fluid, so if you see a posting on a database or website such as Idealist.org, check with the specific organization to make sure the details and deadlines haven't changed. Tailor your cover letter and resume to match each specific internship application. If you're applying for a government internship, remember that many positions require a security clearance, which may take anywhere from eight months to a year. Start your search and application process early.

Just as there are a plethora of job sites and search engines that have bloomed on the Web, the websites devoted to helping you find an internship—at home or abroad—have also expanded. Internships .com and Internabroad.com are examples. Many job websites also contain internship listings and will allow you to refine your search to identify them. But are these broad, more generic internship sites the best resources for helping you find your ideal internship in international education, exchange, and development? In much the same manner as your job search, these search engines are a great tool for seeing the range of options. They will help you get a handle on the great breadth of internship opportunities that exist. They will also allow you to search using several different terms or a combination of terms, or, if you have the patience, to scan *everything* that is listed.

In most cases, however, websites and search engines more closely aligned with your specific internship interests will yield better, more efficient results. For example, if you're interested in an internship with an international nonprofit organization, use Idealist.org. For those interested in international education, the NAFSA.org job and internship registry is an essential resource. If internships in foreign policy or on Capitol Hill are your primary focus, try the Foreign Policy Association's job board or look on HillZoo.com. InterAction's publication *Monthly Developments* is a must in the field of international development. Your undergraduate or graduate university e-mail listservs or career center job boards are invaluable sources of internship information.

Of course, direct contact with specific organizations that interest you is irreplaceable. Most organizations list internship opportunities as well as application procedures on their own websites. If an organization with a mission that attracts you does not have internships available, contact them anyway; they may be able to direct you to similar organizations in the field that do.

Selected Resources

All Work, No Pay: Finding an Internship, Building Your Resume, Making Connections, and Gaining Job Experience, Lauren Berger

> Ten Speed Press, 208 pages, 2012

> The author asserts that a resume is not complete without internship experience. *All Work, No Pay* is a resource targeted toward recent college graduates. It includes basic information on internships as well as techniques and even exercises to help recent graduates attain internships that will help them grow and expand their experiences. *Print.*

Devex

> *See chapter 5 in this volume.*

Foreign Policy Association

> *See chapter 5 in this volume.*

Hello Real World! A Student's Approach to Great Internships, Co-ops, and Entry Level Positions, Jengyee Liang

BookSurge Publishing, 146 pages, 2006 (www.booksurge.com)

This book bills itself as an insider's guide to getting and succeeding in internships (with some tips for postgraduation jobs also included). *Hello Real World!* provides the college student with a perspective on how to land an internship or first job, as well as how to excel in it. This book also includes tips for employers on how to structure an effective internship or entry-level program for students who are new to the professional world. *Print.*

Idealist

See chapter 9 in this volume.

InternAbroad.com

Website: www.internabroad.com

As a member of the GoAbroad.com family (*see chapter 5 in this volume*), this site is part of a one-stop shopping opportunity for students who wish to travel internationally for many different reasons. Intern Abroad.com specializes in providing resources that specifically pertain to internships. *Web.*

The Intern Files: How to Get, Keep, and Make the Most of Your Internship, Jamie Fedorko

Simon Spotlight Entertainment, 208 pages, 2006 (www.simonsays.com)

A straightforward guide for college students, this book leads you through the process of landing an internship and then guides you to make the most of the experience. *Print.*

Internships.com

www.internships.com

Twitter: @internships

Billed as the world's largest internship marketplace, this site requires an individual to sign up for a free membership in order to access its internship listings.

NAFSA: Association of International Educators

See chapter 5 in this volume.

Vault Guide to Top Internships, Carolyn C. Wise

Vault, Inc., 760 pages, 2009 (www.vault.com)

This guide is written by the founders of the career information website Vault.com. The third edition of the *Vault Guide* provides details on internships at more than 750 companies nationwide. Each internship entry provides information on qualifications, pay, length of internship, and contact information, as well as background information on the company or organization. *Print.*

The Washington Center for Internships and Academic Seminars

www.twc.edu

Twitter: @TWCInternships

The Washington Center's programs combine semester-long internships in Washington, DC, with academic seminars. Positions are available for various fields of study, including international education, exchange, and development. Employers include the federal government, nonprofit organizations, news media, and international businesses. The internships are typically unpaid, although successful interns can receive academic credit.

See the profile of Jennifer Clinton for more information. Jennifer was formerly the chief operating officer and executive vice president at The Washington Center.

— PROFILE —

Jennifer Clinton

President, National Council for International
Visitors, Washington, DC, 2012–present

Career Trajectory

The Washington Center for Internships and Academic Seminars,
Chief Operating Officer and Executive Vice President,
Washington, DC, 2002–12

Telecommunications Industry Association, International Marketing
Manager, Arlington, VA, 2001–3

Overseas Private Investment Corporation, Special Assistant to the
CEO, Washington, DC, 1999–2001

STS Foundation, Program Manager, Alexandria, VA, 1998–99

Academic Background

University of Maryland, College Park, Executive MBA, 2008

University of California, Davis, PhD (French Literature), 2001

Marquette University, BA (Political Science and French), 1994

How do you define your cause?

I define it in two ways. The first is about finding opportunities to be a
bridge among perspectives, people, and ideas. This is what has drawn
me to the international exchange world. The second is about helping
individuals and organizations excel. I have a motto that there's always
room for improvement. Helping nonprofit organizations continually
improve and find new ways to think about being creative and excel-
ling in their field—that's something I'm really passionate about. I've

been able to bring those two worlds together: bridging cultures, people, and ideas, and helping the nonprofit sector to excel.

What drew you to this cause and your field?

When I was in high school and an undergrad, I really had this love for languages and felt that language was a key to bridging cultures. When you learn a language, you learn so much about the way a country, or a set of countries, think and behave. I developed a passion for learning languages that then became so much more. It became learning about cultures and perspectives.

I majored in French and completed a PhD in French literature, and was very interested in teaching French at the university level. That was my initial career path. Are these language skills essential to my job right now? The answer is yes and no. Technically, not so much. Philosophically, yes. You have to make an effort to learn a language, right? Learning a language is about putting yourself out there, being okay about saying the wrong thing, putting yourself in the position where other cultures are dominant. I think that the mindset—of accepting vulnerability, listening, and having the discipline to master something in a way that brings you closer to another person, to other cultures— is what, at the fundamental core, has helped me in my role. The skills of how and why you acquire another language are critical.

How would you describe your field?

Our field is one of building cross-cultural relationships to a particular end. For my current work, the endgame is building a cadre of leaders around the world who have, and want to continue to develop, the proficiency to be respectful of other perspectives and mindsets, and even integrate those mindsets into their own. We hope these leaders in key positions can bring that perspective, that greater respect for global differences, to their jobs when they're making tough decisions. We're building a foundation for the expansion of perspectives for good decision making that ultimately leads to good relations between nations.

How would you describe your career path?

Wind-ey (*laughs*). Early on, I identified for myself three key buckets, or areas of interest: international affairs, education, and nonprofit management. I've used these as my compass. But I knew that not every job was going to be able to hit each of these interest areas. When I moved to Washington, DC, I was very much in the international arena. I worked for an international exchange program, then a government agency (Overseas Private Investment Corporation), and then a telecom trade association.

Then I made the decision to move to The Washington Center, an academic institution that serves college and university students. There was some international work in it, but it was not as much as I had done. That was, for me, a bit of a compromise. I knew I was consciously stepping away from the international world. I was able to focus on higher education and nonprofit management, and really hone those two interest areas. Even though I knew I was sort of compromising, I also knew what my three core buckets were. And when I came to NCIV, I was able to bring the education and management components, along with the international pieces that I had developed early on.

Identify your nonnegotiables, or core beliefs, early on. Be okay with knowing that, over time, not every job is going to fit every single one of those buckets—but that you're developing in each of those. Then, at some point, you will be able to bring them all together. It's taken me a good fifteen-plus years to do that. But I've been very conscious about what my nonnegotiables are. I didn't want to go off the track in some direction that didn't touch one of my interest areas.

Where did you start, and how did it help you get to where you are today?

When I was fifteen, I had an opportunity to go overseas with a basketball team to Sweden. That experience was really defining for me, and after that I took every opportunity I could to have similar experiences abroad. And I began to feel like it was my mission in life to play an ongoing role helping other people have those experiences. I met so many great people—a wonderful summer I spent in the Bordeaux region of France with a set of six Rotary families who took me under their wings and let me stay with them while I was doing an internship. They were the most generous, warm people. I told them that I could never pay them back for what they provided me, but that I would commit myself to paying it forward.

What are the major day-to-day activities of your current position?

It's about setting and implementing direction, looking for opportunities, being creative about the direction we want to pursue, and prioritizing those opportunities. I find that it's also about nurturing relationships and building new relationships. Helping the organization move forward and being thoughtful and strategic about why it's doing what it's doing. I'm challenging assumptions, within the organization and outside, by bringing a new set of perspectives.

When I was in my previous job at The Washington Center, so much of my work was to think about the needs of young people from a professional development perspective. The technical skills were very important. How do you develop a curriculum? How do you educate? I can bring all of that to NCIV. But here, it's been more about the networking and relationship-building piece, while also bringing that academic mindset: What are the skills people need and how can we play a role in building them so that people see themselves growing and developing over time?

I also spend a lot time leading and managing: managing budgets, leading people, managing infrastructure of technology, and communications, and processes, and all of that fun stuff (*laughs*).

What is your best advice for developing effective networking skills?

Networking can be intimidating, especially the superficial "go to cocktail parties and collect as many business cards as you can" type of networking. That's not everyone's cup of tea, and not a lot of people are good at it or even want to be good at it. It's more important to know what drives you, or what your buckets are. I'm big on quality over quantity.

Don't just connect with people for a job or a transaction. People appreciate that long-term vision: How do you cultivate a relationship over time that's aligned with what you care about? People love to talk to others who have similar passions.

I also see networking as being about proactively cultivating mentors. For every internship you do, walk away with two or three people you feel aligned with. Keep in touch with them over time. Ask for input on your resume, send them a holiday card, or invite them for coffee. I like it when people ask me for help by saying, "Here's my list of organizations that really interest me, do you know anybody you could connect me with?"

Do you have a mentor? How has he or she affected your life and career?

My boss at OPIC, Kirk Robertson, is still a mentor to me today. He is a great sounding board; I learned so many lessons from him. My former boss at The Washington Center certainly was. A board member from The Washington Center still is today—I'm in regular touch with her. I've maintained contact with some of my professors, most recently at Maryland, and worked with them on a number of projects. I actively seek opportunities to learn from them, in terms of advice or as a sounding board. For me, they play that role, though I don't even know if *they* know they play that role.

The notion of role models is very important to me. You can have a mentor who you're not necessarily in touch with but who you strive to be like. You want to find people who embody the kinds of values that you have and the ways in which you want to interact with people. I've sought role models who are close to me, as well as those I've never met—perhaps I read about them in a book. They describe how they interact with people and I see that as an opportunity to be mentored, aligning with the type of person I want to be, based on how their career has unfolded or how they conduct themselves.

Do you consider yourself a mentor to others?

Yes, absolutely. During my time with The Washington Center, I had more opportunities on a day-to-day basis to mentor compared to NCIV, a much smaller organization. But I do have a number of young people who intern here or have learned about NCIV and want to do an informational interview. I'm always happy to provide guidance and insight. And some of them have stayed in touch, just checking in every few months to tell me how they're doing and follow up. I think that's great.

How have you maintained a healthy balance between your work and personal life?

I haven't been great at it (*laughs*), but that's part of my nature. I always want to learn and grow, so it's not a matter of work and life being different. My husband makes fun of me for reading the *Harvard Business Review* or management books for fun. So you could say I never turn it off. But for me, turning it off is not really that much fun (*laughs*). I don't have this distinct line between work and life. They bleed into each other, and I'm okay with that because that's what gives me a lot of pleasure. And I think this speaks to the fact that I'm in the right place and doing what I'm passionate about.

Are you involved in community service?

I sit on a board of a local nonprofit called the Academy of Hope. I specifically chose this organization because my mindset has been more international than local, and I really wanted to understand DC politics and what's going on in my local community. This is an organization that helps adult learners prepare and pass the GED and gain critical job skills so they can improve their lives. It's been a great experience to better understand the place where I live.

What lessons have you learned as your career has evolved?

I tend to be a fairly impatient person—working hard and striving to get to the next level quickly. That's been good for me, but at the same time, I still have a long career ahead of me. Know your compass and follow it, but also give yourself the time to learn and grow. Think of it as a marathon, not a sprint.

CHAPTER 8

Volunteer Opportunities

Introduction

When Sherry was in her late twenties and newly married, she spent time at the University of Rhode Island with her husband, who was a faculty member there. In addition to finishing her dissertation and teaching a few courses, she also engaged in several international volunteer activities at the university. She served as the president of a volunteer organization that matched international students with American host families. She also coordinated orientation and cross-cultural training sessions for international students.

Directly after graduating from college, Mark moved to the city of Yanji, in China's Jilin Province, as a volunteer with the Salesian Lay Missioners. His primary duty for his year in Yanji was as a teacher of English conversation at a technical high school managed by Catholic priests. He organized after-school activities for his students (such as "extra English" and guitar groups), chaperoned weekend field trips for students, and taught English in several other venues around the city.

As we discussed in the introduction to the book, idealism is typically a driving force for those interested in a career in international education, exchange, or development. Coupled with this idealism is a desire to serve. Volunteer opportunities give professionals the chance to feed this desire while gaining international experience. Sherry did international volunteer work in the United States, whereas Mark did international volunteer work abroad. We both gained rich experience and new perspectives from these activities, all while satisfying our desires to serve.

It is certainly true that not all people are in the position to take a year or two off from the real world in order to volunteer abroad for no pay. Certainly, the decision to volunteer requires much reflection on your part to discern whether the experience will be both beneficial to your career and feasible within the confines of your life situation (e.g., repaying student loans, taking care of bills, or family obligations).

Yet, as Sherry's experience demonstrates, you do not have to go abroad to volunteer. Certainly, your career in international relations will benefit immensely if you do indeed go abroad at some point. (Sherry later worked as a paid English teacher in Brazil for a year.) But if your situation mandates that you remain in the United States, there are still myriad opportunities for valuable international volunteer experience. Such experiences, whether in the United States or beyond, will help you acquire solid experience in the field, increase your foreign language proficiency, gain further regional expertise, and equip you for future success in multinational and cross-cultural settings.

Sample Volunteer Organizations

American Refugee Committee International

430 Oak Grove Street, Suite 204

Minneapolis, MN 55403

Telephone: 612-872-7060 and 800-875-7060 (toll-free in the US)

Website: www.arcrelief.org

Twitter: @ARCrelief

Founded in 1979, the American Refugee Committee is a nonprofit organization that provides health care and health care training to displaced peoples in developing nations worldwide, including Liberia, Pakistan, Haiti, Rwanda, South Sudan, Thailand, and Uganda. Volunteer positions are categorized by country or service; position descriptions include job qualifications, responsibilities, and time and financial commitments necessary from the volunteer.

Amigos de las Americas

5618 Star Lane

Houston, TX 77057

Telephone: 713-782-5290 or 800-231-7796 (toll-free in the US)

Website: www.amigoslink.org

Twitter: @AMIGOS_Americas

Amigos de las Americas is an international, nonprofit organization that provides volunteer experiences in Latin America for high school and college students interested in public health service and leadership development. Participants live with host families and work with a team of two to three other volunteers in a small community. Participants must have some knowledge of Spanish or Portuguese. Amigos has supported more than 25,000 volunteers during its nearly fifty years in operation.

Art for Humanity (AFH)

635 South 25th Street

Arlington, VA 22202

Website: www.artforhumanity.org

Twitter: @artforhumanity

AFH is a completely volunteer-based charity with the objective of "helping the poor to help themselves." Working primarily in Honduras, AFH distributes used items to families who can then use, distribute, or sell the donated products. Volunteers for the organization may work within the United States at the Arlington, Virginia, office, from their homes, or onsite in Honduras at the university and other facilities established by Art for Humanity.

Catholic Relief Services (CRS)

228 West Lexington Street

Baltimore, MD 21201

Telephone: 877-435-7277

Website: www.catholicrelief.org

Twitter: @CatholicRelief

Catholic Relief Services is the official international relief and development organization of the US Catholic community and works through local churches, governments, and community groups to offer development assistance. Volunteers make a full-time commitment for one week to three years or longer.

See the profile of Tom Garofalo for more information. Tom worked as a country representative for Catholic Relief Services from 1998 to 2008.

Concern Worldwide

104 East 40th Street, Suite 903

New York, NY 10016

Telephone: 212-557-8000

Website: www.concernusa.org

Twitter: @Concern

Founded in 1968, Concern Worldwide works in more than twenty-five countries throughout Africa, Asia, Central America, and Eastern Europe. It engages in long-term development work, responds to emergency situations, and seeks to address the root causes of poverty, working in fields such as health, education, sanitation, natural resources, and emergency relief services. Concern offers volunteer opportunities in the United States ranging from organizing fundraising events to joining an organizing committee for Concern's events. Concern also looks for volunteers with specialized skills, including camera crews, producers, and film editors.

Direct Relief International

27 South La Patera Lane

Santa Barbara, CA 93117

Telephone: 805-964-4767

Website: www.directrelief.org

Twitter: @DirectRelief

Direct Relief International is a nonprofit medical commodities donor founded in 1948 that sends medicine and medical equipment to developing nations worldwide. Direct Relief relies on volunteers for tasks such as clerical and administrative support, program research, editorial work, public outreach, warehouse inventorying, and event hospitality. All volunteer opportunities are offered only at Direct Relief's facilities in Santa Barbara. It does not send volunteers abroad.

Global Volunteers

375 East Little Canada Road

St. Paul, MN 55117

Telephone: 800-487-1074

Website: www.globalvolunteers.org

Twitter: @GloblVolunteers

Global Volunteers is a nonprofit organization that has been working to expand volunteer efforts since 1984. Global Volunteers has programs in seventeen countries that cater to all types of volunteers, including couples, families, LGBT volunteers, seniors, and students. In 1999, Global Volunteers was granted Special Consultative Status with the United Nations Economic and Social Council (ECOSOC), a position that allows it to collaborate on child safety and development in UN efforts against poverty and hunger and in promotion of education. Volunteer opportunities are available for one to three weeks.

Health Volunteers Overseas

1900 L Street, NW, Suite 310

Washington, DC 20036

Telephone: 202-296-0928

Website: www.hvousa.org

Twitter: @HVOUSA

Health Volunteers Overseas works in more than twenty-five resource-poor nations to provide health care, training, and emergency assistance to those in need. Individuals volunteer as overseas health professionals for an average of one month, though both longer and shorter placements are available. Volunteers are encouraged to train local professionals and use local medical equipment whenever possible to create sustainable health practices.

Institute for International Cooperation and Development (IICD)

1117 Hancock Road

Williamstown, MA 01267

Telephone: 413-458-9466

Website: www.iicd-volunteer.org

Twitter: @IICDMA

IICD, founded in 1987, offers work and study programs in Africa (eighteen months) and Brazil (nine months). The programs include training and orientation in the United States, group work on a development project, and development education upon return to the United States. Approximately one hundred volunteers participate in IICD programs each year.

InterAction

See chapter 6 in this volume.

International Executive Service Corps (IESC)

1900 M Street, NW, Suite 500

Washington, DC 20036

Telephone: 202-589-2600

Website: www.iesc.org

Inspired by the Peace Corps in 1964, IESC recruits highly skilled executives, administrators, and technical advisers (often recent retirees) to work on more than 1,000 IESC projects and to share their years of experience and expertise with people in developing nations. Volunteer Experts (VEs) register in IESC's Skills Bank and are recruited to provide assistance on projects in more than 130 countries. Paid professional consultancy positions are also available.

The International Partnership for Service-Learning and Leadership (IPSL)

200 Hawthorne Boulevard

Portland, OR 97214

Telephone: 503-395-IPSL (4775)

Website: www.ipsl.org

IPSL is a consortium of colleges, universities, service organizations, and other related organizations that have united to foster and develop programs linking community service and academic study. It sends approximately one hundred college or university students abroad each year to combine studies with community service.

International Rescue Committee (IRC)

122 East 42nd Street

New York, NY 10168

Telephone: 212-551-3000

Website: www.rescue.org

Twitter: @theIRC

IRC is a refugee relief agency founded in 1933. Every year it sends approximately 300 health care workers to developing countries for short- and long-term assignments. People with previous experience in relief activities overseas are preferred. IRC offers both paid and unpaid positions.

See also chapter 9 in this volume.

Jesuit Volunteer Corps (JVC)

PO Box 3756

Washington, DC 20027

Telephone: 202-687-1132

Website: www.jesuitvolunteers.org

JVC, advocating the values of the Jesuits, a Catholic order of priests, offers volunteer positions both in the United States and abroad. It offers two-year positions in teaching, community organizing, and ministry in Africa, Central and South America, and the Pacific. Voluntary service is based on living simply, keeping faith, doing justice, and building communities. JVC provides insurance for volunteers, covers travel expenses and room and board, and provides a small stipend.

Methodist Global Ministries

The United Methodist Church

475 Riverside Drive

New York, NY 10115

Telephone: 800-862-4246 (800-UMC-GBGM, toll-free in the US)

Website: www.umcmission.org

Twitter: @umcmission

Methodist Global Ministries, officially known as the General Board of Global Ministries, is the international mission agency of the United

Methodist Church. The organization coordinates the work of 135,000 volunteers in seventy countries and forty-eight US states. Methodist Global Ministries administers the Global Justice Volunteers Program, in which young adults (eighteen to twenty-five years old) live, work, and learn in the midst of foreign communities where justice support programs are implemented. The United Methodist Committee on Relief (UMCOR) works in more than eighty countries. UMCOR and Muslim Aid (see the following) have established a formal partnership, embarking on joint projects.

Muslim Aid

PO Box 3

London, E1 1WP

England

Telephone: +44-0-20-7377-4200

Website: www.muslimaid.org

Muslim Aid, founded in 1985 "to alleviate the suffering of the victims of poverty, war, and natural disaster," is a volunteer-reliant collaboration of twenty-three British Muslim organizations. Through their offices in Bangladesh, Bosnia, Cambodia, Indonesia, Iraq, Pakistan, Somalia, Sri Lanka, Sudan, and the United Kingdom, Muslim Aid works in partnership with local governmental and nongovernmental organizations to conduct initiatives in emergency relief, education, health care, orphan care, and economic empowerment. The organization focuses its projects on long-term sustainable development. It lists some volunteer opportunities on its website, many of which are based in London.

Partners of the Americas

1424 K Street, NW, Suite 700

Washington, DC 20005

Telephone: 202-628-3300

Website: www.partners.net

Twitter: @PartnersAmerica

Partners of the Americas grew out of a 1962 call by President Kennedy for citizens of the Western Hemisphere to work together. Partners pairs a US state or area with a region or country in Latin America or the Caribbean (or both). Partnership committees are community based and are composed of volunteers who work with their counterparts to assess needs, access resources, and jointly plan and carry out development projects in health, education, rehabilitation, and other areas. Partners of the Americas has evolved into 120 volunteer chapters linked in sixty partnerships.

Peace Corps of the United States

See chapter 10 in this volume.

Project HOPE

International Headquarters

255 Carter Hall Lane

Millwood, VA 22646

Telephone: 540-837-2100 and 800-544-4673 (toll-free in the US)

Website: www.projecthope.org

Twitter: @projecthopeorg

Project HOPE began practicing "medical diplomacy" in 1958, developing relationships with peoples of different cultures and nations by sharing medical knowledge and treating patients alongside local health professional counterparts. The program sends doctors, nurses, and other health care professionals and educators to more than thirty-five countries. These volunteers work to improve the skills of local health care professionals and train other educators and practitioners.

PYXERA Global

See chapter 9 in this volume.

Rotary International

One Rotary Center

1560 Sherman Avenue

Evanston, IL 60201

Telephone: 847-866-3000

Website: www.rotary.org

Twitter: @rotary

Rotary International is an organization of professionals worldwide who provide humanitarian service, encourage high ethical standards in all vocations, and help build goodwill and peace in the world. Rotary coordinates youth exchange programs for high school students and provides a range of district and global grants (www.rotary.org/en/grants) for students, teachers, and others. Rotary also coordinates such volunteer opportunities as hosting international visitors, group-study and friendship exchanges, global peace forums, and an End Polio Now campaign.

Salesian Lay Missioners

PO Box 30

2 Lefevre Lane

New Rochelle, NY 10801

Telephone: 914-633-8344

Website: www.salesianlaymissioners.org

Twitter: @SLMissioners

Salesian Lay Missioners is a Catholic association that sends volunteer lay missionaries to such countries as Bolivia, Brazil, Cambodia, Ethiopia, India, and South Sudan, as well as to communities in the United States. The Salesians (SDB) are a Catholic society of priests and brothers founded to reach out to poor and needy youth. The order has approximately 17,000 members working in one hundred countries. Volunteer missioners work in Salesian communities in their respective countries, focusing on education and human development among youth.

Mark worked as a volunteer Salesian lay missioner in Yanji, China, serving as an English teacher at a technical high school.

United Nations Volunteers (UNV)

UN Campus

Langer Eugen

Hermann-Ehlers-Str. 10

53113 Bonn

Germany

Telephone: +49-228-815-2000

Website: www.unv.org

Twitter: @UNVolunteers

UNV works to promote and harness volunteerism for effective development. It places participants in developing countries to work with human rights monitoring, nonmilitary peacekeeping, humanitarian, and refugee work. UNV places close to 8,000 volunteers in more than 160 countries for a variety of time periods and assignments.

Volunteers for Peace (VFP)

7 Kilburn Street, Suite 316

Burlington, VT 05401

Telephone: 802-540-3060

Website: www.vfp.org

Twitter: @VFPUSA

VFP is a nonprofit organization founded in 1982 that promotes participation in International Voluntary Service (IVS) projects, historically known as International Workcamps. VFP offers placement in more than 3,000 IVS projects in more than one hundred countries each year, including forty projects in the United States. Volunteers come from diverse backgrounds, and each project typically involves participants from four or more countries. Most projects are short-term (two to three weeks) and do not require any specific professional or language training. The IVP website features a searchable Volunteer Project List, a large repository of volunteer projects around the world.

Selected Resources

Alternatives to the Peace Corps: A Guide to Global Volunteer Opportunities, 12th edition, Caitlin Hachmyer, Editor

Food First, 146 pages, 2008

Alternatives to the Peace Corps is a valuable resource for finding community-based volunteer work. The book includes listings for more than one hundred national and international organizations; guidelines for researching and evaluating volunteer organizations; budgeting and fundraising tips; and a resource section of books, websites, and organizations for further reading and research. *Print.*

Delaying the Real World: A Twentysomething's Guide to Seeking Adventure, Colleen Kinder

Running Press, 240 pages, 2005

This book was written as a guide to encourage recent grads to craft their own life-changing adventures and paths other than schooling followed by office work. The author describes a wide range of alternative paths and includes testimonials by those charting unconventional career paths. *Delaying the Real World* also contains a list of relevant resources, including information regarding travel grants. *Print.*

Idealist

Website: www.idealist.org/volunteer/travel.html

Idealist.org, in addition to its many other functions, offers an extensive list (with brief descriptions and links) of organizations that offer volunteer positions abroad in all parts of the world.

See also chapter 9 in this volume.

Transitions Abroad: The Guide to Learning, Living, Working, and Volunteering Overseas

See chapter 5 in this volume.

VolunteerAbroad.com

Website: www.volunteerabroad.com

A member of the GoAbroad.com family, this site is part of a one-stop shop for students who wish to travel internationally for different reasons and in different capacities, including volunteer work.

Volunteer Vacations: Short-Term Adventures That Will Benefit You and Others, Doug Cutchins, Anne Geissinger, and Bill McMillon

Chicago Review Press, 464 pages, 2012 (www.chicagoreviewpress.com)

This sourcebook (in its eleventh edition) details numerous opportunities for those who wish to spend short periods abroad on service-oriented programs. Volunteer organizations are listed, along with the type of volunteer work to be performed and skills required. The book also contains a variety of brief volunteer journals that illustrate the impact of volunteer service abroad, both on the recipients of the service and on the volunteers. *Print.*

See also chapter 5 in this volume.

VolunteerInternational.org

Website: www.volunteerinternational.org

The International Volunteer Programs Association (IVPA) is an alliance of nonprofit, nongovernmental organizations involved in international volunteer and internship exchanges. Its homepage is equipped with a detailed search function that allows you to search for specific volunteer opportunities abroad. It also highlights tips on the whys and hows of volunteering abroad. The IVPA member list provides names, descriptions, and links for more than thirty international voluntary organizations. *Web.*

World Volunteers: The World Guide to Humanitarian and Development Volunteering, Fabio Ausenda and Erin McCloskey

Universe, 256 pages, 2008

This fourth edition of *World Volunteers* is designed as a resource for those who wish to get involved in humanitarian aid projects throughout the world. Both long-term and short-term projects are listed. In addition, as a resource for those without previous volunteer experience abroad, the book includes information about organizations offering work camps, which can help familiarize volunteers with humanitarian and development work. *Print.*

— PROFILE —

Tom Garofalo

Legislative Assistant, Office of Congressman James P. Moran (D-VA, 8th), Washington, DC, 2010–present

Career Trajectory

New America Foundation, Consultant, Washington, DC, 2009–10

Catholic Relief Services
  Country Representative, Jerusalem, 2005–8

Country Representative, Belgrade, 2001–5

Country Representative, Havana, 1998–2001

Senior Communications Associate, 1995–98

Academic Background

The University of Texas at Austin, MA (Latin American Studies) and MA (Communication), 1994

Georgetown University, BA (Philosophy), 1987

How do you define your cause?

I became interested in Capitol Hill because it fit with what I saw as a pattern that had developed in my professional life in international development. The programs that I most liked working on in international development involved connecting people to the processes of change affecting their lives. Many times it plays out in postconflict situations or times of major transition, such as in Serbia. After the wars, the country was changing the way it provided social services and dealt with vulnerable groups. The new government didn't have a way to engage citizens in the major social policy reforms under way, so Catholic Relief Services (*CRS—see previously in this chapter*), the organization I worked with, was trying to provide a space for that conversation.

We were trying to elicit insights from the affected communities and suggestions on how to reach them more effectively and more collaboratively. Our role was to provide a forum and a way for the people who had not been included in the national conversation to be included. Basically, it's about participation; the quality of participation determines the level of people's sense that they belong to a place, that they have a right to contribute to the national conversation.

After working on projects overseas, I was really interested in looking at the US perspective. Because of the preponderant role the United States plays in the world, we have a decisive impact on other countries. If we fail to advance the quality and scope of our participation here at home and the sense of belonging for people throughout society, then social development in so many other countries will face more setbacks and take much longer, with huge human consequences. They're looking to us as a model. It's kind of a romantic way of looking at my arrival on the Hill and my interest in working in politics. We have a lot of benefits here that other countries don't have and we have a lot of influence. What we do creates ripples of change that play out in developing countries.

What drew you to this cause and your field?

Curiosity, for one thing. I was always interested in the world when I was growing up. My family hosted international visitors, and my parents were active with our local Catholic parish council. When I graduated from college, I volunteered to go to Peru for a year through a Georgetown University program, which really changed my life. I fell in love with the people and the culture of Peru. I lived in a small village and got to know how they lived. I always was thinking, "How is the way we live in the United States affecting them?" The idea of doing something professionally to satisfy that curiosity was really a gift.

How would you describe your field?

I love the interaction that we get in our DC office with people who care about an issue. Sometimes I agree with them, sometimes I don't. But they are trying to affect change. For example, we have groups that come in to discuss human rights in Southeast Asia. Lately, Burma has been changing, Vietnam has been changing, and the question of China's role and our competition with China occupies a lot of attention in Congress. We have a lot of folks in the 8th district in Virginia who were born in the region: in China, Tibet, and Vietnam. It's really great the way that they are trying to affect change. It's not that different from the experience of working with a Serbian organization advancing the rights of people with disabilities, as I did in Belgrade. Their goal is to improve the quality and accessibility of services for the disabled. They were actually participating in the political process, which they had previously been denied.

In a general way, that's what I define as the focus of my career: facilitating the efforts of others to be involved in these political processes that affect their lives so much.

How would you describe your career path?

It's always been very much a work in progress. It often feels like I'm building a bridge while standing on it. I think that's the way a lot of people feel (*laughs*), but I just followed what I thought was interesting. And I was interested in the processes and what the people were trying to do to make them fairer. I think that's the essence of development: participation and fairness.

I wasn't the kind of person in international development who got a big adrenaline rush from emergencies and crisis response. Obviously, when you work for Catholic Relief Services, or CARE, or Save the Children, you will be involved in emergency response and post-conflict work. It's incredibly compelling. And that's what I did at first. I started out in Cuba, then worked in postgenocide Rwanda for a short period. I worked in East Timor as the conflict ended there. There are people who spend their whole lives doing emergency response, and they get really good at it. But that wasn't me. I was always more attracted to governance.

Where did you start, and how did it help you get to where you are today?

The importance of service was always a big component of my family life, the importance of trying to be a part of the community. My whole family went on a church-sponsored trip to work in a very poor community in Appalachia. I was too young to go, but they always had stories about this experience. It probably wasn't the best model of development, but it was something that got my family involved in the lives of others. I think that stuck with me.

What are the major day-to-day activities of your current position?

I'd love to say I spend a lot of time thinking deep thoughts and writing laws, but it doesn't always work that way, especially when you're in the minority party. A lot of my job is serving the constituents. We have a very active and well-informed community in Northern Virginia, and you have to respond to the things that concern them.

Right now we're working on humanitarian assistance to Syria. I'm trying to figure out if there is a way that we can do something, even while the conflict is still raging, to help the administration and to help the civilians who are being harmed by the conflict.

You communicate with the administration to bring focus to issues, you try to develop consensus with staff in other offices. Congressman Moran has a strong interest in gender equity in US foreign policy and asked me to draft a letter to the State Department highlighting the importance of specialized assistance to victims of rape and other gender-based violence in Syria. I worked with NGOs and the staffs of other members of Congress—about fifteen members signed—and that helped to raise the profile of this issue. Usually I'm working on two or three collaborative projects like that.

There's a certain amount of time spent supervising and mentoring. The congressman has made providing quality internships for young people a top priority. We always have interns in the office, and we consider it an important part of the job to help them figure out what they want to do and how things operate in a congressional office.

What is your best advice for developing networking skills?

When I look back, I wish I'd been more courageous in reaching out to people whom I respected or that I wanted to emulate. You shouldn't be shy or hesitate to contact people who have written something that impressed you or done something that you think is intriguing and admirable. Just get into the conversation. I would advise people to get involved in that community, to reach out, to do your best to learn and be involved.

The Hill can be an isolating, alienating place. It's big and can seem impenetrable. So it's really important to network and develop relationships that are not just about transactions, because it can also be a very transactional place (*laughs*). But it's a very big community and a fairly diverse community. You have to make yourself go out of your comfort zone of just being at your desk and writing emails. You need to find people in different communities involved in different issues.

Do you have a mentor? How has he or she affected your life and career?

Yes, I've had mentors I met through academic or professional circles; over time they became friends. In particular, I think of a Jesuit professor at Georgetown who has been a close friend for decades. And I just hit it off with my first boss at CRS. We still talk regularly, and I feel like she's part of my family. Cardinal McCarrick, a CRS board member, has been a mentor to me. I got to know him while hosting his visits to Belgrade and Jerusalem when I was posted there. He was always willing to talk, to ask about my family, to offer advice, and even to ask me for help. I never really thought of these relationships as formal mentoring relationships, but that's what they are.

But I also feel I haven't done a good enough job of cultivating these relationships. My advice would be to reach out for help and counsel when you're looking for work. Do it all the time, and make it a priority.

Do you consider yourself a mentor to others?

I have a big family, and I've developed a kind of mentoring relationship with the ones who are getting to college age and beyond. It's a gratifying thing if somebody, especially a younger person, wants to discuss things with you.

I've also been able to maintain friendships with younger colleagues and interns from different jobs. I don't know if I'm doing it right because I don't tend to reach out to them. I'll feel like I'm interfering. But if they're interested, then that's great. In particular, a couple of the interns who have come through Mr. Moran's office have stayed in touch, and I like it. It's great to talk to them. They're super smart, and I feel honored to write their recommendations or to introduce them to friends who I think might also be able to give them advice.

How have you maintained a balance between work and personal life?

It was more difficult living on my own in other countries. Work can become your whole life. But I'm a pretty outgoing person, and I've developed friendships around the world. It's important to be able to decompress and socialize. Basketball was always a way for me to do that overseas. Regular periods of R&R are helpful.

When I was working overseas, I always went home during the holidays, when things tended to slow down. Interaction with my family has been really important, especially my nieces and nephews. I've been able to maintain really close relationships, even though most of the time I've been far away. And now, with a wife and daughter, I have absolutely no difficulty carving out a very happy but busy personal life outside of work! It helps that my boss and my colleagues are so accommodating.

What lessons have you learned as your career has progressed?

You should be willing to reach out to other people and explore ideas. That's really important to somebody just starting out. A lot of time people think it's not their personality to do this. But they should do their best anyway. I think it's rewarding.

Always ask questions. I don't do that a lot, but I've learned a lot from my wife, who is really fearless about that. It's okay not to know something, to seek to understand something. It doesn't necessarily reveal something bad about you. If you don't know something, that's okay. Asking questions is important. I should have learned this a long time ago . . . (*laughs*).

— PROFILE —

Deirdre White

President and CEO, PYXERA Global (formerly CDC Development Solutions), Washington, DC, 2010–present

Career Trajectory

CDC Development Solutions, Senior Vice President & COO, Washington, DC, 2002–10

Arthur D. Little, Senior Manager, Moscow, Russia and Arlington, VA, 1995–2002

IREX, Director of Russian Operations, Moscow, Russia 1992–95

American Councils on International Education: ACTR/ACCELS, Curriculum Consultant, Moscow, Russia, 1991–92

Welt Publishing, Managing Editor, Washington, DC, 1988–91

Academic Background

University of Pennsylvania, BA (Russian and Soviet Studies), 1988

How do you define your cause?

The work we do as an organization, and the work I've done most of my career, has been geared to improving the lives and livelihoods of people around the world. That's a very broad cause. For quite a while my cause was more limited, specifically to economic development and creating jobs. Over time, I have evolved that definition to go beyond economic development and job creation to include other aspects that improve people's lives. Things are much more interconnected than we like to think in the development community.

What drew you to this cause and your field?

I've always been very interested in things international, in international travel. It probably goes back to my roots. I spent the first year of my life living in Ouagadougou, Burkina Faso. My father was part of President Johnson's campaign to eradicate smallpox. He was a public health official who represented the Centers for Disease Control. I had the international involvement bug from an early age.

On the flip-side of that, my mother was a civil rights attorney. So I think between my father in public health and my mother as a teacher and civil rights attorney, it was inevitable that I would do something focused on helping people who have less.

How would you describe your field?

The field of international development is undergoing a revolution. Probably a slower revolution than it should be having, but certainly there have been major changes in the field in recent years, for a variety of reasons. People are starting to realize that some of the more traditional donor-driven development approaches are not as effective or helpful for the constituencies that they are supposed to serve.

The traditional institutional donors are trying to figure out a better way to have more impact. Also, many other people are becoming interested in development, whether because it's the right thing to do or because it's part of our national and economic security. Some of those new players that are getting involved are corporations. So at PYXERA Global today, we really find ourselves at the nexus where the public, private, and social sectors come together to improve human well-being.

Individuals are also taking a more active role in the challenges we face globally. The ability to work together to resolve global issues starts with individuals who understand and can relate to cultures different from their own. The US Center for Citizen Diplomacy (USCCD), a national organization that recently merged with PYXERA Global, is dedicated to increasing the numbers of Americans involved in international affairs at a people-to-people level. Individuals who consciously reach out to people from other cultures while embodying the characteristics of a diplomat—tact, civility, dedication to mutual respect and dialogue—are acting as "citizen diplomats." USCCD offers citizens access to opportunities for global engagement at a multitude of educational, international exchange, cultural, and faith-based organizations. As individuals cultivate a worldview that is broader than their own country, this has a positive impact on national and economic security at home.

How would you describe your career path?

I was very focused on the educational exchange part of my job at both ACTR (American Councils on International Education: ACTR/ACCELS) and IREX (*see chapter 9 for references to both organizations*). At ACTR I worked on student exchanges; at IREX I focused on scholarly exchange. While I was working for IREX, an opportunity came along to manage the Russian-American Bankers Forum Program. Observing these business exchange programs and how they were changing the landscape in Russia and how building small businesses was really working to create an alternative power source to government . . . I became fascinated with professional development and business creation.

I met with some folks from Arthur D. Little, the management consulting company, because they were starting up their Management Education Institute in Russia. It was just supposed to be just an informational interview, and I ended up with a position offer. I took the job at Arthur D. Little and really shifted more to management education and then to post-privatization restructuring—taking the formerly state-owned enterprises and looking at how to privatize them and how to restructure them so that they could actually survive in a market economy.

What are the major day-to-day activities of your current position?

There definitely is no typical day. Our organization has changed so dramatically during the past ten years that what I do day-to-day has changed dramatically as well. I used to know every single thing that went on in the organization; now I no longer do, and that's a good thing (*laughs*). But sometimes it's a hard thing.

I still do a lot of the operations work, the budgeting and projections. But I also spend a lot of time devising our long-term strategy and making sure we are keeping our clients happy. Twice a year I do formal feedback calls to all of our clients, and that number is growing. I provide a lot of input on the strategic direction of products, particularly the ones that are long term, more complex programs.

I speak at various meetings and panels in DC, around the United States, and internationally. Last year, I spent a lot of time on the road—more than one hundred days. So what am I doing when I'm on the road? Visiting our field offices and project sites, meeting with the client representatives on the ground, attending these conferences, meeting with potential clients, and even sometimes, as I did this year in India, doing hands-on project design.

How have you maintained a healthy balance between your work and personal life?

I think that is the biggest challenge (*sighs*). I'm not doing a particularly good job at it, I must admit. But I think that one of the things we're able to do well as a smaller organization is to be very flexible with people. If we know that people have been on the road a lot and need some down time, we give them down time. If you objectively step back, you'd say I have a better work–life balance today than I did a few years ago (*laughs*).

What is your best advice for developing effective networking skills?

I have never considered myself a good networker. I'm not the person who walks into the room and feels comfortable meeting people. My best advice is: force yourself to do it. Most people don't love being there any more than you do. They welcome having a conversation with someone. Take every opportunity to do it, especially when you're working in a place like DC. There's a luncheon or a breakfast or a presentation that is genuinely of interest almost every day of the week. If your schedule and office allow, get out as much as you can into the community of your peers.

As early in your career as possible, when people start asking you to make a presentation, or to be the face of something, never turn down that opportunity, no matter how small you think it is. You never know what will happen. When you're the one who is speaking, you automatically get to network; someone automatically comes to talk to you.

Do you have a mentor? How has he or she affected your life and career?

Interestingly, yes, one person who really stands out is Steve Hurley. Steve was the person who hired me at Arthur D. Little all those years ago. We both went on to do different things, but we reconnected about six years ago. I see Steve at a quarterly business meeting and talk to him at least on a biweekly basis. He's truly someone who helped me think through difficult issues. He's a great resource.

Do you consider yourself a mentor to others?

Our staff is very young, and there are a number of people who have grown up with this organization. Particularly our vice president, who has been here ten years and she's only thirty-three. I think she and others very much consider me a mentor and feel that I'm open to playing that role. But I am also asked more and more by other folks in the development community, who are ten years my junior, to talk through where they are going with their careers. So outside of the organization, I've started to have more of those opportunities as well.

What awards and honors have meant the most to you?

I had an opportunity to be part of the Bellagio Initiative at the Rockefeller Foundation. Last year they brought together forty-eight people from around the world who they considered to be leaders in the development space. To be considered one of those forty-eight was certainly one of the biggest honors I've ever had.

Are you involved in community service?

I've done community service literally all my life, working at So Others Might Eat as a kid, volunteering at schools, volunteering at the Washington International Center for many years. Any time that I have now goes toward my kids' school. Every year, each of the classes picks an international focus, a country, or a region. I help those classes learn about that country—music, language, customs, and costumes. I spend a lot of time sewing costumes; I'm the seamstress (*laughs*).

What are some lessons you have learned as your career has evolved?

Force yourself to do things that you don't like—networking, public speaking. Finances are not my favorite thing, but I forced myself to learn and to understand fiscal management. We wouldn't be alive as an organization if I hadn't forced myself to learn accounting.

Any final advice?

We find that many entry-level personnel have huge expectations of what their job is going to be. The reality is, you have to . . . I don't want to use the term "earn your stripes," but you have to show the organization and your supervisors that you can excel at the little stuff. Then they will give you more to do. But if you consider the little stuff beneath you . . . at least in our organization, no one considers anything beneath them. Be willing to take on absolutely whatever needs to be done, and do it really well. You will move forward quickly.

CHAPTER 9

Nongovernmental Organizations and Educational Institutions

Introduction

Some years ago, many Americans contemplating a career in international affairs envisioned working for the US Foreign Service. The Foreign Service was the ideal. Conscientious performance would propel those who survived the rigorous recruitment process up a structured career ladder. Ambassador Kenton Keith, who spent more than thirty-three years in the Foreign Service, told us in his profile interview that when he was starting his career, those interested in the international realm also thought about the Peace Corps or the US Agency for International Development (USAID). But that was pretty much it.

Today there are infinitely more choices for those who are pursuing an international career, in the private sector as well as in government. The proliferation of internationally focused private organizations—many of them nonprofit, all of them nongovernmental (NGO)—has created a growing arena for people interested in careers in international education, exchange, and development. The Foreign Service is now only one option among many. As Ambassador Keith told us:

> I think that NGOs may actually have more personally rewarding work to offer, in particular for people who have a passion in one area or another. If your passion is environmental protection, you can have an international career in that. If your passion is educational exchange, if your passion is sports . . . with the proliferation of NGOs and interest groups, it's possible to have a job in international, nongovernmental work that is every bit as rewarding as being in the Foreign Service.

And as globalization increases, there will be more and more opportunities in nongovernmental organizations.

A Gallup survey echoes Ambassador Keith's opinion, reporting that many young people think the private sector offers more opportunity for creativity and attracts better minds than traditional federal programs. Because of this, the government now faces "unparalleled and fierce" competition from NGOs in attracting the United States' best and brightest.[1]

What Is an NGO?

NGO. Nonprofit. NPO. Not-for-profit. Private voluntary organization. Any of these terms might be used to describe the organizations listed in this chapter. But do they all have the same meaning? Despite the explosion of private sector activity over the past few decades—what Dr. Lester Salamon, director of the Center for Civil Society Studies at Johns Hopkins University, calls the "global associational revolution"— confusion still persists.

NGOs and private sector organizations are, broadly defined, organizations that are not government agencies (public sector). NGOs do sometimes work in conjunction with the government—many NGOs listed here are referred to as the private sector partners of the Department of State and other US government agencies, implementing US-government funded exchange and development programs. These NGOs might even be funded (at least in part) by US government grants or cooperative agreements. But they are most definitely not a part of the government.

Nonprofits are also called not-for-profits, or NPOs. These are private sector organizations with 501(c)(3) status.[2] Nonprofits are invariably NGOs; that is, they are in the private sector and not a part of the government. But not all NGOs are nonprofits. Indeed, some NGOs (including some of the sample organizations listed later) have both for-profit and nonprofit arms. For example, an organization might have a study abroad component that has been incorporated as a for-profit and a high school exchange foundation that is nonprofit. Both components are dedicated to the cause of international exchange—they have just been financially and legally structured in different ways for various reasons.

We've also included educational institutions in this chapter as places to seek meaningful work. We've done this to recognize two facts: First, many NGOs in international education, exchange, and development have education and educational programs as key elements in their missions. Sometimes they manage language schools and other types of educational institutions. And second, universities, colleges, and high schools play important roles in the creation and facilitation of international programs. A number of the organizations listed here, such as NAFSA and the Institute of International Education, work directly with US universities on international exchange and education programs. Others, such as AIFS and CCI Greenheart, place international students at US high schools for exchange experiences. Still others, such as Ashoka and Abt Associates, are committed to educating communities abroad as a part of their development work, often with an emphasis on social entrepreneurship.

As mentioned, this issue of nomenclature is confusing. Some thinkers are grappling with how it might be fixed. Peter Hero, former president of the Silicon Valley Community Foundation, asserts that using the term *nonprofit* to describe an entire sector of organizations that work to support issues of public interest for noncommercial purposes is misleading. "What other sector of our society defines itself by what it is not?" he asks.[3] Because of this misnomer, Hero contends, many who work outside of the nonprofit sector view it not as the vibrant, well-managed, and important part of society that it is but rather as a group of "well-meaning but marginal and haphazardly managed organizations." For Hero, referring to the nonprofit sector by a name that better affirms its value and the benefits it provides to the public would go a long way in changing these perceptions. He suggests "public benefit corporations" or "public benefit sector." Management guru Peter Drucker referred to NGOs and nonprofits as the "social sector." Toward the end of his remarkable career, Drucker came to believe that "it is the social sector that may yet save society." A coalition of nonprofits has adopted the term "independent sector" to describe themselves.

Regardless of perceptions or names, what largely distinguishes NGOs (and nonprofits and educational institutions) from corporations and traditional for-profit businesses is that NGOs typically exist for the "public good." They have missions that are meant to improve society in some way. These organizations are also run much more like businesses or for-profit organizations than most people realize. The basic fiscal management tasks for both NGOs and businesses are quite similar: preparing a budget, producing timely monthly financial statements for the board of directors, and approving disbursements. The need for transparency and accountability applies to all sectors.

Sample Nongovernmental Organizations and Educational Institutions

Abt Associates

55 Wheeler Street

Cambridge, MA 02138

Telephone: 617-492-7100

Website: www.abtassociates.com

Twitter: @abtassociates

Since 1965, Abt Associates has worked "to improve the quality of life and economic well-being of people worldwide." They seek to do this by providing their clients—businesses, private organizations, and governments—with high-quality research, consulting, and technical assistance. Abt Associates works in seven practice areas: education; environment; food security and agriculture; housing and communities; workforce, income, and food security; international health; and US health. They have been recognized as a Devex Top Forty Innovator and a Global Top Twenty-five US Market Research Firm. Abt Associates has offices in nearly forty countries.

See the profile of Alanna Shaikh for more information. Alanna serves as director of communications, outreach, and public relations for Abt Associates. She is based in Azerbaijan.

Africare

440 R Street, NW

Washington, DC 20001

Telephone: 202-462-3614

Website: www.africare.org

Twitter: @Africare

Africare, founded by Peace Corps volunteers in Niger and a Nigerian diplomat in 1970, is the largest African American–led organization that works "to improve the quality of life of the people of Africa." Active in the areas of agriculture and food security; health and HIV/AIDS; water, sanitation and hygiene; humanitarian aid; women's empowerment; and resettlement, Africare works to advance community development in thirty-six countries throughout Africa.

AFS Intercultural Programs

71 West 23rd Street, 17th Floor

New York, NY 10010

Telephone: 212-807-8686

Website: www.afs.org

Twitter: @AFS

Created in 1914 as the American Field Service, AFS has expanded far beyond its initial mandate of assisting wounded World War I soldiers. Now the organization implements international exchange programs through a network of independent member organizations in more than fifty countries, coordinated from the AFS headquarters in New York City. Each year more than 13,000 individuals participate in AFS programs. These exchanges "help people develop the knowledge, skills, and understanding needed to create a more just and peaceful world." AFS has regional service centers in Baltimore, Maryland; St. Paul, Minnesota; and Portland, Oregon. American citizens have the opportunity to host international visitors and students through AFS international exchange programs. The AFS website contains categorized exchange-oriented resources targeted toward educators, volunteers, young adults, and international visitors.

AIESEC/United States

See chapter 6 in this volume.

AIFS: American Institute for Foreign Study

River Plaza, 9 West Broad Street

Stamford, CT 06902

Telephone: 203-399-5000

Website: www.aifs.com

AIFS was founded in 1964 and currently has offices in six countries: the UK, Australia, Poland, Germany, France, and the United States. Each year, more than 50,000 individuals participate in various AIFS programs including: college and high school study abroad, au pair placement, gifted education, and camp counselors. These programs enable AIFS to pursue its mission of providing "the highest quality educational and cultural exchange programs to enrich the lives of young people throughout the world."

Alliance Abroad Group (AAG)

1221 South Mopac Expressway, Suite 100

Austin, TX 78746

Telephone: 512-457-8062

Website: www.allianceabroad.com

Twitter: @AllianceAbroad

Since 1992, AAG has worked to bring international students, professionals, and teachers to the United States to experience American culture. AAG has reached more than 10,000 international participants and provided international growth opportunities for more than 800 US businesses and organizations during its twenty-year history. Through partnerships with other organizations such as AideAbroad, AAG also offers a variety of programs for US citizens to travel abroad.

Alliance for International Educational and Cultural Exchange

See chapter 6 in this volume.

Alliance for Peacebuilding (AfP)

1726 M Street, NW, Suite 401

Washington, DC 20036

Telephone: 202-822-2047

Website: www.allianceforpeacebuilding.org

Twitter: @AfPeacebuilding

AfP is a network of organizations and academic centers that works in the fields of conflict prevention and resolution. Members from NGO, governmental, and intergovernmental organizations collaborate to maintain sustainable peace and security internationally. Founded in 2003, the coalition provides negotiation and mediation services, develops professional and organizational capabilities, and seeks nonviolent solutions to problems and pressures of domestic and international relations. AfP builds the understanding of and support for peacebuilding policies in a variety of sectors, including government, philanthropy, media, business, and religion.

American Councils for International Education: ACTR/ACCELS

1828 L Street, NW, Suite 1200

Washington, DC 20036

Telephone: 202-883-7523

Website: www.americancouncils.org

Twitter: @AC_Global

American Councils was founded in 1974 to pursue its mission of creating language immersion and academic exchange opportunities for individuals and institutions. Originally incorporated as the American Council of Teachers of Russian (ACTR), American Councils has worked to advance research, training, and materials development in the fields of Russian and English language learning, as well as strengthen contact between scholars and educators in the United States and the former Soviet Union. In 1987, the ACTR board of directors created the American Council for Collaboration in Education and Language Study (ACCELS) to design and administer exchange and training programs. Changing to its current name in 1998, American Councils now administers more than thirty exchange and training programs, including US government programs and non-US national fellowship programs.

See the profile of Deirdre White for more information. Deirdre served as a curriculum consultant for American Councils from 1991 to 1992.

AMIDEAST

1730 M Street, NW, Suite 1100

Washington, DC 20036

Telephone: 202-776-9600

Website: www.amideast.org

Twitter: @AMIDEASThq

AMIDEAST was founded in 1951 as American Friends of the Middle East to strengthen mutual understanding and cooperation between Americans and the people of the Middle East and North Africa. It provides educational advising, English language training, professional training, and cultural exchanges. Headquartered in Washington, DC, AMIDEAST maintains offices in Egypt, Gaza, Iraq, Jordan, Kuwait, Lebanon, Morocco, Oman, Saudi Arabia, Tunisia, the United Arab Emirates, and the West Bank.

Ashoka

1700 North Moore Street, Suite 2000

Arlington, VA 22209

Telephone: 703-527-8300

Website: www.ashoka.org

Twitter: @Ashoka

Founded in 1980, Ashoka promotes social entrepreneurship by investing in sustainable and replicable solutions worldwide. Ashoka supports nearly 3,000 fellows in more than seventy countries. Candidates are nominated and judged on their creativity, entrepreneurial quality, social impact, and ethical fiber. Fellows receive a stipend for three years, access to a global support network, and partnerships with professional consultants. There are many other ways individuals can work with Ashoka. Individuals are encouraged to apply for opportunities as permanent staff members, volunteers, or interns. Free electronic and print newsletter subscriptions are available.

CCI Greenheart

746 North LaSalle Drive

Chicago, IL 60654

Telephone: 312-944-2522

Website: www.cci-exchange.com

Twitter: @GreenheartCCI

CCI Greenheart began in 1985 with seven students participating in a high school exchange; today, CCI Greenheart sends and receives nearly 9,000 participants each year. Throughout its growth, CCI Greenheart has held to its mission of "promoting cultural understanding, academic development, environmental consciousness and world peace." All participants—whether coming to the United States for high school exchanges, ESL learning, or work experience, or traveling abroad for educational exchange, cultural homestays, or to teach English—are encouraged to uphold the CCI mission, participate in volunteer activities, and promote environmentally sustainable practices.

CIEE: Council on International Educational Exchange

300 Fore Street

Portland, ME 04101

Telephone: 207-553-4000 and 800-40-STUDY (toll-free in the US)

Website: www.ciee.org

CIEE, founded in 1947, provides outbound international education experiences for university students, faculty, and administrators, and study, work, and internship opportunities for people coming into the United States. As part of their mandate "to help people gain understanding, acquire knowledge, and develop skills for living in a globally interdependent and culturally diverse world," CIEE hosts an annual conference on international educational exchange and is a cosponsor of the scholarly *Journal of Studies in International Education Exchange*, among other publications. The organization advocates at the state and federal level on behalf of the educational exchange community and also facilitates professional training and exchange.

Council for International Exchange of Scholars (CIES)

1400 K Street, NW Suite 700

Washington, DC 20005

Telephone: 202-686-4000

Website: www.cies.org

A division of the Institute of International Education since 1996, CIES was founded in 1947 to assist in administering the Fulbright Scholar Program. Working with both US and foreign colleges and universities, as well as international Fulbright Commissions in more than fifty countries, CIES has sixty program officers and staff at its headquarters in Washington. The Fulbright Program is one of the nation's flagship programs in international exchange. Since its establishment in 1946, nearly 300,000 participants have traveled as Fulbrighters.

Cultural Vistas

440 Park Avenue South, 2nd Floor

New York, NY 10016

Telephone: 212-497-5300

Website: www.culturalvistas.org

Twitter: @CulturalVistas

In 2011, the Association for International Practical Training and CDS International merged to become Cultural Vistas. Both organizations were recognized as leaders in the exchange field. Cultural Vistas offers exchange programs to and from the United States that are geared toward different ages and objectives including: Teach USA, Placement USA, the Congress-Bundestag Youth Exchange for Young Professionals, and Internships Abroad. All programs are designed to achieve the Cultural Vistas mission: "to enrich minds, advance global skills, build careers, and connect lives through international exchange." Cultural Vistas also serves as a private sector program agency partner to the US Department of State in the administration of the International Visitor Leadership Program.

EF: Education First

1 Education Street

Cambridge, MA 02141

Telephone: 800-992-1892

Website: www.ef.com

Founded in 1965, EF has helped individuals become global citizens through cultural exchanges, language learning, degree programs, and educational travel. EF believes that "in order to learn you need to experience." It provides exchange experiences to students from more than 200 countries. While EF offers English learning tools for individuals and companies online, it also maintains a global network of 25,000 teachers, 9,000 staff, 400 schools, and more than 50 international offices.

FHI 360

2224 East NC Highway 54

Durham, NC 27713

Telephone: 919-544-7040

Website: www.fhi360.org

Twitter: @FHI360

In 2011, Family Health International acquired the Academy for Educational Development (AED) programs and created a new entity, FHI 360. Employing more than 4,000 professionals, FHI 360 works to provide high-quality research, education, and services in family planning, STD/HIV prevention, and family health. It also serves as a private sector program agency partner to the US Department of State administering various exchange programs. Although headquartered in North Carolina, FHI 360 has offices in Washington, DC; New York; Boston; Bangkok; and Pretoria, and works in every US state and more than sixty countries around the world.

Friendship Force International (FFI)

127 Peachtree Street, Suite 501

Atlanta, GA 30303

Telephone: 404-522-9490

Website: www.thefriendshipforce.org

With 377 clubs around the world, FFI annually involves approximately 5,000 participants in exchanges that feature homestays on six continents. FFI was founded by President Jimmy Carter and Wayne Smith in 1977 as a nonprofit organization dedicated to providing short-term programs for participants to connect with peoples of other cultures. This global network of citizen diplomats was nominated for a Nobel Peace Prize in 1992. FFI coordinates exchanges managed by its network of local, volunteer-run clubs from its headquarters in Atlanta.

Sherry served on the board of directors of FFI, gave the keynote address at the 2012 FFI World Conference in Hiroshima, and is a member of the FFI International Advisory Council.

The German Marshall Fund (GMF) of the United States

1744 R Street, NW

Washington, DC 20009

Telephone: 202-683-2650

Website: www.gmfus.org

Twitter: @gmfus

GMF is an organization that works to build relationships and improve cooperation between Europe and the United States. Founded in 1972 through a gift from Germany as a permanent memorial to Marshall Plan assistance, GMF has provided coordination, resources, and scholarships to individuals and organizations who are working in the field of trans-Atlantic relations. GMF programs include the Brussels Forum, a summit of high-level business, academic, and political leaders from Europe and America, and the Balkan Trust for Democracy, a ten-year, $30 million grant initiative that supports good governance in Southeastern Europe.

Heifer International

1 World Avenue

Little Rock, AR 72202

Telephone: 855-9HUNGER (855-948-6437)

Website: www.heifer.org

Twitter: @Heifer

Heifer's goal of ending poverty and hunger "all started with a cow." After World War II, American farmers sent cows to Europe to help rebuild war-torn countries. Today, Heifer supplies individuals and communities in nearly fifty countries with various farm animals and craft/farming tools to help alleviate poverty and to create economic viability. Heifer works with the understanding that individuals and communities benefit more from receiving sustainable items than from monetary handouts.

The Hunger Project (THP)

5 Union Square West, 7th Floor

New York, NY 10003

Telephone: 212-251-9100

Website: www.thp.org

Twitter: @HungerProject

In 1977, THP was founded to help stem the rise of world hunger. It set itself apart by becoming a strategic, rather than relief, organization. THP believes the best way to end world hunger is to empower men and women through three critical elements: building self-reliance, empowering women, and forging partnerships with local government. THP works with partner counties—including Germany, Japan, and Sweden—to help end poverty and hunger in countries in Africa, Asia, and Latin America.

Institute of International Education (IIE)

809 United Nations Plaza

New York, NY 10017

Telephone: 212-883-8200

Website: www.iie.org

Twitter: @IIEglobal

Founded in 1919, IIE is a nonprofit organization committed to "promoting closer educational relations between the people of the United States and those of other countries, strengthening and linking institutions of higher learning globally, advancing academic freedom, and building leadership skills and enhancing the capacity of individuals and organizations to address local and global challenges." IIE is best known for its work administering the Fulbright Program as a private sector partner of the US Department of State. The Fulbright Program has provided financial support for individuals engaged in international scholarship since 1946. IIE provides a wide range of services to and manages or administers programs for many corporations, foundations, government agencies, and international agencies. The organization's highly respected annual publication *Open Doors* reports statistics on the number of international students in the United States, as well as the number of Americans who are studying overseas. IIE also produces a wide array of publications on study and training abroad and financial resources. In addition to its New York City headquarters, IIE has an office in Washington, DC, three regional centers within the United States, and offices in eleven international locations.

See the profile of Allan Goodman for more information. Dr. Goodman serves as president and CEO of IIE.

InterAction

See chapter 6 in this volume.

InterExchange

161 Sixth Avenue

New York, NY 10013

Telephone: 212-924-0446

Website: www.interexchange.org

Twitter: @InterExchangeUS

Since 1987, the nonprofit InterExchange has been working to create American cultural experiences for international visitors from more than sixty countries. InterExchange brings participants to the United States through four programs: Au Pair USA, Career Training USA, Camp USA, and Work & Travel USA. InterExchange also offers similar programs for American citizens to go abroad. Working Abroad Grants and Christianson Grants are available to subsidize programs for some participants.

International Education Service (IES)

15332 Antioch Avenue, Suite 145

Pacific Palisades, CA 90272

Telephone: 310-395-9393

Website: www.ies-ed.com

IES assists students from all parts of the world in finding the right school, college, university, or English language program in the United

States. IES partners with more than 500 educational institutions and helps promote them around the world, to the benefit of both potential students and the institutions themselves. IES offers each student a tailored placement based on previous education, experiences, and current needs.

International Relief and Development (IRD)

1621 North Kent Street, 4th Floor

Arlington, VA 22209

Telephone: 703-248-0161

Website: www.ird.org

Twitter: @ird_voices

IRD is a nonprofit organization that works to improve the lives of the most vulnerable through inclusion, engagement, and empowerment. IRD works by alleviating immediate needs, such as repairing roads, then by improving infrastructure, such as redesigning the transportation system. Since 1998, IRD has provided $3.5 billion in humanitarian assistance to more than forty-two countries in Africa, Eastern Europe, Southern Asia, and the Americas.

International Rescue Committee (IRC)

122 East 42nd Street

New York, NY 10168

Telephone: 212-551-3000

Website: www.rescue.org

Twitter: @theIRC

Founded in 1933 to bring relief to victims of both human conflicts and natural disasters, IRC is composed of units that focus on issues such as trafficking and water sanitation. IRC works to increase awareness and to pressure organizations into taking action to tackle major global problems. Present in more than forty countries, IRC provides major humanitarian relief and engages in advocacy.

Intrax Cultural Exchange

600 California Street, Floor 10

San Francisco, CA 94108

Telephone: 415-434-1221

Website: www.intraxinc.com

Twitter: @IntraxCenters

Founded in 1980, Intrax is a cultural exchange organization that works "to inspire a lifetime of cultural understanding, global awareness, and citizen diplomacy." It includes four program branches: AuPairCare; Intrax, an intern, study, and work initiative; Ayusa, a high school exchange program; and ProWorld, which facilitates the placement of volunteers abroad. Every year, Intrax programs enable more than 21,000 participants to travel to more than one hundred countries. Headquartered in California, Intrax has offices in eight countries including Peru, Germany, and Singapore.

IREX

1275 K Street, NW, Suite 600

Washington, DC 20005

Telephone: 202-628-8188

Website: www.irex.org

Twitter: @IREXintl

Founded in 1968 as the International Research and Exchanges Board to foster exchanges between the United States and the Soviet Union, IREX specializes in international education, media independence, social development, and the free flow of digital information. IREX's staff of more than 400 professionals is present in more than one hundred countries, promoting education at all levels, advancing independent media management, and developing civil society through professional training, grant initiatives, scholarly research, and exchange programs.

Mercy Corps

45 SW Ankeny Street

Portland, OR 97204

Telephone: 503-896-5000

Website: www.mercycorps.org

Twitter: @mercycorps

Founded in 1979, Mercy Corps is a global aid agency engaged in transitional environments that have experienced some shock: a natural disaster, economic collapse, or conflict. Although Mercy Corps provides significant emergency relief in times of crisis, it believes these places in transition present a key opportunity to change the system for the better. With a 95 percent local staff, Mercy Corps works at the community level to make these changes sustainable in nearly fifty countries.

Meridian International Center

1630 Crescent Place, NW

Washington, DC 20009

Telephone: 202-667-6800

Website: www.meridian.org

Twitter: @MeridianIntl

Meridian International Center promotes international understanding through the exchange of people, ideas, and the arts. Established in 1960, Meridian designs and implements exchange, technical assistance, and training programs for people from more than 140 nations. For example, Meridian is the largest program agency (private sector partner) implementing the US Department of State's International Visitor Leadership Program. Meridian also works to promote a free exchange of ideas and the arts through efforts such as art for Cultural Diplomacy, which mounts exhibitions around the world to highlight relevant topics.

See the profile of Ambassador Kenton Keith for more information. Ambassador Keith served as senior vice president of Meridian International Center.

Mobility International USA

132 East Broadway, Suite 343

Eugene, OR 97401

Telephone: 541-343-1284

Website: www.miusa.org

Twitter: @MobilityINTL

Mobility International USA (MIUSA) was founded in 1981 by Susan Sygall and Barbara Williams to foster inclusion of individuals with disabilities in international exchange. Many exchange organizations cannot accept people with disabilities because they cannot accommodate their needs abroad. Since opening in 1981, however, MIUSA has sent more than 2,000 individuals from more than one hundred countries on cultural exchanges. MIUSA also uses advocacy, grassroots leadership, and training to promote their cause of international disability inclusion. In 2001, MIUSA launched Building an Inclusive Development Community (BIDC). This project, sponsored by USAID, works internationally to promote inclusion and understanding of people with disabilities.

NAFSA: Association of International Educators

See chapter 6 in this volume.

National Council for International Visitors (NCIV)

1420 K Street, NW, Suite 800

Washington, DC 20005

Telephone: 202-842-1414

Website: www.nciv.org

Twitter: @NCIVNetwork

NCIV's mission is to promote excellence in citizen diplomacy. NCIV, founded in 1961, is a national network of individual members, private program agencies located in Washington, DC, and more than ninety community-based organizations throughout the United States. A full list of contact information for NCIV member organizations can be found in the membership section of the NCIV website. Member organizations design and implement professional programs and cultural activities and provide home hospitality opportunities for international leaders, specialists, and students. NCIV members provide services to distinguished leaders who participate in the US Department of State's International Visitor Leadership Program and other international exchange programs. NCIV provides leadership development and nonprofit management training while developing its members' capabilities to work with foreign delegations.

Now president emeritus, Sherry served as the executive director, then as president, of NCIV from 1996 to 2011. Mark worked as a program associate for communications at NCIV from 2005 to 2007. For more information, see the profiles of Jennifer Clinton and Peggy Parfenoff. Jennifer is the current president of NCIV, and Peggy is the executive director of WorldChicago, an NCIV member organization.

One To World

285 West Broadway, Suite 450

New York, NY 10013

Telephone: 212-431-1195

Website: www.one-to-world.org

Twitter: @OneToWorldInc

One To World, founded in 1977 as Metro International, works to create global citizens by bringing the future leaders of the world together. One To World works with Fulbright recipients and other international students in the greater New York area to promote international understanding. Events, excursions, and other activities give international students opportunities to explore American culture. These students reciprocate by sharing their culture through presentations in New York public schools. Through these interactions, One To World strives to create transnational understanding and cooperation.

Oxfam America

226 Causeway Street, 5th Floor

Boston, MA 02114

Telephone: 617-482-1211 and 800-776-9326 (toll-free in the US)

Website: www.oxfamamerica.org

Twitter: @OxfamAmerica

Oxfam America is a nonprofit organization affiliated with Oxfam International that works to end global poverty by saving lives, strengthening communities, and campaigning for change. One of seventeen members of the international Oxfam Confederation, Oxfam America works in more than ninety countries in Africa, East Asia, and Central and South America. Oxfam takes both an "on the scene" approach to development work, with employees working on the ground through regional offices abroad, as well as a broader policy role with employees who engage in advocacy and public education in the United States.

People to People International (PTPI)

911 Main Street, Suite 2110

Kansas City, Missouri 64105

Telephone: 816-531-4791

Website: www.ptpi.org

Twitter: @PTPI

People to People was founded in 1956 after President Dwight D. Eisenhower hosted a White House Summit on Citizen Diplomacy. In pursuit of its mission to promote peace through understanding, more than 80,000 families and individuals from 135 countries have participated in humanitarian, cultural, and educational programs. If you are unable to go abroad, People to People offers the opportunity for individuals to begin a Community Chapter. Community Chapters are centered on a project or goal that ten or more people embrace, such as the Global Landmine Initiative or hosting international visitors.

PYXERA Global

1030 15th Street, NW, Suite 730 East

Washington, DC 20005

Telephone: 202-872-0933

Website: www.pyxeraglobal.org

PYXERA Global (a new name adopted in 2013—the organization was formerly known as CDC Development Solutions) was commissioned by the White House after the fall of the Berlin Wall in an effort to develop private enterprise in the former Communist Bloc. The organization was known at its founding as the Citizens Democracy Corps. Since then, PYXERA Global has worked to create sustainable economic development in more than eighty countries using public, private, and volunteer resources. For example, PYXERA places corporate executives as short-term volunteers on development projects abroad. PYXERA also utilizes unique expertise in five practice areas to promote economic development. These include global citizenship and volunteerism, supply chain demand, tourism development, access to finance, and stability and economic recovery.

See the profile of Deirdre White for more information. Deirdre joined PYXERA Global in 2002 and is currently the president and CEO.

Save the Children

54 Wilton Road

Westport, CT 06880

Telephone: 800-728-3843 (toll-free in the US)

Website: www.savethechildren.org

Twitter: @SavetheChildren

An alliance of more than twenty-eight organizations that work in approximately 120 countries, Save the Children is committed to creating lasting, positive change in the lives of children in the United States and around the world. Established in 1932, Save the Children reaches out to all people—parents, community members, local organizations, and government agencies—in order to improve the lives of more than 64 million children worldwide annually.

Sister Cities International (SCI)

915 15th Street, NW, 4th Floor

Washington, DC 20005

Telephone: 202-347-8630

Website: www.sister-cities.org

Twitter: @SisterCitiesInt

Representing 600 communities in the United States and 2,000 communities in 136 nations, Sister Cities is a global network devoted to citizen diplomacy. Since its founding in 1956, Sister Cities has created ties between US cities and partner communities abroad. Sister Cities supports its local organizations from Washington, DC, and hosts a number of events and programs to achieve its goal of building international bridges between communities.

Think Impact

50 South Steele Street, Suite 328

Denver, CO 80209

Telephone: 303-377-3776

Website: www.thinkimpact.com

Twitter: @thinkimpact

Think Impact is an organization, founded in 2010, that seeks to end poverty through market-based solutions and social entrepreneurship. It has offices in Ghana, Kenya, Rwanda, and South Africa. In emphasizing the power of the individual, Think Impact has made significant strides in reducing poverty and creating infrastructure in African communities. Individuals and organizations are encouraged to learn more and help the mission of Think Impact through one of five projects: Institute, Summit, Xtreme, Huddle, and Unleash. Individuals may also sign up for a free e-newsletter.

US Institute of Peace (USIP)

2301 Constitution Avenue, NW

Washington, DC 20037

Telephone: 202-457-1700

Website: www.usip.org

Twitter: @USIP

Established and funded in part by Congress, USIP is dedicated to the peaceful resolution of conflicts worldwide. By teaching others and through its own efforts, USIP provides support in zones of conflict such as Afghanistan, Nigeria, Iraq, and Sudan. Officially established in 1986, USIP sponsors programs and awards grants to promote peace through training, nonviolent conflict resolution, educational programs, and building institutions that support civil society throughout the world.

Winrock International

2101 Riverfront Drive

Little Rock, AR 72202

Telephone: 501-280-3000

Website: www.winrock.org

Twitter: @WinrockIntl

Winrock International works to "empower the disadvantaged, increase economic opportunity, and sustain natural resources" for people in the United States and around the world. It was formed in 1985 by the merger of three Rockefeller family-related organizations, including The Agricultural Development Council. Winrock works in more than 120 countries on nearly sixty different project themes. The website includes a job board for all open positions within Winrock International. Opportunities to become a volunteer are also available; since 1991, volunteers have traveled to fifty-six countries and completed 4,400 assignments.

World Learning

1 Kipling Road, PO Box 676

Brattleboro, VT 05302

Telephone: 802-257-7751 and 800-257-7751 (toll-free in the US)

Website: www.worldlearning.org

Twitter: @WorldLearning

Originally founded in 1932 as the Experiment in International Living, World Learning is a nonprofit organization that advances leadership through education, exchange, and development programs in more than seventy countries. The organization has four main components: the Experiment in International Living, the School for International Training (SIT) Study Abroad, the SIT Graduate Institute, and International Development and Exchange Programs (IDEP). World Learning offers exchanges for high school students to fifty countries and for college and university students to more than sixty countries, as well as other academic programs through SIT. With more than 1,000 employees in the United States and abroad, World Learning also manages various international development projects. The Visitor Exchange Program of World Learning helps implement the US Department of State's International Visitor Leadership Program, as well as other professional and citizen exchange programs.

Sherry participated in a World Learning Experiment in International Living (EIL) program to Germany in 1963, then led an EIL program to the former Soviet Union in 1969 (see chapter 1 in this volume). She served on the World Learning board of trustees for twelve years. See the profile of Adam Weinberg for additional information. Adam served as the president and CEO of World Learning from 2009 to 2013, and executive vice president and provost from 2006 to 2009.

Youth For Understanding USA (YFU)

6400 Goldsboro Road, Suite 100

Bethesda, MD 20817

Telephone: 240-235-2100

Website: www.yfuusa.org

Twitter: @YFU_USA

YFU, formed in 1951, has offices in more than sixty countries and more than 4,500 participants each year. YFU USA organizes Youth For Understanding high school exchange programs in the United States. Because YFU is volunteer based, there are ample opportunities to get involved. Individuals may apply for volunteer positions such as area representative or international student volunteer, or they may volunteer for certain tasks involving administration, recruitment, or orientation.

Selected Resources

Advisory List of International Educational Travel and Exchange Programs

Council on Standards for International Educational Travel, 2012 (www.csiet.org)

Produced since 1984 by the Council on Standards for International Educational Travel (CSIET), the *Advisory List* provides valuable information on many of the international exchange programs available to young people. This information includes countries served by participating exchange programs, as well as organizational contact information, background, and operational details. These programs are ranked according to their compliance with CSIET standards, with ratings of "full listing," "provisional listing," and "conditional listing." This classification offers parents, students, and employment seekers a comparative perspective on the key organizations in the field of international youth exchange. *Print.*

AidSource

See chapter 5 in this volume.

AlertNet

Website: www.alertnet.org

AlertNet was started in 1997 by the Thomson Reuters Foundation as a free resource for humanitarian news. Since its creation, AlertNet has enrolled more than 500 NGO members from ninety-five countries. The website, which receives an average of 12 million visits per year, contains breaking news, blogs, a job board, and training opportunities. All resources are free online to individuals, but membership—which includes the benefits of a membership directory, publishing news, and job openings—is reserved for NGOs only. *Web.*

Charity Channel

Website: www.charitychannel.com

As part of its mission "to create a place where nonprofit professionals can connect, learn from each other, share information, and work together to advance the cause of philanthropy," Charity Channel provides a wide array of resources designed to benefit the entire nonprofit community. These resources are made available by experienced professionals in the field who volunteer their time and efforts. The website features forum discussions, nonprofit-specific news feeds (including one dedicated to international issues), electronic newsletters, book reviews, interviews with experts in the field, and limited job listings. While the site does ask subscribers to pay a few dollars to support maintenance and resource costs, the $2 or $3 monthly fee is not mandatory; Charity Channel "will not turn away any individual without the means to pay." *Web.*

The Chronicle of Philanthropy

Website: www.philanthropy.com

The Chronicle of Philanthropy is a news source for nonprofit leaders, fundraisers, grant makers, and others involved in philanthropic enterprises. It publishes a biweekly print newspaper. Included in the publication are listings of upcoming events, workshops, and seminars, a directory of services, and job listings. The newspaper is useful for gathering information and gives greater insight into the trends in philanthropy and grant making. *Print and Web. Please see entry for Philanthropy.com.*

Dave's ESL Cafe

Website: www.eslcafe.com

Dave's ESL Cafe has become a popular resource for individuals who are interested in teaching English abroad, as well as for those currently teaching abroad. The website offers resources such as employment opportunities, forums, and an ever-expanding "cookbook" on methods to teach certain subjects. The website also offers resources for students including slang and idiom dictionaries, grammar lessons, and quizzes. *Web.*

DevEx

See chapter 5 in this volume.

Global Health Hub

Website: www.globalhealthhub.org

Based on volunteer efforts, Global Health Hub is a unique resource of original news and commentary on global health and development. It gathers its information from traditional sources like news posts and academic journals, as well as blog posts and Twitter feeds. The Hub also utilizes social media by offering hashtags on Twitter that allow individuals or companies to connect directly. Job opportunities, for example, can be found on Twitter by searching for #GHDjob. *Web.*

Idealist

Website: www.idealist.org

The most well-known and popular site for nonprofit job seekers, Idealist is an international consortium of more than 77,000 nonprofit organizations. In addition to posting job and internship openings, organizations on Idealist also present information about their mission and their work, upcoming programs, events, and campaigns, as well as downloadable materials. The Idealist website also features articles about activism, the nonprofit sector, and other related issues. *Web.*

The Idealist Guide to Nonprofit Careers for Sector Switchers, Steven Joiner

Hundreds of Heads Books, 252 pages, 2010

The Idealist Guide, written by the staff of Idealist (see the previous resource), is geared to individuals who wish to move into a career in the nonprofit sector. This book offers advice on entering the nonprofit field, from information on how to begin job searches to the jargon used in the industry. *Print.*

IIE Network Membership Directory 2011: Directory of International Educators

See chapter 5 in this volume.

International Development Career List

Website: www.alannashaikh.com/products/index.html

Hosted by Alanna Shaikh (see her profile for more information on her career), this resource contains much more than just job listings. The website contains valuable career advice, discussion, and various opinions from the author. Individuals can subscribe to a weekly newsletter for $3 a month or for an adjusted rate for six months ($14.95). Individuals are encouraged to send questions and remarks to Alanna to be answered in the newsletter. *Web.*

NAFSA Job Registry

See chapter 5 in this volume.

National Directory of Nonprofit Organizations

Taft Group, 2012 (www.gale.com/taft.htm)

Now in its 27th edition, this directory provides the names, contact information, and annual budget of approximately 260,000 organizations—180,120 of which have budgets in excess of $100,000. Entries in both volumes of this publication cover all twenty-two of the US Internal Revenue Service (IRS) 501(c) subsections, as well as IRS sections 501(e), 501(k), and 4947(a)(2). *Print.*

The Nonprofit Career Guide: How to Land a Job That Makes a Difference, Shelly Cryer

Fieldstone Alliance, 300 pages, 2008

A finalist in the Career Category for the 2008 ForeWord Book of the Year Award, *The Nonprofit Career Guide* is tailored to individuals who wish to be successful in the nonprofit sector. This includes a multitude of profiles from individuals of all backgrounds and enables the reader to explore many career paths. *Print.*

Nonprofit Oyster

Website: www.nonprofitoyster.com

This nonprofit-specific employment site allows users to conduct state, topic, and position-specific searches of organizational vacancies free of charge. Resume writing and posting services are also available. The site assists you in creating an anonymous career profile that subscribing employers can search and vet. These services, along with e-mail job alerts that automatically notify you of available positions that match your declared interests, are available for a membership fee. *Web.*

Opportunity Knocks

Website: www.opportunityknocks.org

Opportunity Knocks is similar to Nonprofit Oyster, but its free nonprofit job search engine allows for much more specificity, including searches targeted according to keyword, company name, topic area, position, employment type, salary, and location. Registered users can also save searches for future reference. Electronic resume posting and editing, automatic job notification, and application organization services are also available. The site is maintained by fees charged to nonprofit employers in exchange for job posting and evaluation services. *Web.*

Peace and Collaborative Development Network (PCDN)

Website: www.internationalpeaceandconflict.org

Created in 2007, PCDN acts as a professional networking site for individuals and organizations involved in development and conflict resolution. Its mission—to create "horizontal networking"—has been supported by more than 27,000 members. Donations for membership are requested but not required. Once an individual or organization has been processed as a member, they can access the many blogs, forums, events, and job postings on the site. *Web.*

Philanthropy.com

Website: http://philanthropy.com

Provided as an online service of *The Chronicle of Philanthropy*, philanthropy.com contains nonprofit-specific resources that are useful to job seekers, young professionals, and chief executives alike. This fact is reflected in the site's range of free services, which include a nonprofit question hotline, a collection of research and overviews of developments in the field, and a diverse collection of articles—updated weekly—covering topics from "getting the right degree for an overseas career" to "how charities cope when their boards need a makeover." Electronic synopses of articles from *The Chronicle of Philanthropy* are also available at Philanthropy.com, with full articles from the print edition accessible only to paid subscribers. *Web.*

Search: Winning Strategies to Get Your Next Job in the Nonprofit World, Larry H. Slesinger

Piemonte Press, 104 pages, 2004 (www.slesingermanagement.com)

This book has been described as "essential" for any person wanting to get a foot in the door of the nonprofit world. Slesinger, founder of an executive search firm that specializes in nonprofit recruitment, shares his job-staffing expertise in *Search*. He offers strategies for those who are seeking a job in the nonprofit sector and provides advice on how to draft a resume, prepare for an interview, and follow up after interviews. *Print.*

SECUSS-L Listserv

Website: www.secussl.info

Started in 1991 out of the University of Buffalo, SECUSS-L is the only national electronic list dedicated to education abroad. While the listserv is intended for campus and overseas advisors and program administrators, individuals may register for free. Postings circulated via SECUSS-L include international education and exchange job openings, as well as a variety of other information. *Web.*

Union of International Associations Job Board

Website: www.uia.be

Union of International Associations is an apolitical, nonprofit, and independent research institute based in Brussels, Belgium. It was formed in 1907 and is best known for its *Yearbook of International Organizations* and other publications. The website contains a job board for positions around the world. *Web.*

Notes

1. *Within Reach . . . But Out of Synch: The Possibilities and Challenges of Shaping Tomorrow's Government Workforce*, a report by the Council for Excellence in Government and the Gallup Organization, December 5, 2006.
2. The designation 501(c)(3) is a subsection of the US Internal Revenue Code, which lists provisions granting exemption from federal income tax to various charitable, nonprofit, religious, and educational organizations.
3. Peter Hero, "Language Matters: It Is Time to Change Our Name," October 2001. This article originally appeared in the Association of Fundraising Professionals October 2001 newsletter and can now be accessed in the articles archives at www.kirschfoundation .org.

— PROFILE —

Adam Weinberg

President, Denison University, Granville, OH, 2013–present[1]

Career Trajectory

World Learning, Brattleboro, VT
  President and CEO, 2009–13
  Provost/Executive Vice President, 2006–9

Colgate University, Hamilton, NY
  Dean of the College, 2002–5

Associate Professor, 1995–2005

Academic Background

Northwestern University, PhD (Sociology), 1994

Cambridge University, PhD, 1994

Bowdoin College, BA, 1983

How do you define your cause?

In some ways, I'm a good, old-fashioned populist. I grew up in a family that believed that you worked for your community and neighbors as part of your everyday life. So my cause has always been citizenship. How do we create communities and countries where people can come together, learn to work with people they like, sometimes learn to work with people they don't like, often learn to work with people they don't know, to identify and solve their common problems?

My cause is to build a stronger global civil society. Because it's more and more clear to me, the older I get, the problems we face are not because we don't have the answers—it's because we can't seem to get organized to do what needs to be done. Nation-states won't get it done; private industry doesn't have the incentive to get it done. It's going to have to be people coming together to get it done.

What drew you to this cause and your field?

Like everybody's biography, it's not one thing but how multiple things came together. One clearly was the influence of my family: my grandfather and my father. Both of them would define themselves as nonpolitical people, and yet they were probably the two most political people I've ever met. But they were political in a nonparty sense. They were people who got up and went to work every day, did different things for the underdog, and contributed to their community. They were both people who were never too busy to do something for a neighbor or a friend.

I often tell people that I've spent the last twenty-five years trying to finish two classes I took at Bowdoin College my junior year: one with William Whiteside, who introduced me to John Dewey and American Pragmatism, and the second with Craig McEwen, who introduced me to a new way of thinking about the law—the law wasn't about punishing or power, but about repairing relationships. It was the influence of my education, the places I went, my family, and my early experiences as a young professional. I saw up close the power of what happens when people come together, even when they don't like each other, and are willing to put their differences aside to identify and solve common problems.

How would you describe your field?

I'm an educator at heart. That's what I believe in and care about. I do not believe there are panaceas in life. There are many things that need to happen for the world to move forward. Education is one of the most necessary and is the area in which I have the most to contribute. I'm an educator, and that's how I define my field.

You understand your career better in retrospect, and the common thread for me has really been civic education. How do we retool academic institutions to help young people develop both the capacity and commitment to engage in public work as part of their everyday life? That's what gets me up and keeps me intellectually and personally motivated.

How would you describe you career path?

My close friends have said that watching my career path can give one whiplash (*laughs*) because in each phase I was going in a certain direction and then took a sharp turn. I was ready to go to law school. Then one night, sitting around with a group of friends, someone asked a really silly question: "If you could do anything with your life, what would it be?" I said, "I'd like to become a professor." So I woke up the next morning thinking, "If that's what I want to do, then why am I headed to law school?"

When we think about careers, we often ask the wrong questions. The answers are the easy part; it's getting the questions right that's difficult. The question isn't, "What do I want to do with my life"—because that begs you to identify a profession. The question should be: "What kind of life do I want to live?" I've always been willing to take advantage of exciting opportunities to follow my passions. If you make decisions that way, there tends to be a good match between your skills and interests and a given job.

How have you maintained a healthy balance between your work and personal life?

I made the decision when our first child was born that I wanted to do three things. First, I wanted to be successful professionally. I cared about my passion. Second, I wanted to be a very active and engaged father. I actually spent the first year of our first child's life at home with her. And third, I wanted to have an egalitarian marriage as defined by our generation. That didn't leave time for anything else. So in a way I'd say, yes, I managed to blend work and family really well. But all my hobbies went out the window.

In my early forties, I had a major health scare that came out of nowhere. I made some radical lifestyle changes for which I will forever be grateful. I took up yoga, took up meditation—what people now call mindfulness—which I've loved. It's become another passion in life, and I've had time to explore it.

I took my first VP-level position early in my life. I would not have survived this long in VP roles, or presidency roles, if I had not found balance because these jobs will eat you up. Unlike when you're in more junior roles, where your job is to get work done, in a senior role your job is to make good decisions, or reasonable decisions in unreasonable circumstances. Being centered and balanced is crucial to doing a good job.

What are the major day-to-day activities of your current position?

They fall into a couple buckets. One is the crisis of the day. World Learning operates with more than 1,000 employees in seventy countries. Universities have their own complexity. The nonprofit world in general—whether it's the academic world, or NGO world, or the exchange world if you're running an organization of size and any history—you're not running a business, you're almost the mayor of a town. A mayor is probably a better analogy than anything else. But it's inevitably dealing with the crisis of the moment.

The second is what I call good management, which is doing the blocking and tackling for your team. You hire good people; you make sure they have good plans that are aligned with what is good for the organization. Part of my job is coaching the team, keeping them aligned and successful.

The third is most important because if you don't do it, then nobody else will do it. And that's the long-range visioning that's connected to resource development. Where is your sector going over the next three to five years, so that you can position your organization to be healthy and thrive in that environment?

Are you involved in community service?

We all have an obligation to make sure our fields stay healthy, so I serve on the boards of the Alliance for International Educational and

Cultural Exchange and InterAction (*see chapter 6 for both*), and the board of Vermont Campus Compact. We have to see ourselves as a community of organizations and as working collectively to shape the world in ways that promote our missions.

What is your best advice for developing effective networking skills?

I have some close friends who are just masterful at going to a cocktail party and walking away with fifty business cards and then following up. Their LinkedIn is going all the time. But that's not me.

You build your networks by doing good work with people. I've tried to develop deep relationships with trust and respect, as opposed to a lot of thin relationships. There's not a right or wrong here, but I think matching the style of networking to your personality is important.

My view on networking has really been to work with people I admire and trust and to develop projects that move the needle forward to make the world a better place. And you'll find over time, while you may not know as many people, your reputation flourishes. The people you do know will move mountains to open doors for you.

As an example, when Denison University recruited me and we got to the final stages, it was interesting to me how many Denison board members knew Colgate or World Learning board members. The network was very small. And I was equally surprised with how many Colgate board members, whom I hadn't seen in eight years, dropped what they were doing to give me a positive reference. That's not because we were connected on LinkedIn; it was because we had gone through some difficult times together at Colgate and really moved the institution forward. We developed respect and relationships by working together. Those relationships paid off.

Do you have a mentor? How has he or she affected your life and career?

I have multiple mentors. Rebecca Chopp, the president of Swarthmore College, has been and continues to be a great mentor for me. Harry Boyte, one of the most important voices in the civic education movement, continues to be a mentor. And there have been many, many other people along the way. Coaches, board chairs, friends.

One of the first things I did when I became the president of World Learning was to seek out two or three people who would serve as mentors and coaches. I called them almost weekly in that first year. The reason they were good mentors and coaches is because they didn't tell me what I wanted to hear, and they didn't give me praise. They were really willing to tell me what I wasn't doing right and what I wasn't hearing. They were willing to pay attention and be authentic and real. It was crucial for me.

Do you consider yourself a mentor to others?

I try. But you'll have to ask them if I'm successful at it (*laughs*). Yes, it's clearly something I enjoy. I consider management to be coaching, which is really a different word for mentoring.

What lessons have you learned as your career has evolved?

Don't let the baby ducks peck you to death. One of the mistakes people make is letting little issues eat them up emotionally. We spend lots of time thinking about how we're going to respond to an e-mail, when we should be thinking about how to stay focused on the big issues.

Be authentic; be real; stick with your passions.

Don't be afraid to take some risks. I've made career moves that other people thought were unwise. But I was focused on following my passions and living the kind of life that I wanted to live.

Any final advice?

Stay focused. There is such temptation to reinvent strategy every other day.

Find good mentors and make sure you always have people in your daily orbit who will tell you what you need to hear and what other people are saying. I love the Wayne Gretzky line: "Skate where the puck is going, not where it's been."

Lastly, and for me this is crucial, in a world that increasingly tries to reduce everything to transaction, remember that it's really the relationships that matter.

Note

1. The interview for this profile took place when Adam Weinberg was president and CEO of World Learning.

— PROFILE —

Peggy Parfenoff

Executive Director, WorldChicago, Chicago, IL, 2001–present

Career Trajectory

LPC Group, Marketing Manager, Chicago, IL, 1999–2001

City of Chicago, Department of Cultural Affairs, Director of Development, Chicago, IL, 1994–99

Academic Background

Northwestern University, Kellogg School of Management, MBA (Marketing & Public Nonprofit Management), 1998

Central College (Pella, Iowa), BA (Communications & French), 1990

How would you define your cause?

I'm working to position our organization as a part of the citizen diplomacy movement, to make that our larger cause. We're all working as a network, an organization, and a staff to make our community and our world a better place through citizen diplomacy.

What I like about working in the nonprofit sector is that we're all motivated by this same cause, of bringing people to see Chicago and to interact with their counterparts in America and to exchange opinions. When I'm interviewing to fill positions, I look for people who are passionate about international affairs. If you tell me you're interested in international work but there's nothing on your resume that says you've ever been out of the country or that you've ever worked on projects with people from overseas . . . I need to see evidence that you've traveled or had some international experience. You need to demonstrate that you really want to be in this field and that you believe in this cause.

What drew you to this cause and your field?

I knew I wanted to work in something that was meaningful and would make a difference in the world. Earlier in my career, I got a job at a consulting firm and realized that I didn't believe in what they were doing. I realized I needed to work in something that I thought was making our world a better place.

I'd always loved things international; I loved travel. I worked in the arts for a while as well. When this opportunity at WorldChicago came up to marry internationalism to some of my other interests, I jumped at it. Coming into it, I hadn't realized how much I would enjoy being in the field and how much I value a job that is different every day.

How would you describe you career path?

It was not planned. It wasn't a strategic path to get from point A to where I am. But somehow I was always drawn to nonprofits, always drawn toward a cause and bettering our world. When I was in graduate school, I remember driving home one night with somebody and talking about my work and what I was going to do next. He looked at me and said, "Don't you want to make money?" It had never actually occurred to me to look at it that way. It is more important to be doing something interesting and meaningful.

What are the major day-to-day activities of your current position?

Every day is different with a new project or program. I spend probably 20 percent of my day on e-mail. I also meet with my staff to coordinate the projects and programs we're doing together. Then there's the administrative side: taking care of human resources, as well as budgeting and fiscal management.

For example, on Monday, I'll work on planning our trip to Brazil as part of our SportsUnited exchange program grant with the US Department of State. I'll start a grant proposal for an exchange to Indonesia. I'll study the backgrounds of the Legislative Fellows who are coming in a few months—I've got to place four of them with host organizations. I'll follow up with Chicago Public Schools to see if they'll take one, and with the City Commission on Human Relations to see if they'll host another. Then I'll check in with my Open World exchange program participants from Russia who are in town right now. That's what my Monday will look like.

How have you maintained a healthy balance between your work and personal life?

You're constantly juggling both sides, work and home, especially when you have children. You're probably never going to be as good as you want to be, but you've got to come to terms with that. I think it's maybe even more difficult to be the mother you expect yourself to be, because your expectations are based on such a high standard. Sometimes you have to be okay with buying the cookies instead of making them.

That's a continuous struggle. I try to look at it as a biweekly or monthly cycle. If I had to work three nights one week, can I be home every night the next week to put my son to bed?

What is your best advice for developing effective networking skills?

Smile, hold out your hand, and approach someone standing alone and introduce yourself. Everyone standing alone wants to talk to someone. Ask them questions about their work. And in this field, if you don't know what to say, ask where they've traveled lately, or what international project they're working on. Those are my go-to questions.

Even if you don't get a job from that person, you might need that person later to meet with your visitors, to help you on a project, or to introduce you to the right person within their organization. In this regard, networking is key.

Do you have a mentor? How has he or she affected your life and career?

When I was working for the city of Chicago for seven years, there was a woman who took me under her wing; gave me more responsibility than I thought I could handle; pushed me to take on larger roles. She was someone I could always connect with. I would sit down with her once a week and review challenging issues. Watching how she approached tasks and how she analyzed the challenges was enormously helpful. She served on the board of the International Visitors Center of Chicago (the former name of WorldChicago) and suggested that I submit my application for the executive director position. I owe this job to her.

Are you involved in community service?

I'm joining the board of the National Council for International Visitors (*see chapter 9*). I've served on a lot of school committees and boards and organized fundraisers. We actually made a lot of changes to our preschool fundraiser because of what I learned from my work. You can take your skills from work and really make a difference at other organizations. I'm also starting to do volunteer activities with my son, so that he has hands-on volunteer experience. He is very engaged with the international visitors I bring home as well.

What lessons have you learned as your career has evolved?

Working for nonprofits requires a certain amount of patience. We can be nimble and flexible because we're a small organization and not trying to turn a big ship. But some decisions—when you're getting a consensus from the whole board of directors, for example—can take months. You need patience to let that roll out.

Don't burn your bridges because you're going to have to work with that person again.

Good writing skills are essential in every job, regardless of what you do. You need to sound professional in your e-mails, in your letters, even in your tweets.

Get as much diverse experience as you can. Go outside your comfort zone and take on a new project because it's going to build new skills.

I've found that many of the benefits of my work are not financial but rather come from the interaction with people, from being out in the community, from people recognizing our organization and wanting to be a part of it. Also, interacting with people from around the world and sharing cultures—revealing first how we are different, but then, in so many ways very much the same—is really gratifying. Those are very satisfying things that give me compensation in a nonmonetary way. That's the best part of my job.

CHAPTER 10

US Government

The Executive Branch

Even in the age of economic strictures and significant budget cuts, the executive branch of the US government offers many exciting career paths with competitive salaries and impressive benefits packages. Some US government departments and agencies are almost totally devoted to international affairs, whether responsible for the conduct of US foreign policy (US Department of State), US foreign assistance (US Agency for International Development, or USAID), or military policy and national security (US Department of Defense). From the Census Bureau to the National Oceanic and Atmospheric Administration, almost all other government agencies have jobs with an international focus. One young friend was recently hired as a protocol officer for the Secretary of Homeland Security. Another serves in the Foreign Agricultural Service (FAS) at the US Department of Agriculture. Yet another is employed by the US Department of Education International Resource Information System (IRIS). These positions, and many more, are all a part of the mix in the executive branch.

The Legislative Branch

The legislative branch of the US government offers a wide array of job possibilities at entities ranging from the Congressional Budget Office to the Library of Congress. One friend has had an exceptionally rewarding career as an analyst at the Congressional Research Service.

Capitol Hill also offers opportunities for meaningful government work that is international in scope. The oft-repeated maxim that all politics is local should probably be lengthened to "all politics is both local *and* global." The distinctions are increasingly blurred. Members of Congress are compelled regularly to deal with international issues. They are expected to be knowledgeable about a large number of complex trouble spots overseas. Thus, representatives and senators need globally experienced people on their staffs to handle their international affairs portfolios. Furthermore, Capitol Hill also offers opportunities to work directly for internationally focused groups such as the Senate Committee on Foreign Relations and the House Committee on Foreign Affairs.

For example, we have a mutual friend with a passion for both international affairs and the politics of Capitol Hill. She was able to combine these interests first as a staff member for the Senate Committee on Foreign Relations, then as a legislative aide for Representative Jim Moran (D-VA), and subsequently as a staff member on the Senate Appropriations Subcommittee for State and Foreign Operations. Later, she worked as a legislative aide for Senator James Webb (D-VA), when he served on the Senate Committee on Foreign Relations. Each of these positions has allowed her to consistently have an impact on international affairs without ever having to work off of the Hill.

Tom Garofalo, profiled earlier, is another example. Tom spent much of his career in international development, working as a field representative for Catholic Relief Services in such places as Jerusalem, Belgrade, and Havana. Eventually, he wanted to take his passion for social development via governmental participation to a new level and saw working directly in the US legislative process as his next step. He now works for Representative Moran as a legislative aide, helping the congressman on international issues as varied as gender violence in Syria to Chinese and Tibetan immigration issues in the 8th district of Virginia.

As these cases demonstrate, the US government remains a source of excellent globally oriented job opportunities. Although the application process can be daunting, salaries are still competitive, and benefits are excellent. For those captivated by international relations and who are comfortable working in a more structured environment, pursuing a career in the federal government can be worth the elaborate application procedures and security clearances that are an inherent part of the hiring process.

We would be remiss if we did not highlight the fact that there are increasing numbers of internationally oriented government jobs at the state and local levels. This trend will inevitably accelerate. Whether helping a governor attract foreign investment or working for the mayor of a large city organizing visits for foreign delegations, there are rewarding careers to be had. One of our colleagues served as chief of staff for Senator Patrick Leahy and then became secretary of agriculture for the State of Vermont. In both positions he has worked on many issues with international ramifications.

Another colleague serves as chief of staff for Senator John McCain in his Phoenix District Office. He, too, handles a wide range of international issues. One of Sherry's friends is a state senator from Iowa. He is a committed internationalist and works hard to expand Iowa's exports, welcome international students, and foster other vital connections to the rest of the world. He has taken what some would consider a domestic role and turned it into an opportunity to serve as an effective ambassador for his state and country.

Sample Government Departments and Agencies

Peace Corps

Paul D. Coverdell Peace Corps Headquarters

1111 20th Street, NW

Washington, DC 20526

Telephone: 855-855-1961

Website: www.peacecorps.gov

Twitter: @PeaceCorps

The Peace Corps was established by Executive Order by President John F. Kennedy in 1961 and authorized by Congress with the passage of the Peace Corps Act to promote world peace and friendship. The Peace Corps employs approximately 8,000 volunteers in developing countries in project areas such as agriculture, education, business development, health care (HIV/AIDS awareness), and information technology. Until recently, every assignment was a twenty-seven-month commitment, including accrued vacation. In 2010, however, short-term assignments became available. These Peace Corps Response assignments place individuals who either have ten years of work experience or have previously completed a full Peace Corp assignment on three- to twelve-month postings. The Peace Corps attempts to match country placement with volunteer requests, but placement in the country of choice is not guaranteed. Most assignments require a bachelor's degree and additional experience; knowledge of a foreign language is not required, and language training is provided. The minimum age for becoming a Peace Corps volunteer is eighteen—there is no maximum age. All expenses are paid during service, including complete medical and dental care and a variety of other benefits.

The Peace Corps offers a number of services for returned volunteers, including *Hotline,* a free, semimonthly, electronic bulletin of employment and educational opportunities. The organization also provides a variety of career resources, including job-hunting tips and techniques, a guide to graduate school programs that give special consideration to returned Peace Corps volunteers, and a list of job links highlighting government agencies that seem most appealing to and most interested in hiring returned Peace Corps volunteers.

See the profile of Karl Dedolph for more information. Karl served as a Peace Corp volunteer in Togo from 2001 to 2003.

US Agency for International Development (USAID)

Ronald Reagan Building and International Trade Center

1300 Pennsylvania Avenue, NW

Washington, DC 20523

Telephone: 202-712-4810

Website: www.usaid.gov

Twitter: @usaid

USAID is an independent federal government agency that advances US foreign policy objectives by supporting and implementing economic growth, agriculture and trade, global health, democracy, conflict prevention, and humanitarian assistance. The organization receives its overall foreign policy guidance from the US secretary of state. For young professionals, USAID offers a Junior Officer program that gives entry-level candidates the opportunity to become tenured employees. The USAID website careers page lists position vacancies in several different areas, including the civil and foreign services, and describes opportunities in USAID's various fellowship and internship programs.

US Department of Agriculture (USDA)
Foreign Agricultural Service (FAS)

1400 Independence Avenue, SW

Washington, DC 20250

Telephone: 202-401-0089

Website: www.fas.usda.gov

Twitter: @USDAForeignAg

The Foreign Agricultural Service of the US Department of Agriculture works to improve foreign market access for US products, build new markets, improve the competitive position of US agriculture in the global marketplace, and provide food aid and technical assistance to foreign countries. FAS has the primary responsibility for USDA's international activities—market development, trade agreements and negotiations, and the collection and analysis of related statistics and market information. With approximately ninety-eight offices in 162 countries, the organization describes itself as a relatively small agency by US government standards. The FAS website provides various career services, including international development-related position openings in FAS, in the USDA as a whole, and in various international organizations concerned with agricultural trade.

US Department of Defense
International Military Exchange Training (IMET)

Defense Security Cooperation Agency

2800 Defense Pentagon

Washington, DC 20301

Telephone: 703-601-1646

Website: www.dsca.osd.mil/home/international_military_education_training.htm

The International Military Exchange Training Program began shortly after World War II with the goals of developing defense cooperation between participating nations and the United States and spreading American core values, such as civilian authority over the military. Every year, the program accepts approximately 7,000 students from more than 130 countries to study at American military education institutions. In these exchanges, students are exposed to both technical training and civilian education.

National Defense University (NDU)

300 5th Avenue, Building 62

Fort McNair

Washington, DC 20319

Telephone: 202-685-4700

Website: www.ndu.edu

Twitter: @NDU_EDU

The National Defense University works to educate the military and civilian leaders of tomorrow. NDU is comprised of four colleges: the National War College, with a focus on international security strategy; the Industrial College of the Armed Forces, emphasizing the management of resources; the Joint Forces Staff College, providing education on joint, multinational, or international initiatives; and the Information Resources Management College, with a focus on the information aspect of power.

National Security Education Program (NSEP)

PO Box 20010

Arlington, VA 22209

Telephone: 703-696-1991

This federal initiative, established in 1991, provides undergraduate and graduate students with the opportunity to gain critical area and language education, most notably through the Boren Undergraduate and Graduate Scholarships and the National Language Service Corps (NLSC). Students who participate in these programs must work in public service for one year within three years of the completion of their education. This program has supported more than 2,000 NSEP award recipients who have served the US government.

US Department of Education

International Affairs Office (IAO)

400 Maryland Avenue, SW, Room 6W108

Washington, DC 20202

Telephone: 202-401-0430

Website: www.ed.gov/international

The International Affairs Office, located in the Office of the Secretary of Education, coordinates all international activities and acts as liaison to international organizations, ministries of education abroad, and the diplomatic community in the United States. The IAO focuses its efforts on three areas: "(1) improving education systems through international benchmarking and comparative research; (2) conducting education diplomacy; and (3) promoting foreign language and cultural studies." The IAO website offers information on partnerships with interagency, bilateral, and multilateral corporations, as well as a schedule of events.

US Department of Labor

Bureau of International Labor Affairs (ILAB)

200 Constitution Avenue, NW, Room C-4325

Washington, DC 20210

Telephone: 202-693-4770

Website: www.dol.gov/ilab

Twitter: @USDOL

ILAB is responsible for all internationally focused activities conducted by the US Department of Labor. It is a center for federal research and policy regarding global issues in trade, immigration, economic interdependence, human trafficking, and child labor. The mission of ILAB is "to create a more stable, secure, and prosperous international economic system in which all workers can achieve greater economic security, share in the benefits of increased international trade, and have safer and healthier workplaces where the basic rights of workers and children are respected and protected." The Bureau's international efforts are accomplished through liaisons, short-term travel, and grants to foreign organizations. The ILAB website contains links to employment information and opportunities throughout the Department of Labor, including the Office of Child Labor, Forced Labor, and Human

Trafficking (OCFT); the Office of International Relations (OIR); and the Office of Trade and Labor Affairs (OTLA), all of which are subdivisions of ILAB.

US Department of State

Bureau of Educational and Cultural Affairs (ECA)

2201 C Street, NW

Washington, DC 20521

Telephone: 202-632-2805 (Academic inquiries) and 202-632-2805 (Private sector)

Website: http://exchanges.state.gov

Twitter: @ConnectStateGov

The Bureau of Educational and Cultural Affairs works to foster mutual understanding between the people of the United States and the people of other countries. It sponsors such exchange programs as the flagship International Visitor Leadership Program (IVLP) and the Fulbright Program, newer programs such as Sports Diplomacy and the National Security Language Initiative, and other exchange programs for students of various ages, as well as scholars, diplomats, and other professionals. Career opportunities in ECA can be accessed on the Department of State's main career page, http://careers.state.gov.

The US Department of State also sponsors a number of internships, fellowships, and other programs. These opportunities provide highly qualified college or university juniors, seniors, and graduate students with the chance to gain firsthand knowledge of US foreign affairs. Available programs include the Fascell Fellowship Program, Presidential Management Fellows (PMF) Program (*see the profiles of Sarah and Amit Mathur and Karl Dedolph for more information—all three were PMF fellows*), Stay-in-School, Student Internships, and the Summer Clerical Program.

Office of Language Services

2401 E Street, NW

Washington, DC 20241

Telephone: 202-261-8811

Website: http://languageservices.state.gov

This division of the Department of State maintains a roster of approximately 1,000 interpreters and English Language Officers, assigning them to accompany visiting international and American leaders on a freelance contractor basis for periods of up to a month. The office also provides interpreting services to many other government entities.

Foreign Service

2201 C Street, NW

Washington, DC 20521

Website: www.careers.state.gov

Twitter: @doscareers

Foreign Service Officers help formulate and implement the foreign policy of the United States by serving as the frontline personnel at all US embassies, consulates, and diplomatic missions—in 294 locations worldwide, including Washington, DC. Foreign Service Officers follow one of five career tracks: management, consular, political, economic, or public diplomacy. The Foreign Service also employs specialists in fields such as medicine, office and information management, and human resources.

To become a Foreign Service Officer, individuals must take the computerized Foreign Service Officer test, which includes questions on topics ranging from US government, society, and culture to world history and geography, to mathematics and English grammar. This exam is accessible several times per year in locations around the world. Those who receive a passing grade on the written test are asked to send in materials for the Qualifications Evaluation Panel. Success here will bring candidates to the final stage: the Foreign Service oral exam. Only after passing these tests is a candidate eligible to become a Foreign Service Officer. The number of yearly new appointments is based on position availability, funding, and the hiring needs of the Department of State.

See the profiles of Ambassador Kenton Keith and Sarah and Amit Mathur for more information. Ambassador Keith served in the Foreign Service for more than thirty years. Sarah and Amit have just begun their Foreign Service careers and are currently serving at the US Embassy in Seoul, South Korea.

Selected Resources

America's Other Army, Nicholas Kralev

CreateSpace Independent Publishing Platform, 254 pages, 2012 (www
.americasotherarmy.com)

America's Other Army takes an in-depth look at how the US Foreign Service is directly contributing to United States security and prosperity. Based on interviews with more than 600 diplomats, the author describes the daily lives and diverse—sometimes dangerous—assignments undertaken by US Foreign Service Officers. *Print.*

Avue Central

Website: www.avuecentral.com

Avue Central is a free federal employment service. It offers private and secure access to a listing of thousands of federal jobs worldwide. This website will help you understand the federal hiring process and navigate—or even circumvent—some of the frustrating rules and regulations that can delay review of your federal job application. Avue Central also allows users to search and apply for federal jobs directly through its site. *Web.*

Brad Traverse Jobs

Website: www.bradtraverse.com

Twitter: @DCPolicyJobs

Brad Traverse Jobs is a comprehensive resource for individuals interested in working in and around Capitol Hill. Individuals must register with the site for a small fee (waived for federal and military personnel). Once registered, individuals are given access to a job board with more than 3,000 postings. *Web.*

Career Diplomacy: Life and Work in the US Foreign Service, Second Edition, Harry W. Kopp and Charles A. Gillespie

Georgetown University Press, 320 pages, 2011 (www.careerdiplomacy
.com/cd)

Career Diplomacy, written by two distinguished Foreign Service Officers, offers advice to those interested in joining the US Foreign Service community. The authors describe what to expect at all levels of a foreign service career. This second edition of the book highlights some of the major initiatives that have occurred since the first edition in 2008, most notably the controversial move to create an "expeditionary Foreign Service" to work in fragile states. *Print and ebook.*

Careers in Government

Website: www.careersingovernment.com

Careers in Government (formerly Jobs in Government) was launched so job seekers interested in public sector careers can identify opportunities more readily. Careers in Government features a searchable job bank of federal openings, a list of participating government agencies, and the ability to search for open government jobs by city and state. *Web.*

Congressional Quarterly (CQ)

Website: www.cq.com

Congressional Quarterly is a nonpartisan publication that has reported on Congress and politics since 1945. In addition to its flagship publication, *Congressional Quarterly* also produces *CQ Weekly* newsmagazine (print); *CQ Today*, a legislative news daily; and a number of specialty e-newsletters, such as *CQ Homeland Security* and the *CQ BudgetTracker*. These publications, along with a regularly updated list of Capitol Hill job openings, can be accessed on the *Congressional Quarterly* website. *Web.*

DipNote Blog

Website: http://blogs.state.gov

DipNote is the official blog of the US Department of State (DOS) with the purpose of offering public access to information on the many aspects of the DOS. It includes a section on the "foreign policy issue of the day," as well as regional topics from around the world. It also includes the ability to inquire and comment on various topics. *Web.*

Federal Resume Guidebook: Strategies for Writing a Winning Federal Electronic Resume, KSAs, and Essays, Kathryn Troutman

JIST Works, 448 pages, 2011 (www.resume-place.com)

The process to apply for and successfully obtain a federal job can be mind-boggling. The *Federal Resume Guidebook* leads you through the complicated federal hiring process and gives practical tips on how to write the optimal resume for federal positions, as well as how best to describe your KSAs (knowledge, skills, and abilities). The author of this resource is the head of a company that specializes in demystifying the federal hiring employment process. *Print.*

Fed World

Website: www.fedworld.gov

Fed World is managed by the National Technical Information Service, an agency of the US Department of Commerce. It serves as clearinghouse of information disseminated by the US government, including a searchable database of federal job openings. The website also enables users to conduct searches that span the websites of all federal departments and agencies. *Web.*

GovLoop

Website: www.govloop.com

Founded in 2008, GovLoop has the simple mission of connecting government to improve government. Acting as a social networking site for more than 60,000 individuals within the public sector, GovLoop offers blogs, a job board, an online directory, and both in-person and online training. Although membership is free, individuals must still apply and be accepted to be a member. *Web.*

The Hill

Website: www.thehill.com

The Hill is a nonpartisan newspaper written for and about the US Congress. It has the largest circulation of any Capitol Hill publication. In addition to its free website, it publishes sixteen blogs including *The Hill's Congress Blog* (http://thehill.com/blogs/congress-blog) and *The Hill's Pundits Blog* (http://thehill.com/blogs/pundits-blog). Its classified section contains a listing of employment opportunities on Capitol Hill and in government relations, as well as housing and lifestyle opportunities. *Print and Web.*

Hill Rag

Website: www.capitalcommunitynews.com

The *Hill Rag* is a community newspaper based on Capitol Hill that is accessible online for free. While it offers no job listings, the *Hill Rag* gives insight into the culture and community of Capitol Hill, which is an invaluable asset to anyone interested in pursuing a career there. *Web.*

Hill Zoo

Website: http://hillzoo.com

Hill Zoo is a web forum for congressional staff members and the wider Capitol Hill legislative community. The site features event listings in Washington, DC, various advertisements and classifieds (including housing in the DC area), and listings of position openings on and off the Hill. *Web.*

IAWG Dispatch

Website: www.iawg.gov

Published by the Interagency Working Group (IAWG) on US government-sponsored international exchanges and training, this quarterly electronic journal highlights topics, initiatives, and events related to the IAWG mandate: improving coordination and efficiency among federally sponsored international exchange and training programs. The dispatch provides insight into the lesser-known activities of the IAWG member agencies, which include the Department of Commerce, the Department of Defense, the Department of State, the Department of Justice, NASA, USAID, the National Endowment for the Arts, the National Security Council, the Peace Corps, the Census Bureau, and many others. These insights may suggest new and unexpected career opportunities to readers interested in entering or transitioning into the field of international exchange. Subscription is free and available via the IAWG website. *Web.*

Inside a US Embassy: How the Foreign Service Works for America, Shawn Dorman, Editor

American Foreign Service Association, 280 pages, 2011 (www.afsa.org)

Inside a US Embassy is designed to answer such questions as "Who works in an embassy?" and "What do diplomats actually do?" The book takes readers inside US embassies and consulates in more than fifty countries, providing detailed descriptions of foreign service jobs and firsthand accounts of diplomacy in action. The book also includes profiles of diplomats and specialists around the world who serve in foreign service positions, ranging from the ambassador to the security officer to the IT professional. The book contains a selection of "day-in-the-life" entries from seventeen different posts, each describing an actual day on the job in an embassy. *Print.*

Opportunities in Public Affairs

Website: www.opajobs.com

The Opportunities in Public Affairs website publishes a newsletter containing more than 200 job listings on Capitol Hill and in public affairs. Individuals can subscribe for a single issue or up to twenty-four issues (subscription rates vary). A limited number of position openings are posted on the website for free. *Web.*

Realities of Foreign Service Life: Volume 1, Patricia Linderman and Melissa Brayer-Hess

Writers Club Press, 292 pages, 2002

Coauthored by a member of a foreign service family (Brayer-Hess), this book provides reflections and perspectives on the realities of foreign service life as experienced by members of the foreign service community around the world. The writers share their views on a wide variety of topics pertinent to anyone leaving to live abroad, but especially to those who are leaving for extended periods and who plan to raise a family abroad. Challenges to foreign service officers and their families are discussed, including maintaining long-distance relationships, raising teens abroad, dealing with depression, coping with evacuations, readjusting to life in the United States, and many others. *Print.*

Realities of Foreign Service Life: Volume 2, Patricia Linderman, Melissa Brayer-Hess, and Marlene Monfiletto Nice

iUniverse, Inc, 286 pages, 2007

The second volume of *Realities of Foreign Service Life* examines the perspective of twenty-nine members of the US diplomatic community. This second book expands upon the issues discussed in the first volume, while offering new insight into the realities faced by the diplomats and their families. *Print.*

The Resume Place

Website: www.resume-place.com

Founded in 1971 by Kathryn Troutman, author of the *Federal Resume Guidebook* and *Ten Steps to a Federal Job*, the Resume Place specializes in writing and designing professional federal and private sector resumes, as well as in coaching and education in the federal hiring process. Troutman is a recognized expert on federal employment; she created the format and name for the "federal resume" that became standard in 1995. She also created the Certified Federal Job Search Trainer program—the first federal career train-the-trainer program ever—to train career counselors and military career counselors in the federal hiring process. *Web.*

Roll Call

Website: www.rollcall.com

Roll Call reports on congressional news and information and is published Monday through Thursday while Congress is in session (Mondays only during congressional recesses). *Roll Call* provides readers with up-to-date news on the legislative and political happenings on Capitol Hill. RollCall.com is the online version of the newspaper, providing not only the full content of the print edition but also breaking news stories and daily e-mail alerts. Access to the resources on Roll-Call.com is a free service for print subscribers and is also available on a subscription basis. A free job board is available to nonsubscribers at RCJobs.com. *Print and Web.*

Ten Steps to a Federal Job, Kathryn Troutman

The Resume Place, Inc., 172 pages, 2011 (www.resume-place.com)

Anyone who has ever applied for a job in the federal government may have a familiar story: hours spent poring over job openings on websites, many more hours spent perfecting an application for the perfect federal job, and then . . . nothing. No acknowledgment, call, or e-mail, and certainly no job interview. So how can anybody get past that seemingly impenetrable wall of the federal hiring process and obtain a federal job? *Ten Steps to a Federal Job* walks you through the process, giving an insider's perspective on the best strategies for obtaining a US government job, including how to tailor your resume for a federal application. *Print.*

Tom Manatos Jobs

Website: www.tommanatosjobs.com

Founded in 2002, Tom Manatos Jobs is another resource for those who are looking for employment on Capitol Hill. A $5 monthly subscription is required for individuals to access the job board and receive updates on new listings. Tom Manatos Jobs also offers internship and fellowship opportunities. *Web.*

USA Jobs

Website: www.usajobs.gov

USA Jobs is the official employment site of the US federal government. Users can create and store resumes on the site and can also search for open positions in any federal government agency. The site offers federal job seeker services and information, answering such commonly asked questions as how federal jobs are filled, how to build an effective resume, how to interview successfully for a government job, and how to best express your KSAs (knowledge, skills, and abilities). *Web.*

— PROFILE —

Ambassador Kenton Keith

Embassy Inspector, US Department of State, 2010–present

Career Trajectory

Meridian International Center, Senior Vice President, Washington, DC, 1997–2010

US Information Agency (USIA), US Department of State
Director, Near East, North Africa, and South Asia, Washington, DC, 1995–97
US Ambassador to Qatar, Doha, Qatar, 1992–95
Public Affairs Officer, Cairo, Egypt, 1988–92
Senior Cultural Affairs Officer, Paris, France, 1985–88
Deputy Director, Near East, North Africa, and South Asia, Washington, DC, 1983–85
Deputy Public Affairs Officer, Brasilia, Brazil, 1980–83
Special Assistant to Deputy Director, Washington, DC, 1977–80
Public Affairs Officer, Damascus, Syria, 1974–77
Branch Public Affairs Officer, Fez, Morocco, 1973–74
Western Arabic Training, Tangier, Morocco, 1972–73
Branch Cultural Affairs Officer, Istanbul, Turkey, 1968–72
Assistant Public Affairs Officer, Jeddah, Saudi Arabia, 1967–68
Junior Officer Training, Baghdad, Iraq, 1966–67

US Navy, Officer, 1961–65

Academic Background

George Washington University, Graduate Work (Comparative Politics), 1978–79

University of Kansas, BA (International Relations and French; Navy ROTC), 1961

How do you define your cause?

I am still inspired by engagement with people from different societies, especially in the cultural and academic realms. Something very interesting and important happens when people meet in those circumstances. I am particularly interested in helping healthy exchanges at all levels—high school, university, and professional—continue. It is critical in a globalizing world for Americans to know the rest of the world and for the rest of the world to know us.

But my cause didn't appear all of a sudden. I grew up in a Cold War environment, in Kansas City, Missouri. We actually had nuclear attack drills. I realized that our lives were somehow connected to what happened in other parts of the world. Even as a youngster, I knew I wanted to work abroad. I didn't know why, but I knew that. I had the feeling that becoming a foreign correspondent or a diplomat would be a fascinating way to lead my life.

When I went to university, I was advised by a treasured mentor, a man named Cliff Ketzel, my political science professor. He shaped my understanding of this country's relations with the outside world and the possibility of my personal involvement. He's the one who urged me to take the Foreign Service exam.

I went into the Foreign Service after the navy. It wasn't until I got to Turkey that I realized cultural and educational exchanges are extremely powerful tools. They create a mutual understanding among participants. Something magical happened when people engaged at that person-to-person level—something almost totally separate from government-to-government relations. That realization has been an engine for my career and what I have tried to accomplish in government and after.

What drew you to this cause and your field?

Very simple things. I remember once at my church being introduced to an international visitor from Indonesia. I was in junior high school when that took place. Mind you, I went to an inner-city school in Kansas City. We didn't have that many international visitors. But that interaction with this intelligent man who came and tried to get to know us, I thought, was a pretty interesting thing.

I began to think about foreign countries. There was a neighbor who had been in the war and showed pictures of Southeast Asia. That piqued my interest as well.

Then television came. Television brought with it these black and white images of foreign intrigue, and I was fascinated with the fast cars and beautiful women, with living overseas. In high school I began to study French. A teacher who had spent some time in France described a different lifestyle and different attitude. All of that went into the mix.

My parents certainly did not discourage me and my two siblings from pursuing any career we wished. They had a lot of confidence that we would do just fine. They knew that whatever our career paths, we wouldn't be in Kansas City.

What are the major day-to-day activities of your current position?

The US embassy inspections I'm doing now generally last six to seven weeks in the field and require work a couple of weeks beforehand and a couple of weeks afterward. A total of three months or so. It turns out that I'm regarded as good at it. My job as team leader is to evaluate the performance of the ambassador and the deputy chief of mission and to judge the quality of the embassy's interagency relationships. I also make sure that all of the basic elements of mission operations are thoroughly and fairly evaluated. I am not a consular officer, but I need to be satisfied that my consular inspectors are doing a good job.

What awards and honors have meant the most to you?

The first award that meant a lot to me was a Presidential Award I received for work in Egypt trying to get public and private sector cooperation in USIA programming.[1] It meant a lot to me because it was at a time when the US government was spending less and less on cultural programming, and I thought it was more and more important. I was in Egypt with an extraordinary ambassador, Frank Wisner. His leadership created an environment in which the private sector—both American and Egyptian—understood that the embassy wanted and needed their cooperation at a critical juncture in our bilateral relationship. In October 1988, the Egyptian government was opening a new opera house that the Japanese government built for them. We saw this as a moment when American presence would be important as a gesture in support of the Egyptian economic reform policies. We wanted to help American companies in Egypt be viewed by the Egyptian population as good corporate citizens, not as exploiters.

So we raised a million and a half dollars to bring a Houston-based opera troupe to perform *Porgy and Bess* as an opening presentation at the Cairo Opera House. This was one of several projects that created momentum for the kind of public-private partnership that had real payoffs for both the private and public sectors. This was seen as a model, and, on that basis, I received that Presidential Award.

Another honor that gave me a lot of satisfaction and a sense of pride was receiving a *Chevalier* in the French Order of Arts and Letters for my work with the Fulbright Program. When I arrived in Paris as the senior cultural affairs officer, I became cochair of the Fulbright Commission in France. The other cochair was a senior member of the French Ministry of Education, a man who eventually became a senior ambassador. The Fulbright Program had been eclipsed, at that point, by the French government's own academic exchange programs, and they only paid lip service to their participation in the Fulbright Program. Not many resources were devoted to it. My goal was to try to breathe some life into it, which I was able to do with help from many people. We accomplished this by going to French companies and convincing them that it was in their interest to sponsor academic exchanges, that it would eventually benefit the participants, the individual companies, and their country.

Thus the Fulbright Program in France suddenly took on a different complexion. The French got on board very quickly. . . . I worked closely with Jacques Chirac and his team at the mayor's office. He was mayor of Paris at that time [*Chirac held this post from 1977 to 1995*]. I had very close relationships with the minister of culture, the minister of education, and the university system in Paris. In fact, it was the chancellor of the universities of Paris who actually pinned on my *Chevalier*.

Paris was a great canvas for me. It was open, I had resources, and I had a receptive host government. I was in a place with intellectual openness . . . there were a lot of special circumstances that have rarely coincided. I did my best to take advantage of them.

Are you involved in community service?

Board Member, AFS Intercultural Programs

Board Member, Council on International Educational Exchange (CIEE)

Board Member, Partners for Democratic Change

Advisory Board Member, University of Kansas Office of International Programs

Vice President, Washington Institute of Foreign Affairs

Member, American Academy of Diplomacy

President, Association of Black American Ambassadors

I've always believed that African Americans have a perspective that is important in our international relations. It is also vital that we have a voice to share our views with the government; thus my involvement with the Association of Black American Ambassadors. We believe it's important for us to take our collective views and feed them back to the government and to American citizens at large who are interested.

What is your best advice for developing effective networking skills?

I think that the implication of the word "networking" is that you are *part of a network*. In the Foreign Service, you've got to have a wide circle of contacts. That's a different thing from networking for your personal growth. And I would make the distinction there because I've prided myself, in all of my posts, on knowing the people I needed to know.

Networking is a vital aspect of the work that we do, not just because it has to do with connecting with the people who are "influence multipliers," the people you really need to know. I think the most important thing for me, when looking back on my career in the Foreign Service, was knowing the right people. Identifying the important players in the field, identifying the influence builders, and finding the appropriate ways to get to know them. When I was in Egypt and Syria, for example, I made it my business to work with people who were *not* particularly easy to get to know, and who were not drawn to Americans. You have to avoid just taking the easy route. The temptation is to get to know people who are comfortable to be around. That may not be—and, in fact, very often is not—the network you need.

In a Foreign Service career, career planning is as important as networking. You must clarify your goals, recognize the gaps in your experience, and bid on jobs that will bridge those gaps. All of my jobs in the Middle East, in the early part of my career, were small posts. What I lacked in order to reach the next level was management experience at a large post. The opportunity arose for me to go to Brazil as deputy political affairs officer, a major management role supervising branch posts and program coordination. It was a career move that was absolutely critical for me. From there I went on to larger posts and responsibilities.

Do you have a mentor? How has he or she affected your life and career?

Cliff Ketzel, my professor at the University of Kansas . . . he was an iconoclast. Ketzel had been a part of the State Department Reserve. Remember, we're talking about the Cold War, and we all thought it was highly possible that a bomb could wipe out Washington, DC. During an emergency, the country's internal affairs might have to be conducted somewhere other than Washington. There needed to be a group of wise experts who would meet and make decisions. He was in that group.

My time in university was a period when not much was happening. The campus was anything but activist. So for Ketzel to be an iconoclast in that period was quite impressive. But he was somebody who was much loved. He was a good professor, a good lecturer, and he had an effective approach to teaching students.

One day after class, he asked me what I intended to do. I said, "Well, I have my military obligation, but I've always been interested in working abroad." So he said, "I think you ought to take the Foreign Service exam. You ought to take the USIA option." At that point, it all sort of snapped into place in my mind.

Do you consider yourself a mentor to others?

I can honestly say there are people who would consider me a mentor. Half of those who are managing US public diplomacy operations round the world are people I consider my protégés.

If you believe in something very strongly, if you think you have an important mission and you know that you are able to influence others to support that same mission, then it's your duty to mentor. I was in a particularly privileged position to be a mentor because I could recruit, assign, and reward. I see the public diplomacy officers at the State Department and I am very happy that some of my favorite protégés are doing well.

What lessons have you learned as your career has evolved?

A critical lesson I have learned is that all of our exchange programs depend on an asset that we have here: the American citizen. If we weren't sure that the "product" we have to "sell" is a good product, then our exchange programs would sink under their own weight. But in fact, the interaction with the average American is such a positive thing for foreign exchange participants. When you meet them, Americans come across as open, hospitable, and hardworking. People in the United States are remarkably nonjudgmental. International visitors are often bemused that Americans can be working next to someone for over ten years and not know whether that person is a Republican or a Democrat or a Christian or a Jew and frankly *not care.*

It is, on the one hand, very positive that Americans are unprogrammed. On the other hand, foreigners find it strange that Americans don't know anything about the rest of the world. If they knew more, maybe they would be more programmed. But it's not part of our DNA. That's not to say that there isn't prejudice or ethnic difficulty or racism—those things exist. But, as a nation, we are generally tolerant. That's a pretty important thing. It's a great strength.

A lesson I learned in the navy that has served me well is that if at the end of the day you have not achieved what you committed to achieving, that's what will be remembered. No matter how justified you may be in not living up to your responsibilities—you know, even if you fell under a combine (*laughs*)—the fact will remain that it didn't get done. If it becomes a pattern, that will influence your career. I have seen talented people who were not achievers. Something always seemed to come up. There was always some "reason." But at the end of the day, they had failed. I tell people that if you're supposed to get something done by Friday afternoon, don't think that it's okay to work over the weekend and get it in Monday morning. That's not good enough.

Any final advice?

For people interested in foreign affairs, twenty years ago, I would have said you need to explore the Foreign Service, Peace Corps, or USAID. But now, I think that NGOs may have more personally rewarding work to offer, in particular for people who have a passion in one specific area. If your passion is environmental protection, you can have an international career in that. If your passion is educational exchange, if your passion is sports . . . it is possible now, with the proliferation of NGOs, interest groups with deep connections and multiple activities, to have a job in nongovernmental work that is every bit as rewarding as being in the Foreign Service.

Note

1. In 1999, the US Information Agency (USIA), formerly an independent government agency that employed many Foreign Service officers, was absorbed by the US Department of State.

— PROFILE —

Sarah Loss Mathur

Political Officer, US Embassy, Seoul, South Korea, 2012–present

Amit Mathur

Vice Consul, US Embassy, Seoul, South Korea, 2012–present

Career Trajectories

Sarah:

US Embassy, Foreign Service Officer, Riyadh, Kingdom of Saudi Arabia, 2010–12

US Department of Commerce, International Trade Administration, Attorney Advisor, Washington, DC, 2006–9

US Department of State, Bureau of International Narcotics and Law Enforcement, Presidential Management Fellow, Washington, DC, 2005–6

Amit:

US Embassy, Foreign Service Officer, Riyadh, Kingdom of Saudi Arabia, 2010–12

US Department of State, Bureau of East Asian and Pacific Affairs, Office of Economic Policy, Foreign Affairs Officer, Washington, DC, 2006–9

US Department of Justice, Justice Management Division, Presidential Management Fellow, Washington, DC, 2005–6

Deloitte Consulting, IT Consultant, Chicago, IL, 2000–2003

Academic Backgrounds

Sarah:

Boston University School of Law, JD, 2005

University of Wisconsin-Madison, BA (International Relations, Political
Science, Spanish) 2001

Amit:

American University School of International Service, MA
(International Affairs, International Politics), 2005

University of Illinois at Urbana-Champaign, BS (Computer
Engineering), 2000

How do you define your cause?

Amit: I think my cause is very straightforward: to promote and defend
the interests and values of the United States overseas. Like so many
others of my generation, the terrorist attacks of September 11, 2001,
and the Iraq War were formative experiences for me. I felt an urgent
need to be a part of something bigger than myself, to give back in
some way. This meant returning to grad school and switching careers
without really knowing what direction I was going. Taking a leap of
faith, trying different jobs, and experiencing different types of internships led me toward the Foreign Service. It wasn't any sort of immediate shift that led me to the Foreign Service.

Sarah: My cause is to represent the United States overseas, to share
what we as Americans are all about, and to do what I can to make this
world a little better—not just for Americans, but for the rest of the
world as well. We work for a country whose actions have a huge influence on the rest of the globe, and with that comes a lot of responsibility. There's a lot of work to be done, and I want to be able to reach out,
communicate, and try to find common ground.

What drew you to this cause and your field?

Sarah: For me, it began in high school. I became interested in learning more about not just global issues but also the United States' role in the world. I realized the importance of explaining our purpose to other countries, explaining our democratic values, our focus on human rights, and our ideals—even though sometimes we, ourselves, don't live up to them.

I wanted to be able to explain my country to other people. I wanted to meet with people from other countries, find commonalities, and work together on global problems. Eventually it made sense that the Foreign Service was one place where I could work officially for the United States government to do these things.

Amit: Before grad school, I was a management IT consultant in the financial service sector. I realized I wasn't happy doing that type of work. It was a great job, a wonderful experience, and I don't regret it. But it wasn't personally fulfilling, and I was looking for something more.

I thought I wanted to do international law, and then maybe international development. I had an internship at a small development firm that does public-private partnerships and then I joined another company, trying to marry my computer engineering and IT background with international development. But I realized I wasn't a good fit for international development. There are people who are very passionate and do fantastic work in the field, but it wasn't a good fit for me.

After realizing this, I joined the PMF program (*Presidential Management Fellows program—see chapter 10*), which allowed me to try different roles in the government. That's how I got into the State Department, through a rotation in the PMF program. It wasn't until about a year doing multilateral work in the State Department in APEC (*Asia-Pacific Economic Cooperation*) that I said, "I really like this work; maybe I should think about becoming a Foreign Service Officer."

How would you describe your field?

Amit: I'd say the Foreign Service encompasses many different fields, from nuclear nonproliferation to bilateral trade. We can also have an impact in the areas of cultural exchange, education, and development. For example, the State Department operates formal exchange programs that date back to the Kennedy administration and even earlier. Part of my job right now is to conduct visa interviews with South Koreans who are interested in experiencing life in the United States as exchange students.

One of the objectives of each regional bureau in the State Department is to promote educational linkages and economic development in their specific regions and countries. The United States recently signed a free trade agreement with South Korea, which is contributing to shared growth and prosperity. It's helping South Korea continue to develop economically, while at the same time helping Americans back home by opening new markets and enabling American businesses to export their products and services to South Korea.

Sarah: I would describe the field as dynamic. Much depends on what's happening in the news that day or within the bilateral political or economic relationship. We very often are expected to become the experts on a certain subject without much advanced notice. That said, it's exciting to be in on the action and to see US foreign policy being formed and to have some role, however small, in making that happen.

Amit: What can we really do? Where do we add value? We have a convening power among US government agencies and among other countries, and we have a facilitation role to play. The Foreign Service doesn't always have the resources to implement everything, but we do have the power to bring all the right people together, to bring stakeholders together to focus limited resources and energies on a particular problem. And that can be in education, health, economic reform, political reform, the environment—any of those areas. We rely very much on our partners in those fields to help accomplish these goals, to help advance US interests and values overseas.

How would you describe your career paths?

Sarah: An international affairs career for me wasn't completely out of the blue. Prior to college, I knew I wanted to do something in this field. Once I made that decision, even if I didn't know what the end point might be, I made sure to take advantage of as many internships and related courses as possible. For me, internships were important. For example, I worked at my state capitol and for a US senator. I think it was important to be involved in domestic politics. When I graduated with my degrees in international relations and political science . . . well, that doesn't immediately translate into a job, unless you're very lucky (*laughs*). So I had my first State Department internship after college, which opened many more doors than I initially thought it would.

Then I went to law school because I wasn't quite ready to choose a career after college. I wanted to look more into the international legal field. I again worked for the State Department, but this time as a law clerk. I participated in the same fellowship program that Amit mentioned, the PMF (*see chapter 10*), and afterward I worked as an international trade attorney at the US Department of Commerce.

It's important to note that every single one of these internships and positions stemmed from the one before it. Now that I think about it, there was nothing completely random about the path I took. Most of my experiences grew from previous opportunities and learning from the people that I met. Each opportunity helped me find the next step along the way. It's important to dream big and to look forward to what you want to do, but realize you can't get there overnight. Take the opportunities as they're presented to you, and they'll always result in something positive.

What are the major day-to-day activities of your current positions?

Amit: It's important to understand that Foreign Service Officer generalists are expected to be able to perform any type of job at an embassy or in the main Department of State offices in DC. Even though you declare one of the five tracks—political, economic, management, public diplomacy, or consular—you're expected to be able to do any of those jobs. This is one of the things that attracted us to the profession: at any point over the course of our careers, we may be doing a different type of job. Both of us are in the political cone, though right now Sarah is in a political job and I'm doing a consular job.

Sarah: Our next tour, we'll both be doing something different. In my current position, I work in the political section of the embassy, which is divided into three subunits: one covers South Korean foreign policy, another covers South Korean domestic issues, and another focuses on the political/military relationship between the United States and South Korea. My role, in particular, is to meet regularly with South Korean government officials, NGO leaders, academics, and others to learn more about issues on the Korean peninsula and in the region that are of importance to both the United States and South Korea. I also explain US policies and priorities to Korean audiences and work with the government here not only to promote US interests, but also to find shared interests that may serve as areas for cooperation. The reason we and our colleagues are here in Seoul, as opposed to covering the same issues in Washington, is to provide the value added by meeting with people, by having extended conversations and gaining a greater insight into the culture, the politics, and the buzz here on the ground.

Amit: Currently, I'm a vice consul, one of several who are required by law to interview any foreigner who wishes to visit the United States. I'm in the nonimmigrant visa section, where we mainly adjudicate tourist, exchange visitor, and student visas. South Korea is a Visa Waiver Program country, which means that people who want to visit the United States for business or tourism for periods of less than three months don't require a visa. But students and exchange visitors still do. My job is to determine whether applicants meet all the legal requirements for a visa. For example, have they overcome the presumption of immigrant intent?

In the high season, I interview more than one hundred people every day. Within the space of two or three minutes, I need to determine whether that person is qualified under US law to visit the United States. I'm not only facilitating travel to the United States, I'm also doing my best to prevent those who would do harm to the United States from ever reaching our shores.

If you're a Foreign Service Officer, generally you're expected to do at least one consular tour. And consular officers are often the first Americans—the first government officials, for sure—that many applicants meet. They probably come in with preconceived notions, or Hollywood ideas, of what America is and what Americans are like. It's important that the conversation be professional and courteous because, in the applicant's mind, we are the face of the United States.

What is your best advice for developing effective networking skills?

Sarah: The best way to network is to always be open to the people you meet. You never know who is going to have something in common with you, who is going to provide insights on job opportunities or career ideas. I've encountered people who obviously had their networking hats on. It's a little bit jarring. They'll recite their resumes in the first fifteen minutes of a conversation (*laughs*). I think that may be a novice approach.

It's a two-way street. Rather than only trying to get leads from people, make sure that you're also providing assistance or advice when you can. You need to be willing to engage. Always be ready to learn, listen, and take opportunities that you hadn't previously anticipated.

Amit: I actually think that if you're looking for a job, you should be prepared with your two-minute elevator speech if you meet someone . . .

Sarah: And I disagree, but anyway . . . (*laughs*).

Amit: (*Laughs*) Well, if you're looking for a job, and you're actively networking to find a job, you need to be able to explain to someone you meet, in two minutes, who you are and what value you can add to their organization. That doesn't mean reciting your resume; that just means giving them something to help them remember you. All that first meeting does is give you an entry into a broader conversation.

My approach to networking, having joined the Foreign Service, is always to stay in touch with people. To be sincere, approachable, and open. To be in touch with people, even if you don't need anything from them. It's not about calling someone up when you need something, it's about staying in touch with your network. Ask about people's hobbies; remember a certain tidbit about that person that humanizes the relationship. It's not a transactional relationship.

Sarah: Yes, it's a long-term relationship. If you come across as someone who is using the moment, and then you drop off and don't bother to foster the relationship further on, you'll be missing out on a lot of professional opportunities.

Amit: And that person is not going to want to help you.

Sarah: Exactly. It's a small world. People know people. You want to make sure you present yourself in the best possible way at all times. As Amit said, keep your communication open, keep the connections active. That doesn't mean you have to e-mail them every week— maybe just once a year. Especially with tools like LinkedIn, you can just drop a message and say "Hey, how are you doing? Where are you working now?" Just stay out there, stay visible.

Do you have mentors? How have they affected your lives and careers?

Sarah: If you maintain an active network, then ideally you should be able to call on any number of those people for advice as your career evolves. As far as an official mentor, no, I don't have one. But, even yesterday, Amit and I had lunch with another Foreign Service tandem couple who are twenty years further along in their careers. We said, "We'll take you out to lunch if you tell us how you've done it. How did you manage to stay married while in this career, raise two kids, and have all these great jobs around the world?" Find someone who has a career you'd love to emulate and ask them for advice and insights. I think most people are willing to share their experiences.

Amit: Everyone has something different to offer. I've never had a formal mentor either, but I've been lucky to have good bosses. I call on them when I'm looking for advice, and I stay in touch with them and keep tabs on their careers.

Sarah: It's valuable to have diverse viewpoints. A mentor with a capital "M" is great, but they are presenting what worked for them, their specific ideas and experiences. In order to have a successful career, you need to draw upon multiple sources and perspectives to figure out what works for you. There's no one-size-fits-all.

Do you consider yourselves mentors to others?

Amit: I'd like to think so. One of the best pieces of advice I got when I started grad school was: "You're going to network as much as you can, get as much advice as you can, but don't forget to give back. That is your responsibility as you progress up the career ladder." I take that responsibility pretty seriously. When people ask me for advice, I help out as much as possible.

Sarah: Within the Foreign Service there are so many paths, so there is a healthy, mutual exchange of mentoring. We haven't been Foreign Service Officers for very long, but we've already been in a situation where we've been able to convey our experiences to others looking for advice. Even though we've only been in Seoul for six months, we bid for our next post next summer. There's no settling down. You never end up getting too comfortable or taking things for granted in your position because you're always moving on to something else. So guidance throughout your career is necessary.

Amit: The Foreign Service is like a journeyman profession; you have to learn the trade from others and through experience.

What lessons have you learned as your careers have evolved?

Amit: There is no such thing as a perfect career plan. Life tends to get in the way. It's important to have goals that lead you in the right direction toward the career or lifestyle that interests you. It's important to be flexible and open to opportunities. As Sarah said, you never know where a particular path will take you.

Sarah: I agree completely. If you have set in stone what you think your career will be and this is the only way to get there, you may be setting yourself up for disappointment.

Amit: It's also important to define your own success. For some people it may mean having a good work–life balance and making sure you can spend quality time with your family. It may mean getting to the top of a profession or helping that one community in Africa get clean water or build a school. Don't discount any of that, it's all valuable.

How have you maintained a healthy balance between your work and personal lives?

Sarah: It's a work in progress (*laughs*). The important thing is to set priorities. You need to look inside yourself and at your family and see what works for you. There'll always be compromises that have to be made, especially with children. But that's a choice you have to make beforehand and then proceed accordingly.

Amit: It's very challenging. We decided at the outset that we had three rules for ourselves. First, we wanted to make sure that we're serving together. The second is to never compete with one another at work.

Sarah: (*Laughs*).

Amit: And the third—not in any order—is always to put family first. Family will drive our career decisions. That's what we'd like to achieve, and there may be times where one may take precedence over the other.

Work–life balance depends a lot on the type of job you're doing and on your boss. If both of those align well, then it's up to you to have personal discipline, to remember what you have decided is important.

Sarah: Right now we're in a situation where our work–life balance is relatively good. Many colleagues have families, and everyone understands this, even when the office gets a little chaotic. That said, when we take on the next assignments it may be different.

Amit: It's also important to cultivate interests outside of work. Being in the Foreign Service defines us in that it's very much a commitment to a lifestyle.

Sarah: Yes, all our neighbors are our coworkers. Especially in this career, there is much less division between personal and work life, given that we are twenty-four-hour representatives of the US government.

Amit: You're always on.

CHAPTER 11

Multinational Organizations

Introduction

Employment in a multinational organization can be the highest aspiration for many international career seekers. Pursuing employment with these organizations can be intimidating, however, given their size and scope as well as the aura of mystery and intrigue that sometimes surrounds them. These concerns are not completely unfounded; it can be much more difficult to get your foot in the door at a large multinational organization than, say, a smaller nongovernmental organization (NGO). Some multinationals have downsized their staffs or streamlined their structures in response to reduced funding; many have strict hierarchical organizational structures. Most have language and experience requirements that may seem daunting to the entry-level professional. Some have strict nationality quotas. Despite these potential obstacles, however, multinational organizations still offer exciting opportunities for qualified individuals who seek a challenging international career with truly global scope and impact.

The Cultural Context of Multinational Organizations

Fayezul Choudhury, who served as controller and vice president of strategy and resource management at the World Bank, emphasized in his profile interview the importance of "cultural context" when attempting to get a job or begin a career with a multinational organization. Of course, job seekers can still use the same strategies with a multinational that they might with any other organization: submit a resume and hope it gets noticed (although Choudhury warned that this approach may be a bit of a crapshoot because hundreds of resumes pour in each day); find an internship and work your way up; or use a personal connection. These techniques can work with multinational organizations, but Choudhury pointed out that you must approach them in different ways than you might with an organization staffed mostly by Americans.

Networks in multinational organizations often depend on ethnic and national affiliations, rather than collegiate or professional ones. Knowing people is important, just as in an American context, but it is also important to use your relationship with a person in a more subtle way. Although some Americans have no problem receiving a straight-forward request from a job seeker, people of other cultures may not be accustomed to or comfortable with such direct interactions. Because no single rule can guide your actions when it comes to networking at multinational organizations, always ask yourself what cultural variables might be at play.

Each organization has its own culture. Your most accurate interpretation of that culture rests on a combination of the views of respected colleagues and your own observations. A good question to ask yourself during any interview process is, "Can I be productive and comfortable in this culture?"

A Crowded Bazaar, Not a One-Stop Shop

Multinational organizations tend to list job openings and information on their own websites. There are few print and electronic clearinghouses that centralize resources and vacancies in this field. However, many universities with international programs have career resource sections on their websites that contain links and advice for employment in international organizations. Also, conducting a search on a general job-listing website using the terms "multinational organization" or "international organization" should provide focused results.

Sample Multinational Organizations

Inter-American Development Bank (IDB)

1300 New York Avenue, NW

Washington, DC 20577

Telephone: 202-623-1000

Website: www.iadb.org

Twitter: @IDBnews

The IDB was established in 1959 to promote the economic and social development of Latin America and the Caribbean. The IDB, with forty-eight member countries, including twenty-two non–Western Hemisphere members, is a major source of external public financing for member countries in Latin America. It has field offices in twenty-nine countries. Most applicants for professional positions at the IDB have graduate degrees in such fields as economics, engineering, agriculture, administration, or environmental sciences and have at least eight years of relevant work experience. In addition, most positions require fluency in at least two of the four official languages of the bank (English, Spanish, French, and Portuguese). The IDB website provides details for available employment, including junior professional and internship opportunities. Approximately 200 positions with the IDB are filled each year.

International Monetary Fund (IMF)

700 19th Street, NW

Washington, DC 20431

Telephone: 202-623-7000

Website: www.imf.org

Twitter: @IMFNews

The IMF, established in 1945, is an intergovernmental organization that maintains funds for use by member countries, promotes world trade, and aids its 188 member states with balance-of-payments problems. Most of the organization's staff members are in Washington, DC, although the IMF also maintains small offices in Paris and Geneva. The IMF has a professional staff of about 800—two-thirds are economists. The remainder of the professional staff includes accountants, administrators, computer systems officers, language specialists, and lawyers. Details about specific positions with the IMF—including those for experienced economists, support-level positions, and the Research Assistant Program—are available on its website.

Organization of American States (OAS)

200 17th Street, NW

Washington, DC 20006

Telephone: 202-458-3000

Website: www.oas.org

Twitter: @OAS_official

Founded in 1948, the OAS works to resolve hemispheric problems including preservation of regional security and the settlement of political disputes. It endeavors to strengthen economic, social, educational, scientific, and cultural relations among its thirty-five member states. The United States, Canada, and all independent Latin American and Caribbean countries are members. The OAS is headquartered in Washington, DC, maintains offices in thirty-one member states, and has approximately 700 employees. The OAS concentrates on strengthening democracy, human rights, security, and development. Most positions require fluency in English and Spanish; working knowledge of French or Portuguese is desired. Job and consultancy vacancies are posted on the OAS website along with information regarding its internship program.

Union of International Associations (UIA)

Rue Washingtonstraat 40, B-1050

Brussels, Ixelles/Elsene

Belgium

Telephone: +32-02-640-1808

Website: www.uia.org

Twitter: @UIA_org

The UIA was founded in 1907 as the Central Office of International Associations to enhance collaboration among organizations and to serve as a documentation center. It was instrumental in establishing the League of Nations. Its mandate focuses on improving research, awareness, and communication regarding "transnational associative networks," which includes both intergovernmental and international nongovernmental organizations. Its yearbook, now in its 48th edition, catalogues and profiles more than 66,000 organizations. This, along with much more information compiled and organized by the UIA, is available via the organization's website. The organization conducts annual meetings of its general assembly and maintains a small full-time staff.

United Nations Development Programme (UNDP)

1 United Nations Plaza

New York, NY 10017

Telephone: 212-906-5000

Website: www.undp.org

Twitter: @UNDP

The UNDP, funded by voluntary contributions from member nations and nonmember recipient nations, administers and coordinates technical assistance programs in 177 countries. The UNDP seeks to increase economic and social development as mandated by the United Nations. The 7,000-member UNDP staff performs a wide variety of duties related to the design, monitoring, and administration of development projects. Typical requirements include a strong postgraduate academic background with an emphasis on international development, several years of relevant experience in a developing country, fluency in at least two of the six official UN languages, strong commitment to the ideals of the United Nations, and other relevant interpersonal and work skills. Job vacancies within the UNDP, categorized by project area and worldwide location, are posted online at jobs.undp.org. Information on the UNDP's Leadership Development Program, Junior Professional Officers Program, and Internship Program is also available.

United Nations Educational, Scientific, and Cultural Organization (UNESCO)

7, place de Fontenoy

75352 Paris 07 SP

France

1, rue Miollis

75732 Paris Cedex 15

France

Telephone: +33-0-1-45-68-10-00

Website: www.unesco.org

Twitter: @UNESCO

UNESCO is a specialized agency within the United Nations that monitors international developments and assists member states in resolving critical issues. The organization's mandate is to build peace among its 195 member countries and in the world by fostering knowledge, social progress, exchange, and mutual understanding among peoples. UNESCO focuses on education; science and technology; social and human sciences; communication; information and informatics; and culture. The UNESCO headquarters coordinates the organization's 2,000-person staff; the New York liaison office has a staff of twelve to fifteen. Vacant posts within UNESCO, as well as information regarding internships and young professional and associate expert positions, are posted on its website.

United Nations Information Center (UNIC)

1775 K Street, NW, Suite 400

Washington, DC 20006

Telephone: 202-331-8670

Website: www.unicwash.org

Twitter: @unicdc

Founded in 1946, the UNIC mission is to raise awareness of the United Nations and to strengthen internal and external partnerships by enhancing public understanding of the United Nations' substantive impact. The United Nations is comprised of sixteen specialized agencies throughout the world, including the UN Development Program (UNDP), the World Health Organization (WHO), and the UN Educational, Scientific, and Cultural Organization (UNESCO). The UNIC website contains multiple resources for job seekers interested in employment at the United Nations, including links to main UN job vacancies pages and information about UN fellowships and internships.

World Bank

1818 H Street, NW

Washington, DC 20433

Telephone: 202-473-1000

Website: www.worldbank.org

Twitter: @WorldBank

The World Bank was established in 1945 as an international development institution with a mandate to reduce global poverty and improve living standards around the world. Funded by membership subscriptions and by borrowing on private capital markets, the World Bank finances foreign economic development projects in developing countries in areas such as agriculture, environmental protection, education, public utilities, telecommunications, water supply, sanitation, and public health. It is made up of two unique development institutions owned by the Bank's 188 member countries—the International Bank for Reconstruction and Development (IBRD) and the International Development Association (IDA). In its one hundred–plus country offices and its Washington, DC, headquarters, the World Bank employs a staff of approximately 10,000 development professionals. The World Bank's website includes a listing of all job and consultancy vacancies, as well as details on its entry-level programs (Young Professionals Program, Junior Young Professionals Program, and Internship Program).

The World Bank also offers summer employment to a small number of highly qualified graduate students (who have completed one year of graduate studies or have already entered a PhD program) studying economics, finance, human resource development, social sciences, environment, agriculture, private sector development, statistics, and related fields. To qualify for these salaried positions, students must be nationals of a World Bank member country and must plan to attend graduate school in the following fall semester.

See the profile of Fayezul Choudhury for more information. Fayezul is the former controller and vice president of strategy and resource management at the World Bank.

World Health Organization (WHO)

Avenue Appia 20

CH – 1211 Geneva 27

Switzerland

Telephone: +41-22-791-2111

Website: www.who.int

Twitter: @WHO

The WHO is the directing and coordinating authority for health in the United Nations system. It works to extend health services to underserved populations of its member countries and to control or eradicate communicable diseases. The WHO also promotes cooperation among governments to forestall epidemics and solve public health problems. Headquartered in Geneva, Switzerland, with six regional offices (including one in Washington, DC) and 150 country offices, the WHO has a staff of more than 7,000 professionals. The WHO website offers a listing of international job vacancies, internship information, and various resources to aid those interested in applying to work for the organization.

Selected Resources

International Civil Service Commission

Website: http://icsc.un.org/secretariat/includes/joblinks.asp

Although not a resource for listing position vacancies, this website contains links to many multinational organization recruitment and human resource pages that help applicants understand the wide range of positions available. The UN application form and instructions are also available on the site. *Web.*

International Organizations Employment Guide
US Department of State

Website: http://intlorganizationjobs.state.gov/iva/default.aspx

This website from the US Department of State delivers valuable information on employment opportunities and the requirements needed for professional and senior positions in the United Nations and other international organizations. It is best used for gathering information on the types of jobs available and topics such as expected salaries and recruitment procedures. Some information on short-term and long-term positions with the United Nations can also be found. *Web.*

Northwestern University Library

Website: www.library.northwestern.edu/govinfo/resource/internat/igo.html

The Northwestern University Library website houses an extensive and updated list of international government organizations. Links are not limited to the United Nations or UN affiliates, but draw from a large variety of fields (economics, education, peace and security, banks, conservation and agriculture, human rights, women and children, and health). *Web.*

UN Careers

Website: https://careers.un.org

UN Careers is the official job board of the United Nations. Job seekers can search hundreds of openings by category, job network, department, or even duty station. While most jobs require advanced degrees, there are internship and temporary job opportunities. *Web.*

UN Galaxy e-Staffing System

Website: https://jobs.un.org

Galaxy is the UN's official recruitment website. It contains a searchable database as well as a list of available vacancies in various occupational groups. In addition, Galaxy contains a link to the UN Peace Operations recruitment website and an extensive list of field and office job openings. *Web.*

UN Jobs

Website: http://unjobs.org

UN Jobs, an association based in Geneva that is not officially affiliated with the UN, lists numerous positions in approximately one hundred organizations around the world. You can search for jobs by new listings, organizations, duty stations (locations), and upcoming deadlines. Many of the job openings in this privately compiled listing require advanced degrees and several years of experience. Some jobs for recent graduates or those with limited professional experience are available on this site. *Web.*

Worldwide Government Directory with International Organizations

CQ Staff Directories, 1,984 pages, 2012 (www.cqpress.com)

This sizable publication provides contact information (phone, fax, and email) for the leadership of more than one hundred international organizations, as well as 32,000 elected and appointed officials in 201 countries. Anyone interested in working or communicating with multinational organizations and foreign governments will find the publication useful. The directory is available in hard copy or as an on-line resource by subscription. *Print and Web.*

Yearbook of International Organizations

K. G. Saur, 1,740 pages, 2012 (www.uia.org/organizations/pub.php)

Produced under its current title since 1950 (and now in its 48th edition), this six-volume publication of the Union of International Associations is a comprehensive directory containing profiles of more than 66,000 intergovernmental and international nongovernmental organizations. These listings, indexed both alphabetically and topically, include the organization's name and acronym in all working languages, complete contact information, executive leadership information, membership, mandate, history, structure, finances, activities, and publications. The listings also contain an array of statistical data concerning participation, activity levels, issue focus, and budgets. *Print and Web.*

— PROFILE —

Fayezul Choudhury

CEO, International Federation of Accountants
(IFAC), New York, NY, 2013–present

Career Trajectory

The World Bank, Washington, DC
    Vice President, Corporate Finance and Risk Management, 2009–13
    Controller and Vice President, Strategy and Resource
    Management, 2006–9
    Vice President and Controller, 2000–2006
    Director of Accounting, 1995–2000
    Chief, Asset and Budget Accounting, 1993–95
    Chief, Loan Accounting, 1990–93
    Chief Accountant, International Finance Corporation, 1987–90
    Staff Member, Organization Planning Department, 1985–87

Price Waterhouse
    Managing Consultant, London, UK, 1984–85
    Managing Consultant, Lagos, Nigeria, 1981–84
    Managing Consultant, London, UK, 1978–81
    Public Accounting, Audit Assistant to Manager, London, UK,
    1974–78

Academic Background

University of Oxford, MA, Honors (Engineering and Economics), 1974

How do you define your cause?

It's very easy to subscribe to the mission of the World Bank: to help
the world's poorest. I think the important questions are, "Is that what
brought you here?" or "Is that what motivates you here?" Or is it just
comfortable to say that you work at an organization whose mission is

to alleviate poverty, rather than saying you work at a place whose mission is to launch bombs?

I'd love to be able to say that I have a passion to help the world's poor and that's the only reason why I worked at the World Bank. Yet it would be dishonest to say that's the case. The reality is, your career starts with yourself. Do you enjoy your work? Do you enjoy your environment? Do you enjoy the people you work with? Often, though not always, the answer to those questions is a function of "Are you effective in your job?"

A lot of being happy in the workplace starts with how well you do what you do. That's not the only criterion, but I think it's a necessary starting point. The purpose of the organization you work for, for some people, is what motivates them or drives them. For other people, it doesn't drive them or motivate them to the same extent, but it does give them a safe anchor. If you take the World Bank as an example, I would say many of its employees are concerned, even have moral outrage, about the extent of poverty in the world. But for the rest, it's just a job. That doesn't mean they're bad people or aren't concerned about poverty . . . but it's just human nature. It's just a job and they enjoy the work. But if they found another job somewhere else that was better . . .

For people who feel very passionately about something, they can forge a career in that area. But I think the majority of people just need to be comfortable with the mission of the organization—and certainly shouldn't be *uncomfortable* with it. You need to balance your passion with self-interest.

The question is, "Where do you derive your satisfaction?" You need to ask yourself that question very, very honestly and searchingly. I think most people derive their satisfaction from being good at what they do and feeling they are valued. A lesser number of people derive their satisfaction from the mission of the organization, from being a participant in the mission. In the end, I hope there's a *very* small number of people who just don't give a damn and will do anything for money (*laughs*).

Self-awareness is so important in so many aspects of life. It pervades. If I look at contented people, they are typically self-aware. Once you are aware of what motivates you and why, once you know what your capacities are and where your strengths lie, I think then you circle into career opportunities that will be the right fit for you.

What drew you to this cause and your field?

I stumbled into accounting and finance. I didn't particularly have a great interest in this profession before I joined it, but with experience I have come to enjoy it. As for working in the field of development . . . in a nutshell, it is very satisfying to feel that you are contributing—no matter how indirectly—to improving people's lives.

How would you describe you career path?

My college degree was back in the early 1970s when students really didn't think too much about careers. They were too focused on changing the world! I think from the 1980s onward, students became much more focused on careers.

I knew I didn't want to be an engineer, but I didn't really know what I wanted to do. My initial career choice is thus a story of random events. In the summer of 1974, just after college, there was an outpouring of stress relief, mainly involving lots of beer. One evening, a bunch of us were at the pub—it was a lovely summer's evening by the river—and most of my friends were talking about the things they were going to do. It suddenly occurred to me that "Holy moly, I've got to get a job! I'm on a student visa, and I have no idea what I'm going to do with myself."

What is your best advice for developing effective networking skills?

Networking is much more of an American concept. Of course people know people and that's just fine, but a more elaborate and systematic kind of networking happens in the United States. Not long ago, my son was at university and looking for summer internships. They encouraged him to go to the alumni website and see who was working where to identify openings. You would probably not get that advice in other parts of the world. If someone contacted you and said they went to the same college as you, it would probably not open too many doors. It's a very different cultural context for networking.

I think networking is . . . let me put it this way . . . maybe . . . (*long pause*) . . . I guess networking can be helpful, but it depends on the organization. For getting that foot in the door, maybe it's helpful. For most organizations, getting a foot in the door is the most difficult part. What happens at the World Bank is much more ethnic or national networks than anything. Since I'm a Bangladeshi, I'll get a lot of Bangladeshis writing to me with interest in the Bank, and if they are qualified, I will ask our HR people to see if there are any openings . . . (*pause*).

Maybe I'm just arguing against myself here! The only reason I'm being interviewed for this book is because of a network, which shows the power of it all. I think I've probably gone 180 degrees (*laughs*). Networking *does* work, I guess. It should just be a little more subtle than the way it's often characterized.

Networking is knowing people. It's knowing people and being respectful of how much you ask of them. If you meet someone at a cocktail party and ask for something unreasonable, that's probably not a great idea. But if you know someone reasonably well, then you can maybe take the liberty to ask for a little more time or attention.

This whole notion of networking has to be grounded in your own cultural context. Every culture has its own version of it. Often if you're living and working in the United States, what's pushed is the American version of it, and that's something that people from many cultures are saying, "I just can't do that. That's not me." They probably have their own version. If you lined up 10 different cultural types and said, "Here's the assignment. You're trying to get a job at the UN. How would you go about it?" you'll get ten different answers. They would all be forms of networking, but they'd take on different cultural shades.

Do you have a mentor? How has he or she affected your life and career?

Mentoring now is a much more structured thing, but the more structured it gets, I find it works less well. What I've always found is that when you work with someone more senior than you and they have confidence in you, then you become the go-to person. It's mutual interest. I certainly found this as I moved up the chain. Now, when I look at junior colleagues, it's the same thing. You want go-to people, people you know can deliver. I call that implicit mentoring. More formal mentoring works less well.

Mentoring becomes effective when you get a chance to see someone close up. And that's when you can give much more targeted advice. Real mentoring has to go hand-in-hand with career development. I don't think you can really separate the two.

I have been very fortunate in having a number of people whom I have worked for who have given me opportunities to grow, who have counseled and coached me, and who have been my advocates. I guess you would call that mentoring.

What lessons have you learned as your career has evolved?

Nothing irks me more than the person who seeks credit. It's smart to pass the credit to your boss and subordinates. Anticipating problems and solving problems are talents in short supply; those who have trouble-shooting skills get noticed. As you take on more senior roles, influencing skills and persuading skills become more important.

Any final advice?

You spend more hours in the workplace than anywhere else. Make sure you enjoy it!

CHAPTER 12

Business, Foundations, Think Tanks, and Consulting

Introduction

Leading up to this final chapter, we have attempted to provide the broadest possible cross section of the jobs and careers available in international education, exchange, and development. We certainly, however, have not covered *all* the possibilities.

International business, consulting, and research are rapidly growing employment sectors with many intriguing opportunities for globally oriented job seekers. You may find that one of these types of careers in international affairs is best suited to your skills and your cause, perhaps as a cross-cultural trainer for a corporation; as a consultant for a USAID for-profit contractor; as a grants officer for a foundation that funds international projects; or as a researcher for a think tank.

All of these positions fall within the realm of international education, exchange, and development. As the private sector continues to expand, as more businesses of varying sizes take their operations international, and as a greater number of consultants with internationally specific skills are needed, the number and kinds of jobs that can be characterized as international will grow. We present this final chapter as an attempt to broaden your view and highlight a few of the possibilities that lie beyond what we have presented in the previous eleven chapters.

There are a multitude of international employment opportunities in the business sector, particularly as more and more multinational corporations become involved in training and development activities that were previously confined to the nonprofit world. As the boundaries between government, business, and the social (nonprofit) sector blur, there is an urgent need for those who are skilled in forging creative partnerships among these sectors.

In all aspects of international affairs, there is greater use of contractors and consultants than ever before. To retain their downsized, lean and mean structure, organizations and government agencies often outsource tasks that in the past were handled by their own employees. For example, a former staff member of Sherry's founded the International Stability Operations Association (ISOA) in 2001. ISOA member companies are contracted by the US Department of Defense, the US Department of State, and other entities to do everything from supplying meals to US troops abroad to providing security at our embassies. Opportunities to join consulting firms—large and small—for work on internationally oriented projects increase by the day. One benefit to consulting is that you can often work on various topics in a variety of settings and not necessarily be relegated to just one office or a single long-term project.

In recent years, think tanks (the term commonly used to describe public policy research institutes) either have started including international projects in their repertoires or have become completely internationally focused. For example, the Brookings Institution, as a general policy research organization, may simultaneously focus on the future of preschool education in the United States and on perceptions of US foreign policy in East Asia. International projects are a large part of what Brookings does, but it also studies many domestic issues. The Henry L. Stimson Center, however, is focused exclusively on international peace and security.

Not all of these think tanks are on the east or west coast. The Stanley Foundation, headquartered in Muscatine, Iowa, sponsors significant international research studies and symposia. If a more academic, analytical, and research-oriented approach to the fields of international education, exchange, and development sounds appealing to you, consider looking into the ever-expanding (both in size and influence) realm of think tanks.

Similar to think tanks, foundations are not necessarily international and may focus on any number of topics. From social and religious issues to regional educational concerns, a foundation may fund any number of domestically oriented projects, depending on the interests and concerns of the family or group that manages it. However, just as the number of nonprofit organizations, businesses, and consulting firms focused on international issues is increasing, so too is the number of foundations interested in funding internationally focused projects. The Foundation Center maintains a large directory of these organizations that may provide employment opportunities or support research and program initiatives that you wish to pursue.

Sample Business Organizations

Business Council for International Understanding (BCIU)

1212 Avenue of the Americas, 10th Floor

New York, NY 10036

Telephone: 212-490-0460

Website: www.bciu.org

BCIU, although a nonprofit, is composed of internationally oriented companies. BCIU works to expand international business and commerce by promoting dialogue and cooperation between the business and government communities, devoting special attention to commercial diplomacy. BCIU operates in New York; Washington, DC; Houston; London; and several other major cities.

The Conference Board

845 Third Avenue

New York, NY 10022

Telephone: 212-759-0900

Website: www.conference-board.org

Twitter: @Conferenceboard

Founded in 1916, The Conference Board is a global, independent business membership and research association. Its mission is to provide its members with the practical knowledge they need to improve their performance and better serve society. The Conference Board focuses on four major subject areas: corporate leadership; economies, markets and value creation; high-performing organizations; and human capital. There are offices in Brussels, Singapore, Hong Kong, Mumbai, and Beijing.

International Stability Operations Association (ISOA)

2025 M Street, NW, Suite 800

Washington, DC 20036

Telephone: 202-367-1153

Website: www.stability-operations.org

Twitter: @StabilityOps

ISOA, the trade association for the stability operations industry, works to maintain high ethical standards, advocate and enhance dialogue with policymakers, and inform the public of the role of the industry and its impact. ISOA has more than fifty member companies worldwide that adhere to ISOA's code of conduct and work to improve the implementation of stability operations.

National Foreign Trade Council (NFTC)

1625 K Street, NW, Suite 200

Washington, DC 20006

Telephone: 202-887-0278

60 East 42nd Street, Suite 920

New York, NY 10165

Telephone: 212-399-7128

Website: www.nftc.org

Twitter: @NFTC

The NFTC, founded in 1914, is an advocacy and public policy organization that supports an open world trading system and a rules-based world economy. NFTC and its affiliates serve more than 300 member companies.

Organization for International Investment (OFII)

1225 19th Street, NW, Suite 501

Washington, DC 20036

Telephone: 202-659-1903

Website: www.ofii.org

OFII is a professional business association that represents US subsidiaries of companies headquartered abroad through advocacy, lobbying, and networking services. OFII member companies range from medium-sized enterprises to some of the largest firms in the United States.

US Chamber of Commerce

1615 H Street, NW

Washington, DC 20062

Telephone: 202-659-6000

Website: www.uschamber.com

Twitter: @uschamber

The US Chamber of Commerce is a business advocacy association working for the rights of businesses and the maintenance of free enterprise. It represents more than 3 million businesses, as well as thousands of local chambers of commerce and more than one hundred American Chambers of Commerce in ninety-one countries.

US Council on International Business (USCIB)

1212 Avenue of the Americas

New York, NY 10036

Telephone: 212-354-4480

Website: www.uscib.org

Twitter: @USCIB

USCIB works to advance the international interests of American businesses while contributing to economic growth, human welfare, and the protection of the environment. USCIB is the American partner of the International Chamber of Commerce (ICC), the Business and Industry Advisory Committee (BIAC) of the Organisation for Economic Co-operation and Development (OECD), and the International Organization of Employers (IOE).

Selected Business Resources

Directory of American Firms Operating in Foreign Countries

Website: www.uniworldbp.com

Hosted online by Uniworld, *Directory of American Firms Operating in Foreign Countries* has information on more than 200,000 industries in 200 countries. Individuals are able to purchase a customized subscription that can include unlimited access to a certain country or company or the entire database. Nonsubscription options, including downloading and printing lists, are also available. *Web.*

Directory of Foreign Firms Operating in the United States

Hosted online by Uniworld, the *Directory of Foreign Firms Operating in the United States* offers the same subscription options as the preceding entry. *Web.*

Principal International Businesses: The World Marketing Directory

Dun & Bradstreet, 3,355 pages, 2012 (www.dnb.com)

The 2012–2013 edition of *Principal International Businesses* provides information on approximately 55,000 companies in 143 countries worldwide. Updated annually, the guide is organized alphabetically, geographically by country, and by type of business. *Print.*

The Riley Guide

Websites: www.rileyguide.com

The Riley Guide is a free employment and job resources website. The website focuses on International Business Resources and Business and Employer Research, containing links to business directories, industry profiles, and other resources you will find useful when examining the field of international business. *Web.*

Sample Consulting Organizations

Abt Associates, Inc.

See chapter 9 in this volume.

Accenture

New York City office

1345 Avenue of the Americas

New York, NY 10105

Telephone: 877-889-9009

Website: www.accenture.com

Twitter: @Accenture

Accenture is an international management consulting, technology services, and outsourcing company working in many industries. The firm has more than 259,000 employees in approximately 120 countries.

See the profile of Karl Dedolph for more information. Karl is a senior manager at Accenture.

Booz Allen Hamilton

Worldwide Headquarters

8283 Greensboro Drive

McLean, VA 22102

Telephone: 703-902-5000

Website: www.boozallen.com

Twitter: @BoozAllen

Booz Allen Hamilton is an international strategy and technology consulting firm working with corporations, governments, and other public agencies. The firm employs more than 25,000 people on six continents.

CARANA Corporation

4350 North Fairfax Drive, Suite 900

Arlington, VA 22203

Telephone: 703-243-1700

Website: www.carana.com

Twitter: @CARANAcorp

Founded in 1984, CARANA Corporation is an economic development and privatization consulting firm based in Arlington, Virginia. CARANA has worked in one hundred developing countries on more than 250 projects in the fields of agribusiness, social reform, and private and public enterprise.

Chemonics International

1717 H Street, NW

Washington, DC 20006

Telephone: 202-955-3300

Website: www.chemonics.com

Twitter: @Chemonics

Chemonics International, founded in 1975, is an employee-owned international consulting firm that promotes economic growth and higher living standards in developing countries. Chemonics has more than 2,000 employees working on development projects in more than 150 countries.

Creative Associates International

5301 Wisconsin Avenue, NW, Suite 700

Washington, DC 20015

Telephone: 202-966-5804

Website: www.creativeassociatesinternational.com

Twitter: @CreaAssocIntl

Founded in 1977 by four women of diverse educational backgrounds and a commitment to educational excellence, Creative Associates International is a minority company and the second-largest women-owned company that works with the US government. Its mission is to support people around the world to realize the positive change they seek. Creative Associates works to help people in nearly forty countries pursue social, educational, and political development.

DAI

7600 Wisconsin Avenue, Suite 200

Bethesda, MD 20814

Telephone: 301-771-7600

Website: www.dai.com

Twitter: @DAIGlobal

DAI was founded in 1970 as a consulting firm with a focus on social and economic development. Since its founding, DAI has worked in more than 160 countries to create more prosperous, fairer and more just, cleaner, safer, healthier, more stable, more efficient nations around the world.

Deloitte and Touche

New York City office (one of three)

Two World Financial Center

225 Liberty Street

New York, NY 10281

Telephone: 212-436-2000

Website: www.deloitte.com

Twitter: @deloitteus

Deloitte and Touche, as a part of the Swiss firm Deloitte Touche Tohmatsu, is a worldwide organization of member companies providing audit, tax, consulting, and financial advisory services. Deloitte has more than 170,000 employees in nearly 150 countries.

DevTech

1700 North Moore Street, Suite 1720

Arlington, VA 22209

Telephone: 703-312-6038

Website: www.devtechsys.com

Since 1984, DevTech Systems, Inc., has been consulting with nations to improve democracy, economic development, women's rights, and education. DevTech has worked on more than 170 projects on the national, regional, and global levels.

John Snow International (JSI)

44 Farnsworth Street

Boston, MA 02210

Telephone: 617-482-0485

Website: www.jsi.com

Twitter: @JSIhealth

JSI has been working for more than thirty years to improve the health of individuals and communities around the world. With a staff of 500 US-based professionals and 1,600 abroad, JSI has implemented projects in more than 106 countries.

Management Systems International (MSI)

600 Water Street, SW

Washington, DC 20024

Telephone: 202-484-7170

Website: www.msiworldwide.com

Twitter: @MSIWorldwide

Since 1981, MSI has worked to increase democracy and economic development through evaluation consulting. It has worked on more than seventy projects, both long- and short-term, in conflict-prone and fragile states. In 2008, MSI became a subsidiary of Coffey International Development.

Tetra Tech, Inc.

3475 East Foothill Boulevard

Pasadena, CA 91107

Telephone: 626-351-4664

Website: www.tetratech.com

Twitter: @tetratech

Founded in 1966, Tetra Tech has become a leading provider for engineering, program management, and construction management consulting. Today, Tetra Tech has more than 14,000 employees in more than 350 global offices.

Tetra Tech DPK

605 Market Street, Suite 800

San Francisco, CA 94105

Telephone: 415-495-7772

Website: www.tetratechdpk.com

As of October 2008, DPK Consulting became an operating division of Tetra Tech ARD—a wholly owned subsidiary of Tetra Tech, Inc. Tetra Tech DPK works to foster economic development and democratic institutions in nearly fifty countries.

Selected Consulting Resources

Consultants and Consulting Organizations Directory

Thomson Gale, 2012 (www.galegroup.com)

The 37th edition of this directory contains more than 26,000 firms and individuals listed in subject sections for fourteen general fields of consulting. *Print.*

Top-Consultant.com

Website: www.top-consultant.com

This website allows you to search a database of consulting firms by name, industry, sector, and location. A long list of consulting firm advertisements, while tedious to scroll through, provides an overview of some of the larger consulting firms and the work that is available with them. *Web.*

Sample Think Tanks and Foundations

The Brookings Institution

1775 Massachusetts Avenue, NW

Washington, DC 20036

Telephone: 202-797-6000

Website: www.brookings.edu

Twitter: @BrookingsInst

The Brookings Institution is a nonprofit research organization that provides recommendations on various public policy and international issues.

Carnegie Council for Ethics in International Affairs

Merrill House

170 East 64th Street

New York, NY 10065

Telephone: 212-838-4120

Website: www.cceia.org

Twitter: @carnegiecouncil

The Carnegie Council, as its name suggests, promotes ethics in international affairs, including ethical leadership on issues of war, peace, religion in politics, and global social justice.

Center for Strategic and International Studies (CSIS)

1800 K Street, NW

Washington, DC 20006

Telephone: 202-887-0200

Website: www.csis.org

Twitter: @CSIS

CSIS, a nonprofit research organization, provides insight on and policy recommendations for issues of global security and economic issues.

Council on Foreign Relations

See chapter 6 in this volume.

Foreign Policy Research Institute (FPRI)

1528 Walnut Street, Suite 610

Philadelphia, PA 19102

Telephone: 215-732-3774

Website: www.fpri.org

Twitter: @fprinews

FPRI conducts research on pressing international issues, long-term historical and cultural questions, and policies relevant to US national interests.

The Foundation Center

Headquarters

79 5th Avenue/16th Street

New York, NY 10003

Telephone: 212-620-4230

Website: www.foundationcenter.org

The Foundation Center maintains a large database of US foundations and grant makers and the grants they award. The center provides research, education, and training programs regarding many topics related to philanthropy. In addition to its New York headquarters, the center has field offices and research centers in Atlanta, Cleveland, San Francisco, and Washington, DC. Its three major publications are listed in the following section, "Selected Think Tank and Foundation Resources."

The Henry L. Stimson Center

1111 19th Street, NW, 12th Floor

Washington, DC 20036

Telephone: 202-223-5956

Website: www.stimson.org

Twitter: @StimsonCenter

The Stimson Center is a research institution devoted to strengthening international peace and security institutions, building regional security, and reducing the threat posed by weapons of mass destruction.

The Heritage Foundation

214 Massachusetts Avenue, NE

Washington, DC 20002

Telephone: 202-546-4400

Website: www.heritage.org

Twitter: @Heritage

Founded in 1973, The Heritage Foundation is a research and educational institution whose mission is to formulate and promote public policies based on the principles of free enterprise, limited government, individual freedom, traditional American values, and a strong national defense.

The Stanley Foundation

209 Iowa Avenue

Muscatine, IA 52761

Telephone: 563-264-1500

Website: www.stanleyfoundation.org

Twitter: @Stanleyfound

The Stanley Foundation is a nonpartisan nonprofit organization focused on researching issues of peace and security, as well as advocating principled multilateralism.

US Institute of Peace (USIP)

See chapter 9 in this volume.

Woodrow Wilson International Center for Scholars

Ronald Reagan Building and International Trade Center

One Woodrow Wilson Plaza

1300 Pennsylvania Avenue, NW

Washington, DC 20004

Telephone: 202-691-4000

Website: www.wilsoncenter.org

Twitter: @TheWilsonCenter

Established by Congress as a memorial to the former president, the Wilson Center is a nonpartisan research organization that works to provide sound policy analysis on public policy and international issues while bridging the gap between scholars and public officials.

Selected Think Tank and Foundation Resources

The Foundation Directory

The Foundation Center, 2,259 pages, 2013 (http://foundationcenter.org)

The first of this two-volume set gives current data on each foundation that holds assets of at least $2 million or distributes more than $100,000 in grants annually. It also provides information about recent, sizeable grants awarded by each foundation, offering insights into the priorities of particular foundations. The second volume features midsized foundations with programs that award grants ranging from $50,000 to $200,000 annually. Subscriptions to a searchable online database of this publication's information are available on the Foundation Center's website, http://foundationcenter.org. *Print and Web.*

Foundation Grants to Individuals

The Foundation Center, 1,600 pages, 2012 (http://foundationcenter.org)

This publication lists organizations that award grants to individuals in fields ranging from education and the arts to medicine. Listings include detailed information on contact names, eligibility requirements, and the specifics of the application process for certain grants. Subscription access to this list of more than 8,500 foundations and public charities is also available online at http://foundationcenter.org. *Print and Web.*

Guide to Funding for International and Foreign Programs

The Foundation Center, 916 pages, 2012 (http://foundationcenter.org)

Similar to *The Foundation Directory*, this publication is one in a series of smaller, subject-specific guides produced by the Foundation Center. These guides are updated annually with new contact and grant information. *Print.*

World Press

Website: www.worldpress.org

This world news website contains an extensive, alphabetically arranged list (complete with hyperlinks) of international think tanks and research organizations. *Web.*

— PROFILE —

Lobna "Luby" Ismail

Founder, President, and Senior Trainer, Connecting Cultures, LLC, Silver Spring, MD, 1990–present

Career Trajectory

American University, Washington, DC, 1988–90

Intercultural Program Specialist, 1988–90

Program Director, Fulbright Grant Program, 1988

Bunker Hill Community College, International Student Advisor, Boston, MA 1986–88

Academic Background

Lesley College, MA (Intercultural Relations; Intercultural Training and International Student Exchange), 1988

American University, BA (International Service; Minor Arabic and Cross-Cultural Communication), 1984

How do you define your cause?

Growing up as the only Muslim and Arab American in a small, southern, Christian community, I lived connecting across cultures and faiths. At age fifteen, I lived in Cairo, Egypt, with my grandparents and large extended family to learn about my Egyptian heritage. This intercultural experience transformed and shaped me and created my cause: connecting across cultures to build bridges of understanding and respect for one another and break the barriers of fear and bias.

Experiencing a culture outside of one's own during a person's formative years should be a requirement for life. This experience expands, broadens, and deeply influences people's perspectives of themselves and their engagement with the world. This experience also sheds the stereotypes and biases that lead to detrimental assumptions about others. It allows us to no longer label Muslim or American, Arab or Jew, but to see the full person and their humanity. I have trained young people participating in a range of intercultural exchange programs, particularly for the Arab and Muslim teenagers who come to the United States on the Kennedy-Lugar Youth Exchange and Study (YES) Program (sponsored by the US Department of State). When they first arrive, there is an enthusiasm about studying in America, yet apprehension about making friends with Americans. During their year here, however, the students are profoundly changed by their experiences.

What drew you to this cause and your field?

It starts with my roots. My parents came to the United States as international students to pursue their PhDs, settling in a small town, Lake Alfred, Florida, where they still reside today. My parents were invited to the Lions Club, schools, and churches to speak about their culture and faith. As the first-born child, I was their guide to American culture, introducing them to the PTA, pep rallies, football games, and prom.

For my friends, I had to explain my parents' cultural norms. They asked, "Why can't you eat the pepperoni on the pizza?" or "Why aren't you eating right now?' (during the month of Ramadan) or "Why won't your parents let you date?" As the wife of a man whose father was Jewish and mother was Christian, and who became a Muslim, I live with the complexities of identity. From childhood until today, I have strived to serve as a bridge builder between people and across cultures and faiths.

One challenge I face since 9/11 is America's uncertainty and fears regarding the "Muslim world" and "Islamophobia." I have trained hundreds of law enforcement officers, first responders, and community leaders at federal, state, and local agencies on the long history of Muslims in America and on the beliefs and practices of Muslims.

The other challenge I face is my diagnosis with multiple sclerosis, a neurological condition that damages the nerves and impacts my mobility. I renamed my disability "diverse-ability" as I've learned to live, work, and travel through various methods and technologies. I describe my "diverse-ability" as another dimension of diversity and culture. I want to be an example of how to work actively as an individual change agent. I want to examine how to respond to societal intercultural complexities to overcome prejudice.

How would you describe your field?

Intercultural communication, interfaith understanding, and dialogue—those definitely have been my passions. A new area that I'm really excited about, as I mentioned, is finding ways to reduce our unconscious bias against those with disabilities. My multiple sclerosis has become more prominent, so that's actually become, in a sense, a new culture. I am learning to live and deal with its complexities and nuances.

Where did you start, and how did it help you get to where you are today?

My work has also been about the pursuit of my two passions: mind-hood—which is intercultural understanding, intercultural confidence, and intercultural relations—and mom-hood. Finding the balance between mind-hood and mom-hood has been a challenge. I had my first son, Sharif, and I wanted to be home with him. I wanted to be able to be a mother and to be engaged in his life. Connecting Cultures was meant to be a two-year career pursuit to get my son out of diapers and into preschool. Sharif was followed by Zakaria, and my little Laila, and now Connecting Cultures is a twenty-two-year-old business. I love it.

When I started my business I met with my American University professor Gary Weaver. He encouraged me, saying, "Just get out there." I left that meeting with him feeling uncertain, thinking, "What does he mean 'just go out there'? Where do I begin?"

I made simple brochures, printed business cards, and went to schools and volunteered to speak about Egyptian culture. I appeared at Rotary Clubs, women's groups, business luncheons, etc. I volunteered for any opportunity to speak about culture.

Speaking at conferences was a great way to get exposure. Delegates came from all over the United States and around the world. This opened up many doors. Volunteering at organizations that are aligned with your cause or passion can lead you to great opportunities.

What are the major day-to-day activities of your current position?

When I started my business, seeking organizations to work with and networking were critical. Over the years, I learned that every opportunity I received was through people who had known me or from a referral by someone who knows my company and me. Not one dollar was earned by marketing. Today, most of my time is spent staying current on what is happening in the world, reading about cultural conversations and initiatives, and developing trainings that are informative, impactful, and engaging.

What is your best advice for developing networking skills?

To someone starting in the field: it is essential to talk to everyone and anyone. People often ask me how I expanded my business. As I said, I have no marketing strategy. I'm not pounding the pavement. It has all been word of mouth. At the beginning, working out of my home was a detriment. I would only be "out there" when I was conducting a training or speaking. Then I came back to my home office, and there was no networking or socializing. I then was selected for a protégé program with Women of Washington. It connected me to powerful businesswomen and leaders. It inspired me and enabled me to make new contacts.

Another valuable way to network is at conferences. If you don't have the finances to attend, volunteer! Submit proposals to speak at conferences. I could always shape a session to the theme of the conference. Those were great networking occasions. You get this one-hour window to entice them with what you have to say and who you are.

Do you have a mentor? How has he or she affected your life and career?

Professor Weaver has certainly been a mentor. He is the reason I really came to know about the field of cross-cultural training. Taking his class when I was just nineteen years old, learning this science of culture that I never knew, fascinated me. Gary encouraged me to join SIETAR (*see chapter 6*). Also, since Sherry Mueller was my professor at American University when I was an undergraduate, she has supported me through the years with advice, guidance, invitations to events, and much more.

I particularly appreciate female mentors, especially those who have their own businesses. I'm always inspired by women's stories. We always get "his-story" but we rarely get "her-story." There are so many talented women in a wide range of fields.

My biggest supporter, though, has been my husband, Alex Kronemer. He is my business partner, financial supporter, cofacilitator, and friend. My business wouldn't have begun or lasted without him. He believed in me and my vision, supported my decision to resign from my job, and shared the courage and confidence needed to take the risk. It is important to have someone you can trust and is willing to tell you, when needed, "You know what? I don't think this is the best idea."

Do you consider yourself a mentor to others?

I've always tried to let younger people know my experiences in the field: what's great about it, what's tough about it, and where you can get training and experience in intercultural communication, such as the Intercultural Communication Institute.

Particularly after 9/11, I think we need more Muslim Americans who are equipped to provide cross-cultural training. Through the US Department of Justice, we have not only delivered training to law enforcement personnel, but we have also conducted training of trainers. We identified Muslim Americans in the communities in which we were presenting and said, "Let's train you now so you will be able to deliver the same training." These are baby steps but so essential. So many young Muslim Americans don't know it can be a career. But I love it. What's the number one requirement? Passion. If you have the passion for it, then you will find a way to make it possible.

How have you maintained a healthy balance between your work and personal life?

I'm trying to "pause first." I strive to pray and meditate each day. I remind myself of the daily blessings I have in my life to remain grateful. One tip I use is the "OHIO rule"—Only Handle It Once—when reading e-mails or texts, or responding to calls.

Connecting Cultures allows me to be flexible and maintain a lifestyle that accommodates my family and health needs. Social media, texting, and e-mail allow me to "work" wherever I am and whenever I need to do so. Being virtual is important, but it cannot replace face-to-face interactions. I still must make the effort to "get out" and attend various social and business-related events.

What lessons have you learned as your career has evolved?

Passion, passion, passion for what you do is critical. Once you know what field matches your passion, do your best to stay in it.

I know it can be so hard to begin in a field, and it can be even harder to stay in. In the early years, I would look at international job vacancies because I was never quite sure of the status of my business. It was either feast or famine; it was either lots of work or no work. If it wasn't for my husband and his faith in me—and honestly having someone who had a secure income to carry us through—I don't know how things would have worked out.

But there came a time when I stopped looking at the Sunday classified ads. That was a big moment. I had come to trust my business, my skills, and myself. Still, it's not easy sometimes. Part of this is my choice due to my family obligations, but part of it is just how the consulting and training business works. It's important for people to know this, to know that it is never simple, no matter how experienced you become.

Informational interviews were such a key thing to do when I was younger. When I would set these up, people would immediately say, "Oh, we don't have any work here." Then I would say, "Well, I would really just love to know more about you and the work that you do as I explore the field." People usually respond positively to this approach.

When you go down one career path and you find it's not working out, that's okay. That's how you're evolving. I started off doing international development work, and I hated it. It wasn't me. Sometimes you figure out what you want to do by learning about the things you don't want to do.

What awards and honors have meant the most to you?

Being named Mother of the Year by the Multiple Sclerosis Society and receiving the Arab American Woman Leadership Award by the American-Arab Anti-Discrimination Committee both mean a great deal to me. As a woman, being acknowledged by my community along with some reputable women whom I admire is an honor.

Any final advice?

Touching someone's heart is how you can shift someone's attitudes and actions. This field is based on our passion and belief in the power of intercultural relations. Share your story and the stories of others. Remain authentic, persistent, and patient in pursuit of your dreams and desire in this field. Once when we were on a walk and I was moving by riding my scooter, my daughter Laila said, "Mommy, you can't walk with your legs, but you walk with your heart." That's you, and that's me. We're driven by our hearts.

— PROFILE —

Karl Dedolph

Senior Manager, Accenture, Washington, DC, 2011–present

Career Trajectory

Accenture, Washington, DC
    Manager, 2009–11
    Consultant, 2007–9
    Analyst, 2006–7

US Department of State, Foreign Affairs Intern/Presidential
    Management Fellow, Washington, DC, 2005

Peace Corps, Small Business Development Volunteer, Togo, West
    Africa, 2001–3

Academic Background

American University, School of International Service, MA
    (International Affairs), 2005

Gustavus Adolphus College, BA (Economics and Communication
    Studies), 2001

How do you define your cause?

One of my causes has been finding work that challenges me. I've always viewed my career path as building a foundation for the future. I'm getting comfortable with the uncertainty of not knowing what the future necessarily is, but knowing what I'm doing right now is building toward something bigger and better. I have to believe many people are, like me, thinking "I have no idea what I want to do."

The way I've made decisions is to focus on what I'm passionate about. I'm passionate about travel, about cultures, about having a purpose. About doing something *of* purpose.

After the Peace Corps, grad school, and a PMF (*Presidential Management Fellowship; see chapter 10*), which allowed me to explore the federal sector, I still didn't know what I wanted to do, but I came back to this idea of building a foundation for the future. I thought: "There are great consulting firms out there, and they can teach me project management skills that are transferable to any job."

When I joined Accenture, I never anticipated that I'd still be there seven years later. I thought of it as another stepping stone—continuing my education. But it has really turned into my cause because I live and breathe it. I don't have a hard time getting up in the morning.

How would you describe your field?

Especially in the federal space, being a consultant might mean being a contractor: you provide a certain service for the government. Accenture is a little different, although it does provide specific services—for instance, "standing up" and operating a help desk for a client. But my work in management consulting is focused on understanding what a client's issues are and working toward tangible outcomes. Part of being a consultant is finding ways to continually provide value for your client. And your client's needs and concerns change on a daily basis. That creates challenges in how we support them. Working to meet these challenges is very rewarding.

When I first got into consulting, I worried that I was abandoning my passion for international affairs. But whether it was luck or determination, I was assigned to a larger project with a US federal agency with an international presence, where we've worked on implementing and deploying logistics systems globally. I've gone to Moscow, I've gone to Baghdad, all as a part of this project. By working with this client, which I've done now for the past six and a half years, I've been able to draw upon that foundation and feed my passion for international affairs.

But that's not always the case in consulting, right? The clients really determine the work. If your company has work at the Social Security Administration, and you don't have a current client . . . you're probably going to work for the Social Security Administration. You have to be open to doing lots of different things over a period of time for lots of different organizations.

Where did you start, and how did it help you get to where you are today?

In high school I was voted most likely to be the first to make a million dollars. In college I thought I was going to go into business. I majored in economics and communication. I thought I was going to do what everyone else in my peer group did: pursue a business track and get the country club membership. I lived in such a limited box. And then things changed financially for my family. I realized nothing was guaranteed, nor did it have to be prescribed. It opened my eyes to the fact that I didn't have to have this narrow view of the world. At that point I decided I was going to take risks. I was going to stop living in that box.

One of those risks was going abroad: a mission trip to Mexico for three weeks. Then I studied in England, then Australia. All of a sudden in these new cultures, my world was so much bigger. It was instantly addictive. I wanted to go from that guy who was voted most likely to make a million dollars to confusing the heck out of everyone. I wanted to do something that had more significance and meaning.

What are the major day-to-day activities of your current position?

On a day-to-day basis, it's a lot of networking and meetings—both internal and with clients—to determine how to deliver the work. A benefit of working for a larger consulting firm is the opportunity to do many different things. For example, now I'm in our federal practice. We want to know what our strategy is on comprehensive immigration reform. I've been tasked with trying to figure that out. I don't know much about immigration reform, so I've got to form a team with the right skill set. Then we have two weeks to figure it out before we present to the CEO of our Accenture federal practice. That's just cool, right?

Also, I'm now at a place in my career where business development is important, while continuing to provide and deliver value to clients. Identifying new accounts and new opportunities for existing clients is a priority. I'm at a level where I'm expected to be a part of that, whether it's writing proposals, executing a call plan, or nurturing relationships with clients. That's an evolving skill I'm excited to learn and develop.

What is your best advice for developing effective networking skills?

The world does not work on the internet or on paper. It works on relationships. That shouldn't be a surprise to anyone. That's how businesses operate on so many levels. That's how getting a job often happens. And don't think that it's not rewarding for others to share their experiences with you or to want to help. When you're in the day-to-day grind of your job, there is satisfaction in trying to help someone else.

Don't think, in networking, that you can't ask someone else who knows someone else to speak on your behalf. You just have to be connected somehow by a network. You know someone, you form a relationship with that person, and they know someone else. It's how I got my job at Accenture.

Social media is a certain form of networking, but to me, you network in person. You might set up a networking opportunity virtually, but if success is based on relationships, the only effective way to have relationships is in person. That's a piece of advice that I give to people in any kind of work, but certainly in consulting. If the opportunity is there to do it in person, then you do it in person.

Do you have a mentor? How has he or she affected your life and career?

As you network, try to find people that you can learn from. People want to be mentors, to be asked for advice, or even, when the opportunity is right, to form a more formal mentor/mentee relationship.

It's all part of people development. When you have a team of people that work for you, being their supervisor and their mentor at the same time has amazing results both for their work and careers. By mentoring your team, your colleagues feel like they are learning, that you're sharing current challenges with them. They get to be a part of the decision-making process. You enter into this trusted relationship where you can share things without fear of judgment. When you need to assemble a team quickly or need trusted people to help you, the first people that come are those you've been mentoring.

After seven years at Accenture, I have mentors who have helped me in this way. I seek their guidance on a consistent basis.

Do you consider yourself a mentor to others?

There's always hierarchy to some degree—you wouldn't necessarily seek someone who is at your same peer level to be your mentor, so you have to get to a certain level before people start asking you to be their mentor. But then again, working in a collaborative environment like I do, there are opportunities to work and lead within your own peer group. At the end of the day, if you can create a team that is collaborative in nature, as opposed to competitive in nature, everyone wins. Everyone learns.

How have you maintained a healthy balance between your work and personal life?

It's such a cliché question. It's different for every person—you have to strike the balance that's right for you. For me, my family comes first. Period. What I've found as I've progressed in my career is that I have subtracted those other life components that aren't my family or my work.

So do I have a good work–life balance? Yes. But do I get to do everything that I want to? No. I haven't played tennis in three years; I wish I could golf every week; I wish I could go to more sporting events; but those are not priorities. My number one priority is my family; part of my motivation to work is driven by the need to support my family.

Priorities change over time. When I started in consulting, my priorities were totally different than they are now, seven years later. But this line of work has allowed me to evolve and change those priorities, and that's part of the reason that I've stayed—the flexibility that allows me to be home with my family almost every night. I also have a great support network in my personal life that enables me to do my work effectively, to keep a good work–life balance.

What awards and honors have meant the most to you?

I would change it to what *rewards* mean the most to you. In the work that you do, how are you rewarded? And for me, it's on the people development side, where I am able to help colleagues grow their careers and skill sets and watch them evolve, as I evolved over the last seven years.

What lessons have you learned as your career has evolved?

Perception is so critical in the workplace. Differentiating yourself from your peers and advancing in your career often comes down to the perceptions people have of you.

Conclusion

It's Not a Small World after All

EVERYONE HAS A STORY that illustrates how small our world has become. Sherry once ran into a former colleague she worked with in Washington, DC, and hadn't seen in years in a Moscow department store. Mark bumped into a classmate from his university in South Bend, Indiana, on the steps of the Sacre-Coeur Basilica in Paris. When a chance encounter like this occurs, when we see someone who lives close to home in a place so far away, we all have a tendency to exclaim, "What a small world!"

Yet, these chance encounters aside, the reality is that it's *not* a small world after all. Rather, the world of the individual has grown enormously. Each of us is coping with so much more information today than ever before. Most of us encounter far more people and places than our grandparents ever dreamed about. When we're transported by the internet, television, or smart phone to other countries and continents, we aren't any closer to these places than we were before. Instead, the size of our individual world, measured by the amount of information and experiences we have access to, has grown exponentially. We are living in an era of hypercomplexity.

The consequence of this for your job search and career development is that there are more possibilities than ever before. One of the realizations we came to during our collaboration on this book is just how huge the world of the job seeker has become, how much information is out there for you to sift through and evaluate. While editing the lists of resources in part II, we found ourselves amazed by the sheer volume. Career websites and books, job boards and search engines, long lists of organizations, more acronyms than you would ever want to decipher—the amount of information was daunting. And we are the first to admit that the information contained in this book is only selected!

When Sherry wrote her first book on careers in 1998, using the internet for career research was almost an afterthought. Now it is a primary tool for a job search. Even in the last several years, the job search capabilities online have been further transformed and expanded—the emergence of dynamic social networking sites is a good example of this ongoing transformation. Once you've logged on (or opened this book, for that matter), the major challenge becomes: Where do you begin? With so much information out there, how do you know what to use, what sources to trust? How do you deal with "the overwhelm"?

We wish we could give you simple answers to these twenty-first-century questions. We hoped we could conclude with a nugget of advice that would allow each and every reader to easily transcend the overwhelm and find that one career silver bullet that would lead to a dream job. We found this to be an impossible task. We certainly encourage you, as we have throughout, to begin where your interests lie. Locate your cause, discern what drives you, then seek out the resources that match. Yet even this advice, we realize, is complicated. What if you are like Mark and have struggled to find your cause? How do you find the right resource when you aren't even sure what you're looking for? Although we couldn't come up with a single solution for these questions, we do offer some simple suggestions.

The first is acceptance. Accept that, in our information-saturated society, overwhelm is a permanent condition. Whether it is in our job searches or our actual jobs, we will forever be dealing with too much information, too many demands, and too little time. Whatever you cross off your to-do list will always be replaced with an even longer list of tasks. By coming to terms with this fact, rather than trying to deny it or change it, you'll find that you're better equipped to adapt to information overload.

Second, be patient. Especially if you are still in the midst of honing your interests and discovering your cause, give yourself time to locate the organizations and opportunities that are right for you. This may mean allowing yourself plenty of time to page through part II and to consider and research the many resources there. But more often than not, it will also require you to have multiple experiences, whether volunteer projects, internships, or full-time jobs. In the end, as Luby Ismail pointed out to us, the trial—and sometimes error—of experience is often the only way we can uncover what we're truly meant to do.

And finally, take comfort in the fact that everyone else is overwhelmed, too. You're not the only one whose world has grown. Others are bombarded by information and requests as well. Everyone copes with that feeling: "If I can *just* get this one big project done, then everything will fall into place and I'll have more time."

So what can we do when we feel overwhelmed? We can step back from our work and our career deliberations. We can muster the discipline to disconnect. Perhaps we can take a walk or talk to a friend. Maybe grab a beer or watch a movie. We can work out, practice yoga, or play with a pet. We can decompress and unwind in some way, and when we feel energized again, we tackle things with renewed vigor. There is no escape from the overwhelm; there are only strategies to deal with it. And sometimes the best way to deal with the stresses of your job search and career development is to just not think about them for a while.

Another realization we came to during our collaboration is that writing a book is a lot like building a career. Both are continuous journeys. As we discuss in chapter 4, building your career does not end when you land that first dream job. In the same way, our roles as authors were not over when we submitted the final draft of the first edition; or when the first edition was published; or when we moved on to this second edition. We've worked with our publisher to find ways to distribute the book; written on our *Working World* blog; served as panelists for sessions on careers at professional association meetings and at universities; conducted workshops on careers; and considered ways to elaborate on subjects in jointly authored articles.

We've set in motion an ongoing process that has engaged us, helped us distill lessons learned, and clarified our thoughts on a wide range of topics. Just as rewarding careers are avenues of constant learning and growth, how much we learned as the book has developed—from our research and from each other—continues to amaze us. We knew we worked well together, but we were pleasantly surprised at the ease of our cooperation. We quickly agreed on tasks that needed to be done and divided them between us with little discussion. Again, this is parallel to building a career. It is not a process that can be forced but grows naturally from working with people you like and respect and embracing a cause that is meaningful.

In one of the quotes we share at the beginning of the book, Albert Schweitzer predicts that "the only ones among you who will be really happy are those who will have sought and found how to serve." As we examined our own experiences and those of the professionals we profiled, it became clear that tremendous benefits rebound to us when we help others. Sherry remembers hearing management guru Peter Drucker speak at a conference in the early 1990s. In a presentation focusing on nonprofit leadership, Drucker pointed out that volunteers benefit as much from performing the services they render as do the recipients of those services. He reminded his audience that once their basic needs are met, human beings gain great satisfaction from building community and being of service—from making a difference. Thinking of your career as the way you will be of service to those around you is the best advice we can offer.

In the end we must admit that our takes on careers in the fields of international education, exchange, and development are but two in a sea of many. The resources presented are only selected—it was not our intention to provide a comprehensive list of every conceivable organization or reference that could have relevance for you. Rather, our goal was to provide a service—to *be* of service to you as you plan your career. We certainly hope that our work will act as a compass to help you map a professionally and personally rewarding career path. We leave you with a favorite quote from Madeleine Albright that offers reassurance: "You can't plan the future. It just happens and is full of surprises. The key is to love what you're doing and work hard. Everything else will take care of itself." We wish you all the best on your continuous journey.

Index